merry
meet
again

About the Author

Deborah Lipp was initiated into a traditional Gardnerian coven of Witches in 1981, became a High Priestess in 1986, and has been teaching Wicca and running Pagan circles ever since. She has appeared in various media discussing Wicca, including the A&E documentary *Ancient Mysteries: Witchcraft in America*, on MSNBC, in the *New York Times*, and in many smaller TV and print sources.

Deborah has been published in many Pagan publications, including *Llewellyn's Magical Almanac*, *Pangaia*, *Green Egg*, *The Druid's Progress*, *Converging Paths*, and *The Hidden Path*, as well as *Mothering Magazine*. She has lectured at numerous Pagan festivals on many topics.

Deborah is an IT professional with a variety of skills. She lives in Rockland County, New York, with her son, Arthur, her partner, Melissa, and an assortment of cats. Deborah reads and teaches Tarot, designs wire-and-bead jewelry, solves and designs puzzles, watches old movies, hand-paints furniture, and dabbles in numerous handcrafts.

merry
meet
again

LESSONS, LIFE & LOVE ON THE PATH
OF A WICCAN HIGH PRIESTESS

DEBORAH LIPP

Llewellyn Publications
Woodbury, Minnesota

FIRST EDITION
First Printing, 2013

Book design by Donna Burch
Cover art: Author photo on front cover: © John Shaffrey
          Misty forest: © iStockphoto.com/Evgeny Kuklev
          Texture: © Digital Stock
          Wiccan objects: © iStockphoto.com/CreativeFire
Cover design by Ellen Lawson
Edited by Andrea Neff

Interior photos provided by the author, except on page 45 by John Shaffrey, page 145 by Jeff Koslow, and page 225 by the Llewellyn Art Department

Llewellyn Publications is a registered trademark of Llewellyn Worldwide Ltd.

Library of Congress Cataloging-in-Publication Data
Lipp, Deborah, 1961–
  Merry meet again : lessons, life & love on the path of a Wiccan high priestess / by Deborah Lipp. — 1st ed.
      p. cm.
  Includes bibliographical references.
  ISBN 978-0-7387-3478-1
1. Lipp, Deborah, 1961– 2. Wiccans—United States--Biography. 3. Wicca—United States—Biography. I. Title.
  BP605.W53L57 2013
  299'.94092—dc23
  [B]
                              2012038021

Llewellyn Publications
A Division of Llewellyn Worldwide Ltd.
2143 Woodbale Drive
Woodbury, MN 55125-2989
www.llewellyn.com

Printed in the United States of America

OTHER BOOKS BY DEBORAH LIPP

The Elements of Ritual:
Air, Fire, Water & Earth in the Wiccan Circle, 2003

The Way of Four:
Create Elemental Balance in Your Life, 2004

The Way of Four Spellbook:
Working Magic with the Elements, 2006

DEDICATION

In memory of Philip Emmons Isaac Bonewits
1949–2010
With a heart full of love.

Contents

Acknowledgments

I have a remarkably well-documented life. I began keeping a diary at the age of twelve, and kept it up for about ten years. I picked it up again for a few six-month stints at later times. I am assiduous about keeping a magical diary. I also save correspondence and used to write a lot of paper letters back in the day; many dozens, perhaps hundreds, of replies are still in my possession. All of this really helped in reconstructing a chronology of my life.

I was also able to get questions answered from a lot of people who filled in memory and documentation gaps. They include Ian Corrigan, Jeff Rosenbaum, Link, Andras Corban-Arthen, Bill Seligman, Constance, Phaedra Bonewits, and Oberon Zell. Thank you all. Thanks also to the extensive archives of festivals past on Rosencomet.com. Between Starwood and Winterstar, I was able to jog a lot of memories. Special thanks to Neilalien (owner of Neilalien.com, a Dr. Strange fansite), who found a back issue of *Doctor Strange* in his extensive archives that brought back an extraordinary moment in my life.

I am grateful to everyone who allowed their names and stories to be shared in these pages, including my parents and siblings, and my friends Barbara, Joey, Dave, the Laplantes, Emilio, Constance, Tracy, Michael Brown, Izolda Trakhtenberg, Gordon, and Jimahl di Fiosa.

My mother, Paula Gellis, reviewed the material on family background and made corrections. My son, Arthur Lipp-Bonewits, read sections of the manuscript involving him, and sections involving his father that were sensitive to him, and sometimes gave his okay and sometimes asked me to pull back a little, and I appreciated all of that.

During the course of writing this book, I have, time and again, been reminded that life can be far too short. The following people, mentioned herein, have passed to the Summerland. They are all missed: Scott Cunningham, Stewart Farrar, Harvey Goldfisher (my first stepfather), Robin Goodfellow (formerly Stephen Edwards), Dr. Timothy Leary, J. P. McClimans, Patricia Monaghan, Richard Ravish, Steve Ritholtz, John Edward Shaffrey, Bob Shea, Karl Steinmayer, Marion Weinstein, Robert Anton Wilson, and Paul Zimmer. May they each be born again to those who loved them, and may they love again.

Chapter 1

HAIL ARTEMIS!

Me in Massachusetts, 1975

I worship [the Moon] every night. Hail Artemis, Hail O Moon,
for thou art beautiful. Or, when it's cloudy and I can't see her beauty,
Hail Artemis, Hail O Moon, though I see not thy face.

—*Journal entry, November 13, 1976*

I was fifteen years old when I wrote that.

I'm a suburban New Jersey girl, born and bred, but I've taken a lot of side roads on that path. By the time I turned eighteen, I'd had a total of ten different addresses, six of which were in New Jersey suburbs. I'm not an army brat; some were job moves, two were my parents divorcing (sold the home) and remarrying (bought a new one), and some were lifestyle moves.

Wiccans talk a lot about the whole "nature religion" thing, but I try to stay conscious of my suburban roots. There are a lot of us for whom "nature" has usually been the undeveloped patch of woods behind the library—more a shortcut than a hike. Nature matters a whole lot, but so does being true to the lives we actually live. So, amidst writing about being out in the woods, I do like to throw in magic you can do by shopping at the mall.

My parents, Michael and Paula, are from the same neighborhood in Brooklyn, and grew up across the street from each other, yet didn't meet until high school. Both are the children and grandchildren of Jewish immigrants who fled from the Russian "Pale of Settlement" around the turn of the century. Michael's parents were both born in Brooklyn. His mother (my Nana Jean) was the daughter of Hungarian immigrants, and his father (my Papa) was born to immigrants from Odessa and Bratislava. My mother's mother (Nana Ann) was born in Russia, and her father (Grandpa Murray) was born in Poland. If you've seen the movie *Hester Street* you have a sense of the Lower East Side immigrant community that is my heritage, and if you've seen *Fiddler on the Roof* you have a feel for where they came from in the "old country." My family established itself enough to depart those tenements for nicer neighborhoods in Brooklyn, and there my parents were born.

Michael Lipp and Paula Wald were married in 1958 and moved to the suburbs, or, as their New York families referred to it, "the country." Dad had a master's degree in mathematics and got involved in the nascent computer industry. Mom was a petite dynamo who, a year later, when she was all of twenty years old, had her first child (my brother Jay). I was born in 1961, and Roberta in 1965, and in 1966, Michael and Paula divorced.

From that point on, my life was on two different tracks. Michael remarried in 1967, and my mom in 1968. I could add more homes to the ten I first counted if I included the places where Dad lived, where I spent alternate weekends. Mostly, these were just more suburbs, but his five years in Ashfield, Massachusetts, had a profound effect on me.

Let me backtrack, though. Before Massachusetts there was quite a lot of New Jersey.

My mother describes herself as an agnostic, although her Judaism is deeply important to her. Like my mother, I understand Judaism as my culture, my tribe, and my heritage. But this was and is much more true for Mom, who grew up in a community of recent immigrants, in a neighborhood that was, at the time, about half-Jewish. She was very close to her grandmother, a warm, loving presence in her life and a Russian immigrant. These were people who practiced their religion constantly, through dietary restriction as well as prayer, who spoke Yiddish, and who lived their entire lives among other Jews.

By contrast, I grew up in suburbs where Jews were a very small minority and English was the only language. Mom fed us ham sandwiches, and prayers were said only on holidays.

Agnostic might not be the right word to describe Mom. She's first and foremost a pragmatist. She cares deeply about the real world and real people. Her sensibility is that spiritual matters are a distraction from what's really important.

She describes me as being a religious or spiritual person from a very young age. Before I was five, she knew I had spiritual needs that she wouldn't be able to fulfill, because she didn't connect to them.

I was a precocious and strangely mature child. I remember being furious at the age of three that I was being "treated like a child"—furious! I was absolutely sure that I *wasn't* a child, and that dissonance was a constant source of woe. I don't remember any particular religious conversations that I had with my mother or anyone else around that age, but I have no doubt that they were gravely serious.

All of Mom's kids (the three of us from my parents' marriage, and my brother Dan, who is Mom's from her second marriage) went to Hebrew school from about age seven, but I was the one who really adored it. Hebrew school is an after-school educational program affiliated with a synagogue, designed to give an all-around Jewish education, both religious and cultural, and to prepare you for *bar* or *bat mitzvah* (the Jewish coming-of-age ceremony that happens at age thirteen; "bar mitzvah" for a boy, "bat mitzvah" for a girl). We attended twice a week after school, plus Sunday mornings, and were taught the Hebrew language, prayers, religious tradition (what the holidays mean, what the laws of keeping kosher are), and cultural history (Holocaust studies, famous Jews in history, the founding of the State of Israel, and so forth).

We moved to a new town, and changed synagogues, between fifth and sixth grade (1972), so when I was eleven years old, my new Hebrew school teacher was Mr. Cohen. He was an Orthodox guy from Brooklyn who had been ordained as a rabbi but had never worked in that capacity.

As I said, Mom's Judaism is important to her (and so, in a different way, is my father's, and so was my stepfather's), so sending us all to Hebrew school was simply the right thing to do. But for me, especially under the influence of Mr. Cohen, it was a spiritual awakening. I was so effusive that Mom got really tired of sentences beginning with "Mr. Cohen says...." Through him, I was introduced to what living a religious life could mean. For the Orthodox, Judaism is lived every moment of every day. There are prayers upon rising and prayers before eating. There are dietary restrictions that are both complicated and time-consuming to follow. There are fast days and feast days. There are ritual baths, ritual candles, and ritual dishes. I was transfixed by the idea of living such a life. I fantasized that, when I grew up, I would keep a kosher home.

At the same time that my passion for religion was being inflamed, though, so was my social consciousness. From my earliest days, part of my nature was to protest injustice. A child will stamp her foot and say, "That's not fair!," but I translated that into action.

Some of that was, actually, my being a Jewish kid in a Christian suburb, and being asked, for example, to make Christmas trees as an art project, and having to insist that a Chanukah menorah be offered as an option. Or being asked to sing "Silent Night" and "Joy to the World" as part of the Christmas choir in third grade (my mother had to speak to the principal about that one). Part of it was being a girl in a world that still institutionalized sexism in day-to-day life.

At my grade school, girls were not allowed to wear pants to school; skirts were required. But for gym class, we were required to change into pants. So while boys could just play in the clothes they'd worn, girls had to change, which meant we had to get to school earlier.

While this was unfair, I think I was motivated to rebel largely by my lifelong struggle to get myself out of bed in the morning. There were days when my mother would literally drag me by the ankles while I clung to the top of the bed with clawed fingers. If only I'd discovered coffee earlier! Anyway, since it was tough enough trying to get to school on time, getting there early enough to change, with a second set of clothes in hand, seemed cruel and unnecessary.

So I started wearing pants. I was eight years old, and it was my first act of civil disobedience. The school said nothing, and the other girls noticed the school saying nothing, so quietly, girls started wearing pants to school—at least on gym days. My first taste of social leadership was sweet.

Four years later, in July of 1972, my mother brought home the premiere issue of *Ms.* magazine. Today, there's still a lot of sexism in the world, but it's hard for younger people to imagine how recent and pervasive restrictions on women's lives actually were. Not long ago I spoke to a young woman, a college student, who said, "I thought that all ended in the 1950s." Nope. I still remember newspapers running separate job listings for men and women, and "Gal Friday" was an actual title you'd see in those listings. I remember my stepfather insisting that he was absolutely right to pay women less, because they'd quit as soon as they got married. My stepmother took maternity leave in 1970, and when she was ready to return to work, her job had been given away. This was an era when a woman couldn't get a credit card without her husband's signature. So reading *Ms.*, and discussing these issues with my mom, was significant.

At the age of twelve, I was studying Judaism and feminism at the same time, and cracks were starting to form in my ability to believe in both equally. In Judaism, prayer is merely optional for women but necessary for men. Mr. Cohen explained that it would be impractical for a woman with a baby to stop everything and pray at requisite times. (Yeah, but the rule isn't about women with children, it's about *women.*) The first female rabbi in Reform Judaism was ordained in 1972, but with my orientation toward ritual and structure, Reform Judaism didn't appeal to me, and the first female Conservative rabbi was not ordained until 1985. (The Orthodox still do not permit women to be rabbis.)

Then there's the *minyan.* Public prayer and certain other religious functions in Judaism require a *minyan*, an assembly of ten men. Although Reform Judaism always considered a minyan to be a gathering of ten *people,* Conservative Judaism didn't count women among the minyan until the 1980s. Prior to that time, ten Jewish women could not gather to read the Torah. So when I was a girl in Hebrew school, women literally didn't count.

There are outstanding feminists within Judaism, groundbreakers like Sally Priesand, the first woman rabbi. There are theologians and speakers and activists working to make sure women have a vital role in Judaism. I admire those women. Since, at twelve, I was already a bit of an activist, you might think that I'd have chosen to be one of them. But I wanted a religion in which I *inherently* had value. I wanted to be *embraced*, not to have to fight for a place. (Feminist Jewish women probably feel they have a place, and feel embraced by God, and that empowers them to fight. I can only speak from my own experience.) At twelve, without much ability to articulate all this, I simply felt that I didn't have a place, as a woman and a feminist, within Judaism.

I told my mother that I didn't want a bat mitzvah. That was okay with her—for precisely the same reasons I was rejecting it, in fact. A boy was expected to have his bar mitzvah, to say, "Today I am a man," but bat mitzvah, the female equivalent, was entirely optional. Mom had never had one. It was a modern ceremony, still mostly performed in Reform synagogues at the time. If I didn't want to put Mom through the expense of private preparatory lessons and the big party, she was fine with that.

I wasn't rejecting religion, just *this* religion. And at that point I became a spiritual seeker.

Since then, my relationship with the religion of my birth has been complex. I identify as Jewish, just as my mother does. It's my culture, my people, my DNA. It's not my faith, but the prayers resonate with me right down to my bones. Any efforts I've made to reject Judaism have failed, but any efforts I've made to incorporate it into my religious life have also failed. As they say on Facebook, "It's complicated."

I said that my upbringing was on two separate tracks, so now it's time to look at growing up with my father.

In the late 1960s, my dad began making himself into a hippie. He turned thirty in 1967, so he was a little old for it. He became involved with an anti–Vietnam War group, health problems led him to natural foods and alternative medicine, and smoking pot figured in there as well.

When young people think about the sixties and hippies, they often don't know that the counterculture was *always* a minority, and the mainstream majority was never all that accepting of it. You really can't understand that period of history unless you understand that counter-cultural movements (free love, hippie, back-to-the-land, etc.) were unacceptable to most people.

As my father moved further and further out of the mainstream, the divide between my parents and my two different lives became greater and greater.

Again, people might make the assumption that this was a sort of conservative-versus-liberal divide. It was not. My mother's politics were and are liberal Democratic. This wasn't conservative versus liberal; this was normal versus off the deep end.

I should pause here to say a couple of things. First, my perception of the sixties is through the eyes of a young child. I was born in 1961. By 1968 I was a smart kid who didn't know she was a kid, but child I was, and my views on that period are necessarily colored by that. Second, the divide between my parents wasn't fundamentally political. There were a lot of personal differences as well, obviously, and issues far more serious than long hair and reefer. But in looking back at the path that led me to the diary entry that opens this chapter, to worshiping the Goddess and ultimately to Wicca, the political and social issues are the ones worth discussing.

As I said, my father had been involved with the computer industry since 1958. In the 1960s, he was a founding partner (with several other people) of a computer time-sharing company. Around 1972, he got into a dispute with the company president, took his stock options, and walked. He was already thinking of "dropping out," and was looking at rural properties. So he purchased a large, run-down house on four acres, on a dirt road in Ashfield, Massachusetts, and, with his second wife, Nancy, opened a health food store in nearby Greenfield. We kids continued our visitation via four-hour bus rides.

Ashfield is in the northwest portion of Massachusetts, near the Vermont border. It's located in the eastern foothills of the Berkshire Mountains, and the northern part of town, where we lived, has several significant hills. There's an exquisite peace in those hills, a sense of presence and benevolent beauty. Spending time there was unlike any prior experience I'd had in nature.

I walked a lot there, sometimes on our own property. I'd explore the woods or sit quietly in a stand of white birch, a little afraid of getting lost since I knew so little about being out in the country, but enjoying myself nonetheless. I'd walk up Bug Hill Road, past where it was passable by car, with so few neighbors that it was as if I were completely alone. There I found maple trees, pine, birch, hay, streams, frogs, a hum in the air, a swampy odor (a good chunk of land adjacent to my walks is now a nature preserve called Bear Swamp).

The sense of presence I felt there formulated itself into a voice. I never thought I was having a vision, but it was a communication, and it was clear. Nature was alive, and she was female. The sense was unmistakable. It wasn't an idea, or a theory, or a metaphor; it was a feeling as real as if she stood before me in full anthropomorphic glory. She was mountains, she was fields, she was all of what I felt embracing me in those woods.

Dad was into spiritual and personal exploration, in addition to health foods and drugs. For a short while he followed a Hindu guru. He read Sufi stories. He went to a self-actualization center and learned about gestalt therapy. And he introduced me to all these things.

So by the time I was thirteen, I had fallen in and out of love with Judaism, I had been exposed to a wide range of spiritual beliefs, and I had encountered the Goddess of Nature.

In my own mind, then, I began thinking of myself as a Pagan, but I was quite sure I was the only Pagan in the whole world.

The language I used was the language of Greek mythology. When I was first introduced to Greek myths, somewhere around the fourth or fifth grade, I couldn't get enough of them. I read every book on the subject in the library. I then went to Norse mythology, which appealed to me less. Finally, I devoured the library's entire section on fairy tales. But the Greek stories were my favorites. So when I began to make a spiritual and religious connection to nature, Earth was Gaia, the Moon was Artemis, and the loveliness of nature was Aphrodite. (It's possible that someone is reading this with a desire to correct my understanding of Hellenism. Please remember, I was thirteen, maybe fourteen. There was no Internet for my research, and no Pagan community—to my knowledge—from which to learn.)

Around this time, my family endured a bitterly contested custody battle, and in June of 1975, I moved to Ashfield with my father's family.

By that point, my older brother, Jay, was already living there. Dad and Nancy had two daughters and a third on the way. My sister, Roberta, remained in New Jersey with Mom, her husband, Harvey, and their son, Danny. My family tree makes heads spin!

In September of 1975, I started attending an "alternative school." It would be easy to describe it through a sneer of "look at those hippies" cynicism, but, despite a lot of flaws, it was also a tremendous experience. Maple Valley was (and still is, although it's no longer remotely the same) located in Wendell, Massachusetts. It was a tiny school, with about forty students—almost all teenagers—and fifteen staff. Maple Valley was based on the idea that children, especially teens, were human beings capable of running their own lives. Decisions about school goings-on were decided by majority vote, and students and staff had equal votes (the exception being "health and safety, and laws of the larger community," meaning students didn't get a vote on the rule against possession of illegal drugs or on fire safety rules). Class schedules were chaotic, since no classes were mandatory, but at the age of fourteen I knew how to work inside of Robert's Rules of Order, and you can't argue the educational value of that!

The other guiding principle of Maple Valley was communication through openness and honesty. It was education meets community-based democracy in action meets giant therapy group—a contentious, pot-fueled puppy pile.

I had found a haven and a home. Throughout my public school education, I'd felt left out and different and was often lonely. I usually had one close friend, rarely two. Here I was accepted by a crowd, and I had fun. I hung out, had adventures, and generally spread my wings and enjoyed my teens. Not everything I did was smart or safe, but I was growing and changing and becoming myself, and that's not a safe or smart process.

One day we had a candle-making class at school. We used a dipping technique where you dip your candle wick into vats of liquid wax of different colors.

My resulting candle was not attractive. Since it was my first attempt, I didn't know the way colors of hot wax blend, so all my pretty choices ended up creating a kind of mottled puce. It was also a bit lumpy. Yet it was something I'd made myself, and my intention in making it was clear from the get-go: I was going to use this candle to worship the Moon.

When the candle had dried, I brought it home and kept it in my room. At night, I would sneak outside with my candle, face the Moon, light the candle, and recite: "Hail Artemis, Hail O Moon, for thou art beautiful." I would gaze quietly for a while, and then go back inside.

It is amazing to me how much I got absolutely right from the beginning. The things I did then, intuitively, are things I teach today.

You can pick up any random book on Wicca among the dozens available, and it will probably instruct you to make your own tools. A handmade magical tool is imbued with your personal energy, your intention, and your focused will. It is bound to you. The whole time you are making a magical tool, these books will tell you, keep your intention firmly in mind; in this way your tool will be the perfect expression of that magical purpose. Beauty and craftsmanship matter less, these books will continue, than the personal and intimate expression of yourself. It's no different, in many ways, than making a Mother's Day card instead of giving Mom a store-bought one. The message of love and appreciation doesn't even need to be inscribed in a homemade card; it's there in the making.

I'm sure there were candles in the house, but they weren't *magical* candles, made to worship in the night. The same would have been true of store-bought candles. You might be surprised how much harder it was to *find* candles at most stores in the 1970s, but they were around and I could have bought some. Yet I knew that the only way to acquire the candle I needed was to make it myself.

It's funny, because today I buy candles by the dozen, but I also have so many more magical techniques at my disposal. I know how to "dress" a candle, and how to consecrate it, so if I don't hand-dip candles much anymore, I still can personalize and dedicate their energy. I also have other tools on my altar, including homemade ones, but at the time, that candle was my only such tool.

I also dedicated that candle to use solely in worship. In fact, when my girlfriend was hanging out in my room, and found the candle and lit it, I was horrified. I wasn't sure if it was appropriate to ever use it for worship again! Dedicating a ritual tool preserves its energy, which remains undiluted and contained. It's like what happens when you cover a pot: water boils faster, steam builds up, pressure intensifies.

In addition, I maintained secrecy. In truth, this was partly out of embarrassment and fear of being mocked, and had nothing to do with magic or religious devotion. On the other hand, preventing the sacred from being mocked is an age-old justification for preserving the secrets of the Mysteries.

Not everyone uses secrecy as a component of their Pagan or magical work, but it is a time-honored practice. It keeps profane and disbelieving eyes away from the sacred, and preserves the dignity of the moment. Like dedication, secrecy is a container that maintains magical "heat." In addition, secrecy preserves intimacy. Just as a couple might keep little in-jokes or pet names private, and almost certainly keep some or all of their sexual relationship strictly between themselves, secrecy in Pagan worship maintains the intimate relationship of the worshiper and the Gods, as well as the relationships within a coven or other dedicated Pagan group.

Another practice that I've never changed is the use of liturgical language. Catholics who seek out a pre–Vatican II Latin Mass and Jews who dislike the Reform movement's preference for English over Hebrew both understand that changing the language you use, so that everyday speech and religious speech are different, has a power all its own. In English, many people achieve the same effect by using "thee" and "thou," either when addressing deity or throughout ritual. Not everyone likes this, or needs it, or even appreciates it, and I've certainly been in ritual with people who *hate* all that thee-and-thou stuff. But for me, it sets the tone today just as it did in 1975.

I also understood that my worship needed to be committed, regular, and consistent. On an overcast night, when I changed my prayer to "Hail Artemis, Hail O Moon, though I see not thy face," it was the beginning of knowing that, although my worship was connected to nature, it transcended that connection. It wasn't *about* seeing the Moon; it was more than that.

At the time, I thought I was the one and only person in the world who worshiped the Old Gods. Soon, I would learn otherwise.

How to Dress a Candle

Dressing a candle prepares it to be a magical tool and imbues it with the intended purpose of your spell. For magical purposes, an unscented candle is best; you will be adding your own scent in the dressing. If you're dressing a candle, and you like the kind that come in jars, then make sure the candle comes out—some candles are made by pouring the wax into the jar, and others can be slipped out of the jar, dressed, and put back in.

You can blend your ingredients in any ordinary, non-porous dish, or use a dish set aside for magical work.

1. Use a small amount (2 or 3 tablespoons) of pure oil. Olive oil and almond oil are both good choices.

2. Choose a pure essential oil, dried herb, or fresh herb that is aligned with your purpose: lavender for peace, cinnamon for success, rose for love, and so forth. For worship, you can choose a scent sacred to the deity.

3. Then add 1 to 2 drops of essential oil, a pinch of dried herbs, or a small handful of fresh herbs (or flower petals, etc.).

4. If using essential oil, the dressing can be used immediately; otherwise, let the dressing sit for a few hours or overnight to absorb the essence and scent.

5. Consecrate the oil to your purpose (see the next section).

6. Dip your fingers in the oil and rub the oil onto the candle. For blessing or increase, use an *upward* and *clockwise* movement. For banishing or decrease, use a *downward* and *counterclockwise* movement.

The candle is now ready to burn.

HOW TO PERFORM A CONSECRATION

The simplest consecration is done with the power of your *will* and your *word*. Point your athame, wand, open palms, or fingertips at the object and say: "I do consecrate this _____ by the power of _____ that it may _____. So be it."

Examples:

"I do consecrate this dressing oil by the power of
my True Will that it may lead me to success. So be it."

"I do consecrate this candle by the power of
the Lord and Lady that it may aid me in Their worship. So be it."

"I do consecrate this wand by the power of
the Goddess Brigid that it may be a worthy instrument
upon my altar. So be it."

Always state the purpose of the consecration (the "that it may" part), and always say "So be it" at the end—it declares success. Always use a newly consecrated object immediately, in order to seal and release the consecration—for example, briefly light the candle, point the wand, and so forth.

Here is a slightly more elaborate consecration that uses the four elements:

1. Begin by consecrating as before, using just your will and your word, but leave off the "So be it" at the end.

2. Pass the object through incense smoke and say, "I do consecrate this _____ by Fire and Air." Thoroughly cense the object, turning it this way and that so every bit is touched by the smoke.

3. Wet the object with saltwater, saying, "I do consecrate this _____ by Water and Earth." Again, wet every bit of the object. Depending on what you're consecrating, you might be able to submerge the object, or you might use your finger dipped into the water and rubbed on the item, or you might need to place the item in a container and rub the water on the container. To

consecrate oil, you can either use a container or sprinkle a few drops of the saltwater into the oil.

4. Now say "So be it" and use the item.

Chapter 2

WITCHES

1977: Age sixteen

I used to think that radical feminists who call themselves Witches
were crazy, but now I'm not sure. I mean, I worship the Moon and
the Earth Goddess of All.

Journal entry, November 24, 1976

In 1969 a socialist feminist organization formed, calling itself Women's
International Terrorist Conspiracy from Hell: WITCH. It had no relation to Wicca, or indeed to Paganism, Goddess worship, or magic. In
general, the use of the word *Witch* by feminists in the 1960s and early
1970s was strictly a political statement. If goddesses or the Goddess
were mentioned, it was as a metaphor or as alternative history, not as
a serious religious statement. This was true even as Wicca, including
feminist Wicca, was beginning to appear in the United States. It was
simply not visible to most feminists, and even if it was, the metaphor
and shock value were too good to resist.

Witches were, after all, scary women, and feminists scared the patriarchy. Witches were women who had been oppressed and killed by a
society that hated them; feminists identified their own oppression with
that of the Inquisitions. Witches were seen as ugly hags. Anti-feminists
often claimed (and still claim) that the only women interested in feminism were those too ugly to get a man. Ironically, these same oppo-
nents complain about feminists' wanton sexuality, which is kind of
odd—how can they be too ugly to find someone, yet have sex left and
right? The same dichotomous view existed about Witches during the
Inquisitions; Witches were hideous, yet Witchcraft was the product of
insatiable carnality.

WITCH and its Witch metaphor were also about political theater, casting spells on the New York Stock Exchange and all that. So the impression I had from reading about it in *Ms.* was of women dressing up and pretending to be Witches and pretending to cast spells, and it made no sense to me at all. I certainly didn't associate these theatrics with what I was doing secretly in the night.

One day late in 1976, a year, perhaps less, after I'd begun worshiping the Moon, I was in a health food store in Amherst, Massachusetts, and saw a free feminist newsletter on the counter. Amherst was (and is) a very hip town, one of my favorite places. It was something of an enclave for hippies and alternative lifestyles. "Health food store" may make you think of GNC, but at the time, natural and organic eating hadn't yet become interesting to corporate chains; it was strictly mom-and-pop, if Mom and Pop had long hair and Birkenstocks. Community bulletins were available at the front of the store, and this was a way for alternative types to connect. The newsletter was mimeographed, a form of document reproduction that was much cheaper than photocopying in those days. The newsletter had that purplish-blue mimeo ink and was stapled together, conveying the message that someone had put it together in a basement.

When I got home, I opened the newsletter and began to read. There I found a description of a women's group Samhain ritual. I think they called it Halloween. I remember little of the description except that it was explicitly Pagan—the Goddess was invoked—and they sliced open an apple to reveal its sacred mystery to the group.

I was floored. Stunned, shocked, amazed, thrilled, and transformed. My life was made over new. There were *others*.

There was also no way of finding those others. The newsletter had no contact information of any kind—no name, no phone number, no PO Box. I was rarely able to get into Amherst; at fifteen, I got around by hitchhiking or getting rides from people. Amherst was twenty-five miles from home, twenty miles from school, and an eight-mile detour from the route between the two. Many of my friends would have just hitched or found a way there, but I was always nervous about getting lost. I didn't learn routes easily (and still don't—the GPS is my dearest possession), and I became intensely anxious if I didn't know where I was. I certainly was not going to explain to anyone why I wanted to return to that store, since that would have meant revealing my secret.

I read the article about the ritual over and over, and I pored over every inch of the newsletter, trying to solve my problem, but I never did. By the time I got back to that store, there were no more newsletters—not even a later issue—and no one there could tell me about it, or perhaps I was too afraid to ask.

The feeling I had inside was still wonderful; I was still not alone. The people like me, who worshiped the Goddess, called themselves Witches, and now I was determined to find them.

THE MYSTERY OF THE APPLE

Apples are associated with Samhain (Halloween) for the simple reason that Samhain is the final harvest festival of the year, and it occurs at the time of the apple harvest.

During your Samhain ritual, consecrate apples with, or instead of, cakes or cookies. Slice one apple across the core, dividing top from bottom. The center of the apple, sliced this way, is a pentagram. Show the sacred symbol to all. The Mystery speaks of the Gods within the harvest, the life that fills us even as winter approaches, and a promise of returning spring, hidden like a secret within the fruit we eat.

Then pass all the apples around to eat. I like to dip the apples in honey, a tradition borrowed from Judaism to bless us with a sweet season.

Before I found out about Witches, I didn't connect my worship with any kind of magic, but I did discover a kind of magic that had a profound impact on me.

One night my girlfriend and I were hanging out and getting very stoned. We started playing a mime game. I'd form a ball in the air and toss it to her, then she'd reshape it into a hat, take it off her head, and hand it to me. I'd take the hat, make an ice cream cone, offer her a lick, and so on. I don't know how many transformations we effected.

I gradually began to notice the buildup of an energy field around my hands. It felt like a warm cushion. When I brought my hands close to each another, the cushion between them resisted the effort to touch the palms together. The more we played our game, the bigger and stronger this field became.

This is a magical technique I use to this day, and most people find, with a little practice, that it's a simple and easy way to raise power. Draw your hands slowly out, until they are about shoulder width apart, palms facing each other. Gently bring them very near to each other, without letting them touch. Stop when you feel the energy field. If you don't feel it at first, bring them no closer than a quarter-inch apart, then draw them out again. Continue to bring the palms in and out. I like to use a taffy-pulling motion, as if I'm weaving or drawing out the energy. Some people knead and mold, as if the energy were dough. It won't take long before you feel the power you have created, since one source of magical power is the energy from our own bodies.

This is essentially what my friend and I were doing, except instead of weaving or kneading, we were miming, forming a variety of shapes. I was shocked to feel the tingling power between my palms. I was sure there was something I could do with this power, but I didn't know what, or how.

One thing about a democratically run school is that there are a lot of meetings. We'd have a general meeting once a week on Wednesday afternoons, and there were also special meetings and emergency meetings.

The Maple Valley dining room was a lovely space that was designed to accommodate a whole bunch of meetings, classes, meals, and general hanging-out. Like a kitchen in a friendly home, it was where people naturally gathered.

Shortly after my experience playing the mime game, I was sitting behind my friend Lee at a general meeting. There was a built-in bench along one wall of the dining room, and in the corner there was a level above the bench—I don't remember if it was a planter, or a table, or what, but that's where I was sitting, directly behind Lee, so that my knees were at about the height of his shoulders.

I was only half paying attention to the meeting. I began to "massage" Lee's head, moving my hands in stroking motions around his head and hair, without ever touching him. I was seated behind him, so he couldn't see me. I wondered if he could feel it, but I continued, without saying anything, for quite a long time, at least twenty minutes.

After the meeting ended, Lee turned to me and said, "That felt good." I sort of stammered, "What? You felt that?" I was astonished. I couldn't quite believe he'd really felt it. It was one thing to know I could create energy and feel it, but it was quite another to know someone else could feel it too.

So now I had the pieces of the puzzle: I had the Goddess, the worship of Earth and Moon, and I had the sense that there was an invisible, inexplicable energy that could be generated from my body and felt—and I now knew that there were people called Witches who gathered for both of these things.

I desperately wanted a teacher or group. I was easily intimidated. I was scared to talk about these ideas, scared of being mocked or misunderstood. I was, in those days, riddled with fears, anxieties, and phobias. I was too insecure to study on my own. I loved my friends, my school, and the hills I lived in, and this was all really important to me, but my feelings were a jumble. I'm sure a lot of it had to do with the intense emotions of the teen years.

In February of 1977, my father and stepmother decided to move back to New Jersey, primarily for financial reasons. The computer company my father had left in 1972 rehired him; the company president he'd fought with had since departed. After the interlude in the Berkshires, it was back to the suburbs and public school. The change was incredibly difficult for me.

My older brother had collected comic books from the time he could read, and I followed suit. Up until we left Ashfield, the collection was his, but after the move, I got more passionate about them, and began collecting on my own. I discovered that reading the letters sections of comics books was fun and interesting, and that there was a literate audience out there as engaged as I was. I started writing letters to comic books myself, and was absolutely thrilled when I was first published. I got involved by mail with other fans—addresses were almost always published with letters, so we could write to each other—and worked to create my own amateur stories.

One day, in the back of *Doctor Strange*, I saw a remarkable letter. Dr. Strange was a magician and occultist, and in recent months the writers had been exploring a side of him that was less otherworldly and more, well, Pagan. The letter appeared in the August 1977 issue of *Doctor Strange* (which was on the newsstand around March of that year) and said, in part:

> *As a priest of Wicca (a male witch, not a "warlock," if you please) and a follower, since its inception, of DOCTOR STRANGE, I am intrigued by the interesting direction the storyline appears to be taking as regards the depiction of women therein.*
>
> *Our religion is goddess-oriented, and as a longtime reader of Marvel Comics, I have been dismayed at the shallow depictions of women that have been standard. But now it appears change is afoot. The powerful goddess images in the recent DOCTOR STRANGE ANNUAL were very well done and non-stereotypical.*

The letter was signed "Stephen Edwards," with a San Francisco address.

I wrote to him immediately. There aren't words to say how thrilled and excited I was. I told him how I'd been searching and how little I knew, but how I was sure that Wicca was for me. I said I didn't even know there were male Witches, but I was eager to learn. I realized I didn't know how a Witch would sign off, so I quoted the Donovan song "Season of the Witch"—the part about picking up every stitch—to approximate, as closely as I could, what a Witch might say.

I received a reply on May 27, 1977. Stephen told me I could call him "Robin Goodfellow." Not only was it his "Witch name," but he used it legally, and it was even how he was listed in the phonebook. His letter was helpful, thoughtful, and detailed. He explained that Witches didn't ever attempt to convert others, but since I was the one who'd contacted him, and since he sensed my sincerity, he would try to help me.

He gave me an enormous amount of information. He included addresses for Witches I might try to write to, including fairly well-known Pagans such as Margot Adler, Leo Martello, Raymond Buckland, Starhawk, and Z Budapest. At the time, I had no idea what luminaries I was contacting! He listed a number of books for me to read, and discussed the philosophy of Wicca, mentioned some different traditions, and walked me through some of what happened when his coven met. I look back in awe at the effort he went to for a sixteen-year-old stranger. He even explained that a Witch uses "Blessed be" for hello and good-bye, and signed his letter that way. Across the back of the envelope he wrote, "I've picked up every stitch ... so has Donovan."

Some of what he described was "the cone of power," the use of "sky-clad," the principle of "harm none," the use of sacred sexual energy in ritual, the kiss of greeting, the idea of not judging, the idea of different traditions and different ways of practice all being good, and more.

Wow! I was floored, and said in my diary that I really believed Wicca was for me. I sat down that day and began writing letters.

The most exciting connection that Robin sent was Margot Adler. Margot, who today is a journalist on NPR radio, had a show on WBAI radio in New York at the time. WBAI was and still is freeform, listener sponsored, and kind of wild. My mother, an inveterate fan of talk radio, used to listen to Margot's show every day. It was an afternoon show, so I often heard it on the kitchen radio when I got home from school.

I recalled, in my letter to Margot, the time that she was on the radio wishing that she was on a boat, and asked any listener who was on a boat to call and describe it to her. Amazingly, someone did call.

Margot's response to me was warm, but she had only one contact to send to me, and she was about to leave town for some months. She suggested we meet when she got back.

Unfortunately, my search at that point fizzled out. I wrote a dozen or more letters and made several phone calls. I received catalogs for candles and spell kits, and solicitations to spend the weekend with men I didn't know, but usually I received no answer at all. It was all very disappointing. I wrote to Robin again, and he commiserated with me and suggested that I keep at it. He also gave me more information about ritual and the Craft.

My life was about to change a lot. I had gotten involved with a civil rights case that got media attention. As a result, my phone rang off the hook. One call was from a man named Ronnie Keane Jr. On the phone, Ronnie was flirtatious and engaging, and I agreed to meet him.

We had our first date on July 4, 1977. We lived in different towns in New Jersey, and neither of us had a car (I didn't have a license), so we met at the Port Authority Bus Terminal in New York City. In 1977, Times Square was full of huge old-fashioned movie palaces, porn, street hustlers, and greasy spoons. We saw *Star Wars* and got something to eat, then went to a different theater and saw *Annie Hall*. Next we went to Central Park and hung around, getting to know each other.

So, now I had a boyfriend. I wasn't head over heels from the start, and in retrospect I think the idea of being in love, and the whole *sturm und drang* of it, was as appealing as the man himself. But Ronnie was definitely seductive, attractive, smart, and different. He was also twenty-three years old, and, as any sixteen-year-old girl will tell you, *wow,* that's hot.

However, Ronnie was absolutely terrified of Witchcraft, and begged me to drop my quest.

He had a story about having been kidnapped, which was really scary, but I couldn't figure out why he connected it to Witchcraft. I guess the crazy person who'd tried to kidnap him was involved, in some way, with the occult, but I could tell even secondhand that it had nothing to do with the occult I was seeking. Yet Ronnie was insistent, and I wasn't as good then as I am now at not being manipulated. My letter writing and phone calling weren't yielding fruit anyway, so I stopped looking for Witches. I never recontacted Margot after she returned from her travels, and I stopped writing to Robin Goodfellow.

Ronnie and I had a tumultuous relationship. It took me a long time to understand that he was an alcoholic. No one in my family drank. I knew there was such a thing as social drinking, but I didn't have any firsthand experience of it, so I didn't know how to distinguish it from problem drinking. Ronnie's drinking was definitely a problem. There were times when he terrified me, but he always stopped short of doing anything that would push me permanently away. There was one night he was so angry that he punched the bed an inch from my face. Yet I couldn't say he'd hit me. I didn't know how to measure the way he terrorized me, or even how to define it as that.

I graduated from high school at the top of my class. My career goal at that time was to become a midwife. There was a program in Texas that seemed to be exactly what I wanted, but I'd never been far from home on my own before, I didn't know how to get it together to do that, I couldn't figure out how to move myself out there, my parents offered no help, and I had a boyfriend in New Jersey. The easiest thing was to stay, so I attended nursing school in New Jersey. I moved out of my parents' home and in with Ronnie as my permanent residence, and also lived in the dorm.

In nursing school I gradually discovered that my dream of midwifery wasn't going to translate into reality. I am simply not a hands-on, earth-mother type. I thought I was. I *always* thought I was, and that misconception of myself has led me down some strange paths. I would fantasize that I was all Earth Goddess, growing my garden and raising babies, in flowing skirts and sensible shoes, but the reality is that I like to read and write and disconnect from the physical realm for long stretches of time. I am definitely earthy; I'm a Taurus with a Capricorn Moon, for goodness' sake! But I need to balance body, mind, and heart. If I don't give each its due, I become restless and unhappy. As a nursing student, I was walking a path that was too physical, too body-heart, and it wasn't right for me.

Meanwhile, I was discovering that Ronnie's drinking was a destructive force that wasn't normal and wasn't okay. I broke up with him over Thanksgiving break and moved myself entirely into the dorm. He became frantic, calling constantly and harassing the entire dorm. (Back then, pre-cellphones, a dorm would have a public phone for use by all students, so the ringing of the phone all night would disrupt everyone.)

As spring came, just as I was deciding to leave nursing school, Ronnie was getting off the booze. He'd actually gone to my father for help drying out, and once he was no longer drinking, he set out to win me back.

Things moved very fast. Ronnie "sober" (really more like "dry") put all his energy into wooing me and proving to me that he had changed. I knew it was time to leave nursing school and figure out what to do next. By May, Ronnie and I were engaged to be married, and I had left school. I was also working three part-time jobs and planning a wedding.

On July 4, 1980 (our anniversary), Ronnie and I were married at my father's home.

A 1977 Book List

Here are the books that Robin Goodfellow recommended, in the original order he wrote them in his letter. Every one of these was also on the book list of the group I eventually joined.

Witchcraft Today, The Meaning of Witchcraft, and *High Magic's Aid* by Gerald B. Gardner

The Book of Shadows, by Lady Sheba

Woman's Mysteries: Ancient and Modern, by M. Esther Harding

The Great Mother: An Analysis of the Archetype, by Erich Neumann

Witches: The Investigation of an Ancient Religion, by T. C. Lethbridge

Witches U.S.A., by Susan Roberts

What Witches Do: The Modern Coven Revealed, by Stewart Farrar

An ABC of Witchcraft Past and Present, Natural Magic, and *Where Witchcraft Lives*, by Doreen Valiente

Any books by Dion Fortune

The White Goddess, by Robert Graves

Any books by W. E. Butler

Real Magic, by Philip Emmons Isaac Bonewits

Aradia, or The Gospel of the Witches, by Charles G. Leland

Mastering Witchcraft: A Practical Guide for Witches, by Paul Huson

Witchcraft: The Old Religion, by Dr. Leo Louis Martello

The God of the Witches and *The Witch-Cult in Western Europe*, by Margaret A. Murray

Chapter 3

SUSAN

July 4, 1980: Mom, me, and Nana Ann on my wedding day

This letter is in response to a letter you wrote Theos,
in Commack, L.I., regarding the Craft...
(I am a Gardnerian—and have been in the Craft
over 10 years—just in case you need to know
who is writing to you.)
—*From a letter from Susan C., October 24, 1981*

My marriage was a disaster within weeks, maybe sooner.

It quickly became apparent that the main difference between Ronnie wet and Ronnie dry was that dry was less predictable. It seemed to me that, in his drinking days, I could tell more or less how an encounter with him would go: pretty well if he was sober, pretty badly otherwise. He had two different personalities, the one I loved and the one who drank. But now, either persona could appear at any time. His behavior was explosive, sulky, and arbitrary, and I was constantly on guard for shifts in mood. I was in hell.

We'd been married less than a year when I decided I had to leave. It took some planning. The first thing I had to do was get a driver's license, which I'd failed to do in high school. Once that was accomplished, it was a matter of getting my mother to help me move my things out, as well as seeing a lawyer. I did all of this covertly (not the driver's license—he knew about that—but the planning). Perhaps I could have confronted him, but I was frightened. Looking back, I know that I was badly treated, and I had good reason to be afraid. I also know that I was twenty and ill-equipped for personal confrontation. My friends thought of me as assertive, strong, and outspoken, and in many situations that was certainly true. But I also allowed myself to be swallowed up by fear, which wasn't Ronnie's fault. I was as afraid of being manipulated into staying as I was of anything else. In addition to my earthy Sun and Moon, I have a Scorpio Ascendant. Like a scorpion, I have the ability to strike from behind, and that's how I ended my first marriage: by sneaking out rather than facing the confrontation honestly.

Ronnie and I often went to bookstores, to browse or buy. While he perused science fiction, I would go to the New Age / occult section and stare at the titles. Many of the books looked lurid and unsavory. *The Magic Power of Witchcraft* by Gavin and Yvonne Frost had drippy, *Chiller Theater* lettering. *Psychic Self-Defense* by Dion Fortune had a glowing eye, and why did I need self-defense anyway? I had long since forgotten the book list from Robin Goodfellow. I didn't know how to discern good information from bad. It felt like the books in the store were con jobs, and I was an easy mark.

But in the fall of 1981, with my packing already begun, I came across *Drawing Down the Moon* by Margot Adler. Here was a book I could trust, because I knew the author! Knowing that I was leaving Ronnie, I no longer cared about his disapproval. He stared black death at me as I paid for the book, but I didn't let him stop me.

I didn't just read *Drawing Down the Moon,* I swallowed it whole. I had found the Witches I'd been looking for!

Drawing Down the Moon is a remarkable book. For twenty years or more, it was the only one of its kind, a "buyer's guide" to the Pagan community. Today it's joined by a number of other titles, but it's still unique, and for me, it was uniquely helpful.

In addition to providing a smart introduction to Wicca and Paganism, Margot gave me a tour of the variety of Pagans out there. In it, I found Wiccans of a variety of traditions, including Gardnerian, Alexandrian, NROOGD (New Reformed Orthodox Order of the Golden Dawn), traditionalist, Victor Anderson's Faery faith, plus Dianics of several types, including feminist, women-only Dianics, and mixed groups. There were also the Church of All Worlds, the Reformed Druids of North America, Feraferia, several Reconstructionist groups, and even the Discordians.

Because the book was primarily journalism, combining exposition and interviews, I felt like I was getting to know these people. Because it presented so many different styles of Paganism, I felt like I was being invited to choose.

SOME "BUYER'S GUIDE" BOOKS

Here are some books that introduce the reader to the Pagan community, including the one that I first read by Margot Adler. If you are looking for the kind of overview I found so helpful in 1981, any or all of these are a good place to start.

Drawing Down the Moon: Witches, Druids, Goddess-Worshippers, and Other Pagans in America Today, by Margot Adler

Modern Pagans: An Investigation of Contemporary Pagan Practices, by John Sulak and V. Vale

Being a Pagan: Druids, Wiccans, and Witches Today, by Ellen Evert Hopman

Paganism: An Introduction to Earth-Centered Religions, by Joyce and River Higginbotham

The more I read, the more certain I became that Gardnerian Wicca was for me. I wanted ritual with structure, knowledge, and tradition behind it. I enjoyed reading about the Church of All Worlds, and the idea that making up your own Paganism was not only allowed but sacred, but as far as I was concerned, I'd already tried making it up on my own, and that hadn't gotten me very far. I couldn't really see learning from someone who'd done the same.

Maybe that was an unsophisticated view. To make it all up successfully, you need a great deal of creativity, an eye for research sources (which, remember, was much harder before the Internet), and a lot of practice. You also need personal honesty, so when something doesn't work, you can honestly say to yourself, "That ritual sucked," and try something different next time. Without that forthright honesty, practice can never make perfect. At the time, I didn't think through what it was that might make a self-created practice really work. I only knew that it hadn't worked for me, and I didn't care to dive back into that pool.

Gardnerian Craft teaches polarity: that the universe is created, divided, and energized by great polar forces, and that magical power can be derived by using that polar energy. God and Goddess, male and female, light and dark, winter and summer, youth and age: polar forces support, create, transform, and empower each other. We do ritual by dividing the poles and bringing them together—for example, by separating male and female roles, and then ritually uniting them. In all cases, each "opposite" also contains the other. Each pole exists in relation to its counterpart, so that gray is the dark counterpoint to white, but is the light counterpoint to black. Indeed, most polar opposites are actually simply the extreme end points of a long continuum. We use the polar extremes as a magical tool, but they shouldn't limit our perception of reality.

One of the great polarities of the universe is order and chaos. At its best, order is foundation, support, sanity, and structure; at its worst, it's tyranny and stagnation. At its best, chaos is freedom, spontaneity, creativity, and openness; at its worst, it's insanity and messiness. In Paganism, you might call these poles Apollonian and Dionysian. Most people think of Pagan religions as Dionysian in nature—ecstatic, chaotic, and wanton—but in fact, there are paths all along the spectrum.

As individuals, none of us is entirely orderly or entirely chaotic, but most of us have a leaning toward one pole or the other. As kids, some of us were busily making rules (*Don't step on the crack!*), and some of us were busy breaking them (*Cut off G.I. Joe's head!*). I've always been on the side of order, rule making, and structure (and again, I point out my Taurus Sun and Capricorn Moon, signs that orient me toward the solid, the traditional, and the stable).

In Gardnerian Witchcraft, I saw stability, structure, history, and order. It was exactly what I was looking for. Lady Theos, quoted throughout *Drawing Down the Moon* as a Gardnerian source, was one of the voices that resonated most with me while reading. At the back of the book was a resources section, and there I found Theos's address.[1] When I saw that she was more or less local, and that hers was the only address in the eastern half of the United States, it felt like synchronicity, like the bell that rings when things fall into place in just the right way.

I wrote to Theos, who forwarded my letter to Susan C. in New Jersey. At the end of October, I received the letter quoted at the beginning of this chapter, as well as an application to Susan's group. I filled out the application and sent it back immediately, a little embarrassed that I had listed only one book in the "what books have you read" section.

On December 5, 1981, I attended my first Pagan circle, at the Jersey Shore Pagan Way, in Asbury Park, New Jersey.

From the first, I felt at home. I knew it was weird, and yet, it also wasn't. I knew there were robes and knives and candles and incense, and yet, in my journal, I compared it to a ritual at a church, where at least the candles and incense would fit right in.

A day or two before Thanksgiving of 1981, I moved in with Mom in Ridgewood away from my home with Ronnie in New Brunswick. She'd driven to meet me as soon as Ronnie had left for work. We loaded up both her car and Ronnie's with as much of my stuff as would fit, drove to her place (almost an hour away), unloaded, drove back, loaded her car once more, and departed. I'd left Ronnie only a note. For years afterwards, Mom pined for the beautiful antique chairs she'd given me that we'd been unable to fit; they stayed with Ronnie. It wasn't until after I had moved that I attended Susan's circle.

I'd been dating a controlling alcoholic since I was sixteen years old, so in addition to learning Wicca, I was also sowing some long-repressed wild oats. Ronnie didn't like to go out, mostly, I learned later, because he didn't like people to see how much he drank. Now I was free and twenty (which was legal age for drinking at the time) and living not just with my mother but also with my sixteen-year-old sister. Roberta and I hadn't had much of a relationship before, but we became very close and were able to go out and have fun together. We went to the *Rocky Horror*

---

1. I read the first paperback edition of Margot Adler's *Drawing Down the Moon*, published in 1981. In the 1986 and subsequent editions, Theos was no longer listed.

Picture Show in Greenwich Village, and I dated a lot, volunteered, went to the occasional nightclub, and traveled to the Jersey Shore Pagan Way about twice a month.

When I was in nursing school, during the five months or so that Ronnie and I had been apart, I had dated quite a bit. There was one guy named Bob whom I had seen quite often, although it had never been serious. Shortly after I left Ronnie, I called Bob. I think I was lonely and looking for a little feminine validation. I drove about an hour to see Bob, and probably knew it was a mistake before I got back home later that night. I regretted calling him, I regretted seeing him, I regretted sleeping with him. I felt *dirty*. I was overwhelmed by feelings of remorse and self-hatred.

In the back of *Drawing Down the Moon* was something called "The Self-Blessing Ritual" by Ed Fitch, himself a Pagan author and Gardnerian High Priest. It was probably the first structured ritual I ever performed on my own. I put together the ingredients with care and trepidation, feeling desperate for the spell to work. Afterwards, I felt renewed, purified, and at peace. It was an awakening to the power that a simple ritual can have. I reprint it here with Ed Fitch's permission.

SELF-BLESSING

This ritual should be performed during the New Moon, but it is not limited to that phase. Need, not season, determines the performance. There is real power in the Self-Blessing; it should not be used other than in time of need and should not be done promiscuously.

The purpose of the ritual is to bring the individual into closer contact with the Godhead. It can also be used as a minor dedication, when a person who desires dedication has no one who can dedicate him. This self-blessing ritual may also be used as a minor exorcism, to banish any evil influences that may have formed around the person. It may be performed by any person upon himself, and at his desire.

Perform the ritual in a quiet place, free from distractions, and nude. You will need the following:

- Salt, about ¼ teaspoon
- Wine, about 1 ounce

- Water, about ½ ounce
- Candle, votive or other

The result of this ritual is a feeling of peace and calm. It is desirable that the participant bask in the afterglow so that he may meditate and understand that he has called the attention of the Godhead to himself, asking to grow closer to the Godhead in both goals and in wisdom.

When you are ready to begin, sprinkle the salt on the floor and stand on it, then light the candle. Let the warmth of the candle be absorbed into the body. Mix the water into the wine, meditating upon your reasons for performing the self-blessing.

Read the following aloud:

Bless me, Mother, for I am your child.

Dip the fingers of the right hand into the mixed water and wine, and anoint the eyes:

Blessed be my eyes, that I may see your path.

Anoint the nose:

Blessed be my nose, that I may breathe your essence.

Anoint the mouth:

Blessed be my mouth, that I may speak of you.

Anoint the breast:

Blessed be my breast, that I may be faithful in my work.

Anoint the loins:

Blessed be my loins, which bring forth the life of men and women as you have brought forth all creation.

Anoint the feet:

Blessed be my feet, that I may walk in your ways.

Remain ... and meditate for a while.

The Pagan Way tradition got started in 1969, as a form of Pagan ritual available to non-initiates, and was created by Ed Fitch, Joseph Wilson, Tony Kelly, and a number of others. It was intended for those who weren't interested in initiation or weren't really candidates for some reason. Fitch also created an "Outer Court Book of Shadows," to be used as training material for Pagans prior to initiation. While the Pagan Way was a set of simple rituals, the Outer Court was more structured and serious, and actually took members through three degrees of Outer Court initiation, presumably prior to their "Inner Court" (Gardnerian) first degree.

Susan used the Pagan Way material, and called her group a Pagan Way, but in some ways it was much more like an Outer Court, as at least half the members at any given time were serious candidates for initiation.

Prior to the existence of the Pagan Way and Outer Court rituals, there was really no way for an initiated Witch to introduce a prospective initiate to the ritual experience. Covens would often hold classes—in dream interpretation, Tarot, the Kabbalah, or the like—in order to meet candidates, and if the person was suitable, he or she was initiated. In that system, your initiation would be the first Wiccan circle you'd ever been inside of. A first degree was a rank beginner, and second degree was the mark of a mature person in the Craft.

The Pagan Way changed all that. Now, Pagans (which is what a Gardnerian calls a non-initiate—we discourage such people from calling themselves "Witch"; the word means many things, but in our tradition it means "initiate") could learn ritual. They could learn the technology of the magic circle, the nature of the magical tools, how energy moves, and the meaning of the holidays, and they could be in the presence of the Gods. Ultimately, it also meant that the people initiated into a coven were more experienced and more mature; the people to whom Susan gave first degree may well have had the equivalent of a second degree's knowledge and training, judging by past standards.

Both the Pagan Way and Outer Court rituals and rules got passed around, Xerox to Xerox, mimeograph to mimeograph, with various teachers adding, subtracting, and making changes. During the course of our training, we were given copies of the Jersey Shore Pagan Way's rituals only if we were going to be performing the rite (students would lead the holidays, and Susan and her partner would lead regular meetings). We were also given quite a lot of material that Susan had photocopied or typed from a variety of sources—the Pagan Way materials, books, Pagan magazines, and more. At every meeting there were handouts, which we put in our Pagan "Book of Shadows." Susan also had an "Outer Court Book," which was actually several different iterations of the original Outer Court Book, and which she gave to serious students. It was about three inches thick, and some of the pages were so faded (copies of copies of copies) as to be barely legible. Early in my training, I volunteered to retype the whole thing. I type about ninety words per minute when I get a head of steam up, and, working as a secretary in a quiet office, I often had time to type personal projects. I typed about three hundred pages and bound several copies. Typing the material repeatedly really drove it into my head!

My second ritual was Yule. (As I said, the group met approximately twice a month, so this was the second December meeting.) Susan called and asked if I'd give a ride to a friend of hers who lived near me. When I picked up Tim, he asked if we could stop for a six-pack, and by the time we arrived at Asbury Park an hour and a half later, he'd already finished four beers.

Tim's drinking really freaked me out. I had only just escaped from a terrible marriage to an alcoholic, and I wasn't ready to be around that kind of drinking. The ritual was great, but Tim was sauced; he put out a cigarette in an appetizer and passed out in circle. Late that night, before crashing on the floor of the ritual room, I said fervently to another member of the group that I never wanted to see Tim again.

I never did. Tim left before I got up the next morning. (I don't recall if he got a ride from someone else or if he took public transportation.) Soon thereafter, he moved to Alaska. I don't tell this story to judge Tim; he and Susan stayed in touch, and she thought fondly of him. Maybe he had a serious drinking problem, maybe it was just one bad night, or maybe I overreacted. No, the part of this story that is so memorable to me is the accidental magic.

I've encountered true accidental magic only a few times, but often enough to realize it's not exactly rare. It happens only in the heat of the moment, when you feel something with passionate intensity and no thought at all. A perfect, clear desire forms in your mind, and your emotion sends it exactly where it needs to go.

In practicing magic, we learn a great many techniques for emptying the mind of rational thought, for generating intense emotion, for concentrating perfectly on one exact image, and for figuring out exactly where to send that image so it will manifest our goals. But sometimes an intense desire will be felt upon an alignment of all of those factors, and the goal will be achieved. I wonder, indeed, if incidents of accidental magic didn't cause our ancestors to study how magic works. We often assume that magical techniques were derived from magical theory, but inventions often copy nature. We see the webbed feet of ducks and swans, and devise swim fins. We study the way a maple pod spins as it lands, and invent the helicopter. We see the way a thistle burr holds on, and Velcro is the eventual result. So maybe these instances of desire becoming manifest were studied by mages and distilled into their component parts: intense emotion, absolute concentration, and clear visualization.

After spending time with Tim, I intensely, clearly, and without equivocation wanted to *never see that man again*. My second husband always placed great store in the beginner's luck of a new magician, so I guess I had that on my side as well, although I recall a lot of botched spells in my early days.

At the end of January 1982, a family friend had a baby who was born with heart problems. I decided to do a spell to help her.

I had been a member of a Pagan group for all of two months. I had so far acquired very few magical tools. It is commonplace to say that you need no tools except your mind, and that's true … sort of. You don't need a boat to cross a river; you can swim. You don't need a door to get into a house; you can climb through the window, or just hurl yourself into the wall over and over until you break through. But tools help *a lot*.

Ask actors if a costume helps them get into character, and they'll say, "Absolutely!" Especially in a period piece like *Mad Men* or *Deadwood*, the costumes tell the actors who and where they are, which makes acting much easier. Costumes, props, and stage sets help actors, and tools, robes, and ritual help magicians.

Susan strongly encouraged us to do solitary ritual, and I was urgently trying to get it right. I'd spent all those years knowing I wanted to be Wiccan and not knowing how. Susan had provided a pages-long reading list, and I was gobbling up as much information as I could. I'd found a teacher who loved getting it right as well; the difference between a well-performed ritual and a haphazard one was crucial to Susan. We learned proper ritual behavior, including how to respect the boundaries of the circle, and to never leave the circle unless a proper gate was cut. We learned the symbolic meaning of the ritual tools, and were encouraged to find or make our own. We learned why to choose a Pagan name, why to wear a robe, and how to make a robe (there was at least one sewing day that first year). We learned meditation and pathworking, ethics and divination.

At our very first meeting, Susan read my cards, then handed me the Tarot deck and had me read hers. Thus began a lifelong relationship with the Tarot. I was raised in a family of card sharks; all the Lipps are card players. From childhood Go Fish we progressed to Gin Rummy and Hearts. We grew up with Double Solitaire, Spit, 500 Rummy, Oh Hell, and I Doubt It, among many other games. Cards feel natural in my hands. In addition to my other studies, I worked diligently at learning the meaning of the cards flashcard-style—intuition is important, but the memorization has to come first!

For my healing ritual, I didn't have an altar, so I arranged everything nicely on the floor. The things I had were all small, so they fit nicely in a corner. I had a tiny cup made of soapstone, which is woefully impractical for drinking out of, but is useful as a Water dish for a solitary circle. Stick incense gave me Fire and Air, and a geode was my Earth. I used a multi-day ritual from a book on my reading list. The only thing was, after I'd finished, I realized that I had no idea where the points of the compass were from that spot. When I figured it out, I saw that I'd done the circle exactly backwards. I was horrified. The baby was no better, and Susan told me to do the spell again. Today, that baby is a grown and healthy young woman, but I can't take any credit for that!

I drove the hour and a half "down the Shore" (as we say in New Jersey) every other Saturday night. The Garden State Parkway at one or two or three AM for the trip home was deserted, and it wasn't long before I nodded off behind the wheel and had to jolt myself awake. After that, I routinely slept on Susan's couch.

In a lot of ways, that decision, a purely practical one, had a profound magical effect. I learned a lot in class and ritual. Susan thought it was important to spend as much time as possible in sacred space, so, in addition to a class before ritual, a lot of teaching was done in circle; we might discuss what a guided meditation was before ritual, then in circle we'd actually participate in one. Susan favored a Socratic approach to teaching; she'd ask us questions to see what we came up with. No matter what was asked, her favorite response was, "What do *you* think?" Nonetheless, she conveyed a great deal of solid information, and she was often quite strict, which suited me fine.

But over breakfast, it was another story entirely. Susan and I would often go to a local restaurant for a late breakfast, then maybe hit a flea market (Collingswood or Englishtown). She would tell funny stories about other Pagans and Witches, gossip about people and rituals, talk about spells that had gone hilariously wrong or bizarrely right, and muse over her own decisions as a High Priestess. I would have the chance to ask questions I hadn't thought of in class. At the flea market, I might find a cool object, and we'd discuss using it in ritual, and why it might be suitable as such-and-such a tool but not for this or that. It was like a second education on top of the formal classes, and I soaked it all up.

I was lying to my mother about what I was doing at the Shore with my friend Susan. Looking back, I don't know if she would have objected then, or been freaked out, or what. She's certainly fine with it now, and proud of my success as an author. It was simply very hard to tell anyone in those days. I have never liked lying, and I'm not terribly good at it, but it was such a huge leap to take with people. Today, when I meet people and tell them I'm Wiccan, nine times out of ten they've heard of it, and usually know someone else who is or was involved with Paganism in some way, but in 1982, it was more like, steel yourself for a discussion on Satanism. I remember that there was a woman I volunteered with, and when I told her I was a Witch, she said, "I always thought that was evil, but if you're involved, it must be good, so tell me more." I was so touched by that, by her faith in me and her willingness to listen. But it was also true that, even in the more tolerant Northeast, people usually assumed that Wicca was evil, and that was a hard thing to face up to.

I was having huge fun in the Jersey Shore group, as well as learning and worshiping. Susan had a knack for gathering people around her. There were barbecues, road trips, and other events as well as ritual.

The first weekend of April, Susan took me to my first Pagan festival. She had, as I said, a terrific ability to organize that I will always envy. If I tell my coven that I'm going to a festival and suggest that we all go together, not only do I end up going alone, but I can't even get them to feed my cats! But when Susan said, "Let's all go to a festival," by the Gods, her van was full of people.

The event (now defunct) was in upstate New York, near Kingston. The weather was cold—it actually snowed—but there were indoor bunks as well as tenting areas, and people who were tenting piled into the building to get out of the snow.

Susan struck up a conversation with a guy named Steve Ritholtz, who had black hair, thick eyebrows, a beard, and a mustache—the very picture of a New York occultist—and she pulled me over to join in. He was the High Priest of a Wiccan group in the New York area, and some of his people were there as well. Because of the snow and the makeshift indoor accommodations, it was crowded and cozy. We drank into the night. At one point, Susan pointed at me and said to Steve, "She's the one who's going to exceed me. She's the student who is better than the teacher." I was stunned. I'm pretty sure I blushed.

I was initiated as a first-degree Gardnerian a week later, Easter weekend: April 10, 1982. It was three weeks before my twenty-first birthday.

Chapter 4

ISIS, ASTARTE

1982: Photo taken in Ridgewood, NJ, by John Shaffrey

Isis, Astarte, Diana, Hecate, Demeter, Kali, Inanna!
—*Goddess Chant, by Deena Metzger*

My initiation did not go well. Well, that's not quite true. No candles got knocked over, no smoke alarms went off, and no charcoals exploded, sending hot coals scuttling over bare skin. I've been in rituals where each of those has happened, but my initiation wasn't one of them.

There was a moment I will never forget. Before you can enter your initiatory circle, you are challenged, and you must say that you are prepared to endure whatever comes next. In that moment, as I was challenged, I thought, "I have a choice. I can say no." I wasn't taught that beforehand, and the guide who led me in and told me what to say didn't tell me that, yet it dawned on me during the challenge, and it remains always with me: I chose. I said yes. In fact, my guide said I would hear a certain phrase and I should respond with "I do." Today, I instruct guides (the High Priestess herself wouldn't be the guide during an initiation) to say to people, "You will be asked a question. Answer yes or no," without coaching people on the answer. I want them to have the same choice I did.

Despite that moment, afterwards I felt like it didn't "take." I felt no different, and the ritual felt … ordinary, somehow. During the rite, my mind never stopped analyzing what was happening—I never felt a silence of mind. In the years since, I've learned not to worry about the "monkey brain," or ego mind, and what it's thinking. Chattering thoughts will tell me that I'm not in a trance, or I'm just faking, or nothing's happening here. They're just chatter and have no meaning. It's like those stage hypnotists who ask people if they're hypnotized, and the people say, "Not at all. It didn't work on me," and then he gets them to do ridiculous things. The ego mind is that "It didn't work on me" voice, and is every bit as accurate! I didn't know that then, and I didn't trust myself.

I was not yet twenty-one. I had already left a marriage, left school, and left a career choice. I was afraid I was a person who was good at leaving and not good at sticking around. I was afraid I would leave the Craft.

For Beltane, we accepted an invitation from Steve Ritholtz's group. As an initiate, I was attending both the Outer Court Pagan circles and the Inner Court coven circles. Susan taught me to take Pagan circles seriously. There certainly were (and are) people in the Craft who said that if a circle was "just Pagan," it didn't count, but she felt that we were doing magic, we were invoking gods, and we should be as reverent, conscientious, and creative as we were in the coven. In fact, Pagan circles were often *more* creative. In the coven, we studied the Mysteries, worked with inherited materials, and dug deep into esoterica. Much of that material, though, was covered by our oath of secrecy, and we couldn't use it in the Pagan Way. Without access to the esoteric, oath-bound secrets, we were left to our research and imagination to spice things up. We students were all encouraged to write and lead our own rituals; in fact, that was part of our training.

We were also expected to learn from a wide variety of sources. Susan would add bad or contradictory books to the reading list if they had some good material or if they provided good food for thought. She'd distribute handouts with no explanation as to why they were part of our studies, to see if anyone asked. She also wanted us to learn from other Pagans. To that end, she wanted us to attend festivals, and was eager to accept invitations from other groups, like Maxine and Steve's. (Students were required to get *permission* to attend another group's rituals, though.)

Maxine dazzled me. This was my first exposure to another High Priestess doing her thing. I'd been in circles run by students (including myself) functioning as High Priestess *du jour,* and I'd met priestesses when they were off-duty, but this was different.

One thing I took note of was that Maxine took some time to herself before circle, some "do not disturb" time. And when she came back downstairs, not only was she robed for ritual, but she had a full face of makeup and was glammed to the max. I was impressed.

She also said something to me that I still repeat: "Everyone should have a protection spell memorized." It was excellent advice. When I got home, I memorized a spell that I had in my Gardnerian Book of Shadows, which I use to this day. One time, when Susan heard me quoting Maxine, she joked, "How come I never hear you quoting any of the things *I've* said to you?"

Most Beltane gatherings follow the same pattern: a maypole and perhaps other festivities, then a meal, then a more formal ritual. Since this one was held indoors, a fifteen-foot pole was out of the question, but we made do with a May dance around a smaller version. The dance had women going in one direction and men in the other, and when we met, we'd kiss. I was enjoying myself and feeling my oats, and began experimenting with kisses that were more than a peck. It was a little scary, but I felt powerful and sexy.

When we talk about "sacred sexuality" in Paganism, people often think that means intercourse, or orgies, or both. Maybe for some people it does, in some cases, but that's not really the point. Sexuality is an inherent quality of all human beings, and is sacred in all its forms.

If I say to you that intelligence is sacred, you don't assume that means it's sacred only when someone is very smart, or only when someone is actively thinking deep thoughts. Intelligence is part of a human being; even when that human being is zoned out and staring at the TV, or asleep, that person still has intelligence. Just so, that person has sexuality even when celibate. Sacred sexuality is the celebration of the sacredness of the wonderful, erotic life force that flows through us.

I had no intention of sleeping with any of the several men I kissed that day; rather, I was honoring the sexuality of the Beltane season, I was honoring the erotic within myself, and I was having *fun.* We sometimes get so critical of people's sexuality, particularly when it's freely given, particularly by women, that we forget it's supposed to feel good. It was a wonderful experience for me to explore that way, and there were no negative repercussions.

After the dance, there was a break, and people got ready for the ritual. I was looking forward to experiencing Maxine's circle. Unfortunately, that never happened.

From the time I was twelve until my mid-thirties, I had low blood pressure that would sometimes drop precipitously—and me with it. That is, I'd faint. Steve and Maxine's ritual space was an enclosed room, maybe twelve by twelve, and it was holding twice its usual complement. Then the smoky incense got going. Before the quarters had all been called, someone caught me on my way to the ground, and I was escorted out of the ritual to lie down on the couch. It was embarrassing and disappointing, but I had a good time anyway.

A Protection Spell

I can't share the oathbound protection spell I have memorized, but I can offer this one.

Start by drawing a circle around yourself, clockwise, with your athame, index finger, or mind. Say:

In the name of the Lady,

Visualize protective white light coming from beneath your feet and surrounding your entire body. Say:

In the name of the Lord,

Visualize protective white light coming from above your head and surrounding your entire body. Say:

I am safe from all harm!
I am safe from all harm!
I am safe from all harm!
What I say three times is true,
So mote it be!

Stamp your foot and clap your hands once.

A few weeks later, a new member joined the Jersey Shore group. Alan was a little older (he had a daughter in her twenties) and worked on a dairy farm. He had use of the land on weekends—I think he was the caretaker of the place. We began having circles at the farm in June. Three huge trees marked quarters at our ritual site, with a lake in the fourth direction (I don't recall which direction the lake was in). These were my first outdoor rituals since joining the group.

At every ritual, after the ceremony of cakes and wine, we'd pass the cup and a libation bowl, make offerings to the Gods, pour the offering into the bowl, and then drink.

The first time we had a ritual at the farm, I looked over the setup. We were going over things carefully, because it was a bit of a walk from the house to the site, and we didn't want to have to go back *again*. I asked Susan where the libation bowl was.

"We don't need one," she said. "We're outdoors."

It hadn't occurred to me—the bowl was to collect the offerings, which we would bring outside later. When the cup came around, and I poured an offering directly onto the Earth for the first time, tingles went up and down my arm. I felt as if I understood something about my religion in a new way. I was still struggling with the fear that I would leave the Craft, but this was a beautiful moment, and in it I felt connected and reverent. It was small, but it was an awakening.

LIBATIONS

I was taught a strict discipline about libations, and I teach the same discipline. Libations are offerings to the Gods, and so should be done with reverence and respect.

- Everything that we consume in sacred space is given first to the Gods. They are our honored guests, and it is rude to drink before offering your honored guests a drink. From the principle that the Gods get the first of everything, the following logic flows:

- Only new food and drink are used. Unopened bottles, uncut cakes, and so forth, are proper offerings. Open food or drink cannot be brought into a circle.
- The first of everything means that when a bottle is first opened, the first sip from that bottle is poured out to the Gods.
- The first of everything means the first time you personally drink (even from a bottle that has already been offered from), you first pour a libation to the Gods.
- The first of everything means the first time you use a cup, you first pour a libation to the Gods. So if everyone shares from the altar cup, then everyone pours, because it's each person's first sip. Then if everyone fills an individual cup, everyone pours again, because that cup has not yet been offered from.
- Libations are for the Gods and the dead. To toast a living person, raise your glass but do not pour.

It's really not complicated once you get the hang of it.

It was in July that we all piled into Susan's van and drove the eight hours to the Starwood Festival. That was Starwood II, and the festival is still an annual event. That year, and for the next three years, Starwood was held at the Whispering Winds Nudist Camp in Devil's Den Park, outside of New Philadelphia, Ohio. (The nearest town was actually Gnadenhutten, which we ultimately gave up attempting to pronounce.)

It took me years to get the hang of protecting my skin at a clothing-optional event. Shortly after we set up camp, a cute guy came along and visited with us, and before long, he was offering me a back rub. Thanks to his kind ministrations, I fell asleep in the sun, and woke up an angry red color. The second year, we all leaped out of the car (eight hours on the road makes you eager to GET OUT), whipped off our shirts, and went hunting for the sunscreen. We put on the sunscreen immediately, but three of us had sunburnt breasts just from the short time it took to find the sunscreen and put it on.

But back to 1982. Other than a burnt back, I was having an outstanding time. If my first circle with the Jersey Shore Pagan Way was a personal homecoming, then my first Starwood was coming home to my community. Although I'd been to one festival before, this one was much larger, both in terms of the number of people (around three hundred, which was huge for a festival at that time—1982 was the embryonic stage of the festival movement) and in terms of physical space (more than two hundred acres). It was hot during the day and mild at night, so there was easy movement around the grounds for meeting people, going to the swimming hole, walking in the woods, exploring caves, attending workshops, and more. Clothing optional has, to me, always been an environment in which one sheds one's psychic barriers along with the physical shield of clothing. I find it opens doors of communication and friendship. Everything felt right.

Susan loved to socialize, but she invariably chose a campsite far away from the main activity. This first time, I didn't know it was her preference, and I just *couldn't believe* how far we had to walk to everything, including the only showers. Because there were a bunch of us, and because we were far off the beaten path (or unbeaten, pathless field), we were able to set up our own little camp town, with a half-dozen or more tents in a rough circle, a central fire, and a kitchen tent—the works. Alan was incredibly handy at camp and placed himself in charge of preparing breakfast and strong morning coffee, which made him beloved.

One of the important educational experiences I had at that Starwood was attending my first bad circle.

The "Devil's Den" part of Devil's Den Park was a gorge with a small waterfall. At the top was a horseshoe-shaped ledge—not narrow or treacherous—surrounding the gorge, with caves accessible from the horseshoe. I attended a ritual held in the gorge, with the circle defined by the horseshoe itself—an exceptionally beautiful setting. The priestess was fairly well known, and there were thirty or forty people standing there.

There were quite a lot of things in the ritual that I thought were incorrect. I realize now that some of them were merely different. Before the festival movement really got going, most people had little to no experience of rituals other than those done in their home circle. It made you firmer in your personal conviction that there was a Right Way to do ritual, and it also made you ignorant of methods to improve your ritual technique. I was a stickler for doing things right. I still am, in a lot of ways, but then I was still the young woman who had searched so hard for a teacher and for an understanding of how to do what I wished to do. Now that I'd found my teacher and my "how to," I was somewhat rigid about it. This was reinforced by the fact that the public Pagan rituals I saw looked very Wiccan. In those days, it seemed that 85 percent of the Pagan community was some form of Wiccan, or modeled their practice after a basic Wiccan circle structure. If what I was seeing had been explicitly something else, such as a Druid or Voodoo ritual, I wouldn't have been so judgmental.

One thing that bothered me about the ritual in the gorge was that, after the east, south, west, and north were greeted, there was no final acknowledgment of the east. Susan called that a pizza with a slice missing; I came to call it a Pac-Man. It was like the circle wasn't whole, and a circle is all about wholeness! That's an error that bothers me as much today as it did then.

Above and beyond my mental criticisms of what was happening, the circle just felt anemic and flat. I began to notice a feeling at my back, like a breeze. I felt open, exposed. I gradually realized what it was: the lack of energy. Prior to that afternoon, had you asked me if I sensed energy during rituals, I would have said no, and indeed, I would have been a bit ashamed of myself. I longed to see and feel all the cool things people talked about—energy and tingling and auras and all that—but I never did. Yet during this ritual I realized that I'd been sensing energy all along; the warmth at my back that I always felt was actually the circle, and this cool breeze I felt now was its absence.

Realizing that gave me a lot more faith in my own abilities. It also gave me a new method for sensing all kinds of non-corporeal things: just look for their absence. I might not always know when I'm acting intuitively or psychically, but I know what it feels like when my intuition isn't working and my psychic abilities have shut down. I know what a bad circle feels like more than I know what a good circle feels like, and I know what danger feels like more than I know what safety feels like. That one bad ritual in the gorge taught me an enormous amount.

Starwood is famous for its Saturday night bonfire. It was a much smaller affair back then, but since I'd never seen the house-size one, I thought it was great.

Here's something that may surprise you: Festivals, even bonfires, didn't have much drumming until the early to mid-1990s. There were, perhaps, a total of three drums at this fire; music was made mostly by chanting.

I stood at the fire, chanting and swaying. I wanted to throw off my clothes and dance around the fire, but another thing that the community hadn't yet worked out was appropriate festival garb. As a result, I was wearing a hooded, over-the-head robe with a light cloak around my neck. I felt tangled up, like, *how am I supposed to get this thing off*? It was far too hot to dance around a fire with those layers on, and I ended up giving up the project and staying where I was, chanting, lost in the fire.

The chant was: *Isis, Astarte, Diana, Hecate, Demeter, Kali, Inanna!* For years afterwards, I thought that "Kali" lasted for about twice the beats it actually does. The name kept extending, stretching, longer and longer: *Isis, Astarte, Diana, Hecate, Demeter, Kaaaaaaaaaaaaaali, Inanna!*

Isis, Astarte, Diana, Hecate, Demeter, Kaaaaaaaaaaaaaaaaaaaaaaaaaaaaaa aaali, Inanna!

And then there she was, filling the sky: Kali, with her many arms, fierce, penetrating eyes, and glorious crown. She was transparent, as if etched on the sky. She was the size of the bonfire, floating above it and looking right at me.

Kali lowered her hands, placed them on my head, and said, "You belong to me. You're mine now."

I don't know how long I stayed at the fire. When the vision ended, it ended, and then I was back to myself—a little bit strangled by the cloak around the neck of my robe, and a little warm, yet still lost in the beauty of the experience. Eventually I went back to camp and to bed.

When I got up the next morning, Alan, already preparing breakfast, took one look at me and said, *"Now* you're initiated."

That's how it went for days, maybe weeks. People would look at me and know I was different. "Did you lose weight?" "Did you get new glasses?" "Did you get a haircut?" Everyone tried to pinpoint how I'd changed, but only I and those closest to me knew that I had changed because my Mother Kali was with me. Even my posture was better. I felt strong.

I knew little of Kali at the time except that she was a Hindu goddess. My studies about her and about Hinduism were inspired by my vision, not the other way around. I was close to being a blank slate that night at the bonfire.

Years later—in 1988 or '89—I visited the New York Ganesh Temple (Sri Maha Vallabha Ganapati Devasthanam), and there was a carved idol of Kali unlike any I'd ever seen. It was exactly as she had appeared in my vision. I burst into tears. I told the temple employees that I'd had a vision of Kali and wanted to learn more about worshiping her. The first man was impressed and brought me to the head Brahmin of the temple, who was more cautious. He questioned me in detail about my vision, and when I was through explaining, he brought me to another Brahmin, saying, "This woman is a chosen daughter of Kali, and we're going to help her." Validation by that Brahmin meant a lot to me, and indeed, he did help me.

I never became a Hindu per se. Worship of Kali became part of my life, but it remained a Wiccan life.

Chapter 5

THE DESCENT OF THE GODDESS INTO THE UNDERWORLD

May 1985: With John Shaffrey

[The Goddess] replied, "I love thee not. Why dost thou cause all things
that I love, and take delight in, to fade and die?"
"Lady," replied Death, "it is age and fate, against which I am helpless."

—*The Legend of the Descent of the Goddess into the Underworld,*
from What Witches Do, *by Stewart Farrar*

I met John Shaffrey on a volunteer team while working on a four-month
project. The team would go to a diner after we were done each week.
When the stint was over, early in 1983, John phoned and asked me out.

We were living in very different worlds. John was a shy computer
professional. He explored self-actualization and New Age ideas, but his
day-to-day life was considerably more "normal" than mine. He was a
geek long before geek was cool. I was working in Manhattan, hanging out with the *Rocky Horror* weirdos, practicing Witchcraft, going to
poetry workshops, and generally living a more youthful and wilder life
than he was, which makes sense, as he was almost twelve years older
than I.

In time, I came to adore him. John was six feet four, with deep blue
eyes, sandy brown hair, and pale Irish skin that turned pink in the sun
or when he laughed. He had a Clark Kent handsomeness about him.
A Virgo, he lived quietly, dressed in slacks and button-down shirts, and
detested medicine and doctors of all kinds. (His father was a doctor,
and it was not a good relationship.) His medicine chest contained a
razor and a bar of soap. Period.

As different as we were, there was something extraordinary between
us, something magical. There was an "us" that we were blessed with.

Both of us believed that our connection was a gift from a higher place, and felt it was important to honor that.

We dated for a short time—perhaps three months. I loved what we had, and I also knew he was the kind of guy I "should" love, but I found myself pulling away. I think, because of our connection and because he looked good on paper, I pushed myself too hard into a relationship, and it backfired.

We went back to being friends, and it was a precious friendship. The sense of blessing never left us, but now, because we'd almost blown it, we were even more careful to honor how we felt about each other and what we had together. We said to each other that there was never anything wrong with "us"; there were just my issues, and his issues, and each of us as individuals with the capacity to damage us. That "us" thing was sacred, and we treated it as such. We saw each other regularly but not often—maybe dinner and drinks every two or three months, plus frequent phone calls. We'd talk about everything, and especially about our inner work. Our love for each other grew.

The work we were each doing in our lives was powerful. Susan was pushing me into more of a leadership role in the Jersey Shore group, with an eye toward having me start my own group. I was also in therapy, and becoming stronger and more self-possessed in a number of ways. John was becoming less shy and, to my observation, far less fragile. He seemed less a hermit and more a person with an introverted nature who wasn't confined by that nature.

I have often recommended therapy for students of the occult, and I've gotten a lot of pushback on that. Some people really object to it, and it's not for everyone, but to me it's important, for a lot of reasons.

Initiation is a rebirth, almost by definition, and what happens is, you go through your entire life cycle in microcosm. You become a child, go through adolescence, mature … the whole deal. Many of the unresolved issues from your life, then, get relived in the context of your occult life. There were times, while I was in therapy, living with Mom and working with the Jersey Shore group, that I would have really negative judgments about Susan. But then I'd realize that I was thinking or feeling the *exact same things* about Mom. Therapy allowed me to see that connection and to place the responsibility for those feelings squarely on my own shoulders. My "mother stuff," projected onto my real and spiritual mothers, was my own problem, not theirs.

It was also true that, as I did this work, I was better able to see intuitively, to sense energy, and more. It seemed like many of my senses were bound up in blocking the things I didn't want to know. We all have some secrets we keep from ourselves, some shadows, fears, or bad memories. But the mind doesn't discriminate; its walls are not delicate or discerning. When I blocked bad memories, some of my senses were too busy blocking stuff to be used for sensing stuff, *and* I was blocking things other than the original target. The more peace I made with my inner demons, the more my magical abilities grew.

Then there's the whole group thing. The drama. The whining. The attention-grabbing, back-biting, schoolyard antics of a group of people who cannot work in harmony, because it's not merely that they're projecting their mommy issues onto the High Priestess, they're actively reliving *all* their family dynamics. The things that go wrong in every workplace and on every team can go wrong in a Pagan group as well, and an understanding of what really motivates people is a powerful tool.

Shortly after John and I ended our romance and became friends, I got involved with another guy, "F." F. was an Italian guy from Brooklyn who was earthy, funny, and sexy. I'd been with a long string of tall intellectuals, and no one really understood my short, blue-collar boyfriend. We had a lot of fun for about a year and a half—fought like crazy, made up like crazy—but in the end it was just a poor match.

John and I saw each other the entire time I was involved with F., and our friendship, though platonic, grew more intimate. I knew that John wanted more than friendship, and was, in a sense, waiting for me, but I was afraid of screwing up and hurting him again.

Not long after F. and I broke up in October 1984, John and I were on the phone, and he told me he was thinking of moving to Arizona.

"Don't leave me," I said.

It was a blurt and a surprise, and we were both silenced for a moment. It didn't take me long to realize that this wasn't something friends said to each other, that it characterized a different sort of relationship. Because we talked about everything, we talked about this. We again talked about honoring what we had, and agreed to maintain the status quo.

Around January, I started reading the book *Seth Speaks* by Jane Roberts. In the 1980s, "channeling" was strangely trendy, with a lot of New Age publishing going on. J. Z. Knight, who channeled an entity named Ramtha, was especially popular. But Jane Roberts predated all of that by twenty years, and her *Seth Material* books were the first of their kind in modern times. Seth was a non-corporeal entity channeled by Roberts. After she wrote two books about Seth based on recordings of him speaking, Seth came through and announced that he was writing a book, and that Jane's husband, Robert, should take notes. That book was *Seth Speaks*.

There was always a fierce divide between the New Age and occult movements, but I found these particular books (which were on the reading list provided by Susan) deeply influential. While reading *Seth Speaks,* I had a series of psychic experiences unlike anything I'd ever known.

By this time, I was living in Queens, New York. One morning, as I was about to leave the apartment, a huge, booming voice spoke from above, saying, "WAIT! DON'T LEAVE!"

I went back, took everything out of my purse that I didn't absolutely need that day (I was one of those New Yorkers who carried everything I owned in my purse), and said, "Can I leave now?" The voice said yes, so I headed off to work.

I was robbed that night.

Somehow, it was the best kind of robbery possible. I sort of blamed myself, as I had left my purse unattended for a few minutes. I got a ride home from someone, since all my subway tokens were gone, and I managed to wake my roommate when I got there, since my keys were gone as well.

When I arrived at work the following morning, all my possessions were sitting on my desk. Someone had found my wallet in a trash can and, since my business cards were in it, had brought the contents of my purse to my office. The only things missing were the purse itself and the cash. I had my ID, my wallet, my keys, and the subway map I carried with me. It was pretty amazing, and I never even got to thank my anonymous Good Samaritan, who was gone before I arrived.

One thing I *didn't* get back was *Seth Speaks*, but my roommate had a copy, so I picked up where I left off. While I looked for a new purse, I temporarily "moved in" to a small purse I used when I traveled.

ANTI-THEFT SPELL

This spell uses a pin to prevent a purse or wallet from being stolen. The pin represents sharpness. The visualization is that, should a thief touch your purse or wallet, OUCH, the thief will be pricked by the magical pin (not the physical pin, which, if set up to prick a thief's hand, would also get *you*). Any thief who comes near your purse or wallet will feel compelled to pull away.

If you're a person who switches bags a lot, you can charge several pins at once and use one for each bag.

This spell requires a great deal of worked-up emotion. You should precede it with meditation, visualization, and maybe additional power-raising (movement, drumming, Om-ing).

Warning: This spell may make your bag unpleasant for anyone other than yourself to hold or carry, so don't plan on having someone go get your bag for you when your hands are full!

1. Consecrate a pin (or one pin per bag/wallet) to the purpose of this spell.

2. Place the pin(s) on the altar, and point your hands or athame at it, saying in a loud, commanding voice:

> *Stop, thief!*
> *You cannot touch!*
> *You cannot approach!*
> *I command you, thief, to stay away!*

It is too sharp to touch!
It is too painful to come near!
No thief can approach!
No thief can come near!
Only I can approach!
Only I can come near!

3. Hold the visualization clearly in your mind, pouring the energy into the pin. You may repeat part or all of the spell as many times as you like. When you are ready, end with:

   So mote it be!

4. Place the pin inside your purse in such a way that it won't prick you or come loose. You might stick it into the leather of the strap or into the zipper pull. It should be there permanently but be pretty much invisible.

Less than a week later, I was visiting my stepfather. I'm not sure why I had my car with me, since that's kind of unusual in Manhattan, but I did. I parked, put my keys in the outside pocket of my purse, and was about to get out of the car when the voice (which I had begun to think of as "Seth") spoke a second time.

"WHERE ARE YOUR KEYS?"

"In my purse, dummy," I replied, and got out, locking the car behind me.

With the keys in it. They had worked their way out of the pocket of my unfamiliar and too-small purse and were on the floor between the driver's seat and the door. Of course, I didn't know that at the time. I had a nice visit with my stepfather, Harvey (ex-stepfather, technically), and realized my keys were missing only when I started to leave, around midnight. I went back in, slept on the couch, and in the morning hailed a cop, knowing that many had slim jims and could break in.

So much for sassy backtalk to non-corporeal entities.

"Seth" spoke to me one last time.

As agreed, John and I were maintaining the status quo. I met some-one and began dating him in a noncommittal way. I had actually told this guy about John, and he was baffled as to why I wasn't with him. But breaking up two and a half years earlier had been incredibly painful, and I didn't want to go through that again. I didn't want to hurt John, or risk what we had.

Valentine's Day 1985 came on a Thursday. I spent the night with my new guy. The next morning, I was walking on Third Avenue toward the subway at Grand Central Terminal when Seth's booming voice filled the sky:

"YOU IDIOT! YOU DON'T WANT *HIM*. YOU WANT *JOHN*."

"All right! Okay!" I said. No more sassing. And by the way, I shouted. Out loud. So that Manhattanites could all see the crazy lady shouting at the voice in her head. Believe me, I knew it was weird, but by now, I'd had plenty of evidence that this voice was worth listening to.

At the very end of *Seth Speaks*, Seth says that he's implanted things in the manuscript so that a person reading it will have experiences of a psychic nature. To which I said, "Aha, knew it all along."

John had planned a wonderful Valentine's Day for us on Saturday. He arrived with a bouquet and a box of chocolate bottles. We had a nice lunch, and then picked up a newspaper. There are places in Man-hattan where you can get the Sunday *New York Times* on Saturday (gen-erally missing the front page but otherwise intact), and that's what we did. The paper was so we could decide what show to see. We had a couple of false starts, failing to get same-day tickets, but then selected *The Fantasticks*.

With several hours on our hands before the show, we went back to my apartment and cuddled up on the couch to do the Sunday cross-word puzzle. He stretched out, and I lay next to him, tucked under his arm so we could both see the puzzle. All of a sudden, the feeling between us shifted, and I said, "If we move *at all*, the status quo is over."

The Fantasticks, known as the "world's longest-running musical," opened at the Sullivan Street Theater in New York City in May of 1960 and closed in 2002. I had seen it at the age of twelve, owned the soundtrack, and adored it. It is, in part, the story of two young lovers whose love is based solely on fantasy and romantic notions of what love is. Their fathers, next-door neighbors, have engineered this romance by feigning a feud, knowing that forbidden love would be irresistible. However, once the "feud" is ended and Luisa and Matt are free to be together, there is no fantasy and the couples break apart. Matt leaves to seek his fortune, and Luisa runs off with a romantic stranger.

In the end, the two return home, both battered, world-weary, and wiser, realizing that the joys they'd sought elsewhere could be found in loving each other. They sing the duet "They Were You" in recognition of this.

Sitting in the theater with John, tears streaming down my face, I knew that this was our story, that I'd sought "rainbows far away" when the thing I wanted was right next to me all the time.

When I told John how I felt, his reaction surprised me. He said that he knew I was the last person he'd ever love, that if we were together, we'd be together forever, and he wasn't sure he was ready for that. Maybe he should sow some wild oats first. After all, I'd been sowing oats left and right, and he hadn't. Wouldn't that be weird? I said I would wait for him.

That was annoying! Here I'd declared my true love to someone who I knew loved me back, and he wanted me to wait! I didn't have to wait long, and within a couple of weeks, we were together.

In some ways, it was idyllic. In others, we were two imperfect people trying to figure out how to be together, and doing an imperfect job of it. Yet our love for each another was profound, and we were exquisitely happy. John told me he intended to marry me, but he wasn't ready to be formally engaged (but yes, I could consider him my "future fiancé").

In February, I did a Tarot reading on our relationship. It had a series of really positive, romantic, balanced cards: the Emperor and the Empress, side by side, the Four of Wands…just great cards all around—until the outcome. I used a layout that had two outcome cards: the outcome, and what follows (the outcome of the outcome, so to speak). The outcome card was the Three of Swords: heartbreak. The "what follows" card was the Nine of Swords: grief.

It didn't make sense. Everything was perfect in the reading; there were no cards leading to sorrow. I decided it was unreadable, put the cards away, and thought nothing of it.

On Tuesday, June 18, John and I attended a New Age workshop that a friend of mine was conducting. She led a guided meditation in which we were told that someone approached us and gave us a gift, a fairly common sort of open-ended instruction allowing the person meditating to find their own path in the meditation journey. In my journey, Anubis, the jackal-headed Egyptian god of the Underworld, approached me, took off his head, and gave it to me.

On Thursday, June 20, I dreamed that I was at John's funeral, wearing a white suit. I was asking people to speak about John, but no one would because they were all too grief-stricken.

On Friday, June 21, 1985, John Shaffrey died of a heart attack. He was thirty-five years old.

Here's one for the list of stupid psychic tricks: My car died at the same moment John did. I had a bad cold and had stayed at John's instead of going to work. I'd driven into town for lunch and was about a quarter mile from John's home when the car just stopped. Unable to get it started, I walked the rest of the way, and planned to call AAA later. When I got to the house, the phone was ringing. It was the hospital telling me to come right away. John was dead on arrival, but they didn't tell me that over the phone.

After the doctor gave me the news, I called Mom. She came to the hospital at once. I couldn't face driving into Queens, so we took the few outfits I had at John's and she set me up to stay with her. She took me back to my car the next morning, and it started with no problem. At some point, we realized that I didn't have anything appropriate to wear to a funeral, so she took me shopping. I was out of my head and utterly dazed. She was kind of guiding me passively around, handing me clothes to try on, letting me model them for her. I don't know how much of a role I played in the final purchase decision, nor do I know why she thought it was proper to wear a white suit to a funeral, but she handed me a white suit, it fit beautifully, and that's what I purchased.

No one spoke for John at the funeral. There was a Jehovah's Witness wake to suit John's mother, and a Roman Catholic mass to suit his father. He'd have hated both. Both were insert-name-here ceremonies. There was no personal eulogy.

On Tuesday, June 25, I spoke with John for the final time. It was early morning, around dawn, and I was sleeping fitfully. All of a sudden, John was there.

"What happened?"

"John, sweetheart, you died."

"*Really?* I'm *dead?*" Nothing could have convinced me more thoroughly that it was really John. No one else would have said it that way.

"Yes, darling, you're dead. Why did you die?"

John showed me in images, his spirit being thrust out of his body by a forceful push between the shoulder blades, accompanied by a nonverbal *Out!* as his body began to fall to the ground.

"I miss you," I said.

He said something like, don't come here, some kind of warning that I should not commit suicide, that we'd see each other when it was time, and then it was over.

Chapter 6

PERSEPHONE

January 1985: In Mom's kitchen

PERSEPHONE
by Deborah Lipp
May 1986

I am made pure
by my white wailing gown
In my white wedding grief
I am yours.

On our wedding day
I carried my bags to
your new hometown
It is starless, unfamiliar
Here, only I am alive.

I am chaste Persephone
my white lips hold your kisses
my dry womb holds your pleasure
my husband you bring me no joy
I am too arid to be untrue.

But the taste of you…
feeding me…pomegranate seeds
Too sweet
not nourishing;
our nuptial opiate.

    I close my eyes and hear
        your shy giggle
        maybe I nag a little
        maybe see
        your long delicate fingers

expressing your point on air
I can feel
the shudder
as you trace the line
of my chin
eyes neck and breast
suddenly grab
I lay my head against
the soft blanket of your chest
I close my eyes and am
happy, drugged.

Red juice running down my throat;
my grief.

The period of my life following John's death was strange and sad, transforming and, in a weird way, productive. The immediate grief was a kind of madness, in which time compressed and expanded randomly. Sometimes I was able to leave the apartment, but not often. One friend would call me, tell me stupid jokes until I laughed, and then get off the phone quickly, knowing I really couldn't talk. When I went back to work, my hours were sporadic. I'd arrive late and leave early. Sleep was a problem. I took to doing huge jigsaw puzzles deep into the night.

Grief is an emotion as singular as love or anger. People describe it as an amalgam of feelings: loss plus sadness plus whatever ... but that's simply not true. It's its own thing, an island unto itself, and for a while, I lived there.

Grief is also predictable. The acute period lasts no more than six months, and a year later, most people are a lot better. Not that they're "over it"—that takes years to approximate, and the loss never goes away— but they're *better*, as in functional, able to live life outside the shadow of pain. For some, though, grief is a trigger. The sorrow floods the brain chemistry, and sometimes, instead of recovery, you get depression. I had an underlying depression that I'd never acknowledged or addressed, and instead of coming out of grief, I dove deeply into clinical depression.

The strange part was, during the months leading up to my depressive breakdown, there was a joyous part of it, and that makes the story hard to tell. The year 1986 was a time in my life in which fun and wonderful things happened, in which elaborate jokes were played, in which I engaged fully with my friends and with the Pagan community. Most of that was a kind of mania. I've never been bipolar, but for that year I was often full of manic energy, a kind of happy coat of paint slapped over my sadness. I wasn't happy in any real sense of the word. I was drinking far too much, and I was sleeping around, irresponsibly and randomly. I was generally trouble waiting to happen.

But there were also genuinely good things that happened in 1986. I met my second husband and started my own Pagan Way. It was the year of the Flamingo Tradition.

So, in writing about this period of time, I'm telling two very different stories: one about grieving and depression, and one about playing and being productive. Both are true, and happened in parallel.

When we look at our lives, we find spots that divide life in two. "My life before I had a child/My life after becoming a parent" is a common demarcation, and I have that one, too. But the two demarcations that matter the most to me are these: "Before the Craft/After the Craft" and "Before John died/After John died." I tell the story of my love and loss in detail because it was a fundamental turning point in my life and made me who I am today. In Wicca, we ask the initiate if she is willing to "suffer to learn." John's death was the hurt, the suffering, that filled my heart and forced me to learn.

Like a lot of spiritual people, I had believed that everything happened for a reason, that the universe flowed from a kind of logic—in short, that there was a plan. That belief ceased to be acceptable to me when John died. Someone telling me it was for a reason was likely to get their head snapped off. *What* reason? It made no sense.

I couldn't touch my Tarot cards. It felt like my hands were burning up when I held them. Part of this was due to the simple knowledge that

I'd seen the cards predicting this death, and I'd ignored them. But part of it was because of a deep psychic sensitivity I'd suddenly developed.

I visited a psychic who told me that my third chakra—my solar plexus—had been attached to John and was now ripped. As wacky as that sounded on one level, on another level it resonated—I had a wound. Psychic input such as ritual or Tarot physically hurt. It was many years before I could attend rituals other than those with my home circle without feeling battered by the random psychic energy floating about. A Gardnerian circle has the advantage of being tightly contained: the circle is cast, and the energy stays within and flows in a gentle and constant clockwise stream. Public rituals sometimes raise no energy at all, but often they raise it without the tight container. I was suddenly able to feel the chaotic movement of energy this way and that, and it made me ill.

I asked *why*, over and over, and got no answer. I told Susan I needed a leave of absence. I wasn't sure the Craft was for me. I felt abandoned by the Goddess. I suppose I felt entitled to some sort of protection from her. I know how immature that sounds (and is!), but it's also a common, even banal, response to death.

About four months into my leave of absence, Susan called and asked if I would help her. It was October, and the local paper wanted to do a "Real Witches at Halloween" story. She appealed to me to participate in the interview because, she said, I was so articulate and could handle this better than anyone else in her group. The vanity plea worked. I took the train to meet with the reporter and several members of the Jersey Shore Pagan Way. (By then, living in the city, I no longer had a car.)

The reporter wanted to know why the Craft appealed to us, what it meant to us, who the Goddess was in our lives. In answering his questions, my deep love for my Gods came to the fore; the very act of speaking opened the floodgates that I'd kept dammed up. I was back for good.

In truth, Susan had planned the whole thing, knowing that if she could just get me talking, I'd get back in touch with my true feelings for Wicca.

The loss I'd suffered still left me with a dilemma, and I dove into the Craft itself to work my way through it. The Legend of the Descent of the Goddess (known by a variety of names) was given to me as a handout when I first joined Susan's group. It appeared, with slight variations on the wording, in several of the books on my reading list: *Witchcraft Today* and *The Meaning of Witchcraft* by Gerald Gardner, *What Witches Do* by Stewart Farrar, *The Grimoire of Lady Sheba* by Lady Sheba, and even a version in Starhawk's *The Spiral Dance.*

The Legend of the Descent of the Goddess into the Underworld

This version of the Descent is from *What Witches Do* by Stewart Farrar. This was given to me as a handout when I first joined the Jersey Shore Pagan Way:

In ancient times, our Lord, the Horned One, was (as he still is) the Consoler, the Comforter. But men know him as the dread Lord of Shadows, lonely, stern, and just.

But our Lady the Goddess would solve all mysteries, even the mystery of death; and so she journeyed to the underworld.

The Guardian of the Portals challenged her: "Strip off thy garments, lay aside thy jewels; for naught mayest thou bring with thee into this our land."

So she laid down her garments and her jewels, and was bound, as all living must be who seek to enter the realms of Death, the Mighty One.

Such was her beauty that Death himself knelt, and laid his sword and crown at her feet, and kissed her feet, saying: "Blessed be thy feet that have brought thee in these ways. Abide with me; but let me place my cold hands on thy heart."

And she replied, "I love thee not. Why dost thou cause all things that I love, and take delight in, to fade and die?"

"Lady," replied Death, "it is age and fate, against which I am helpless. Age causes all things to wither; but when men die at the end of time, I give them rest and peace and strength, so that they may return. But you, you are lovely. Return not; abide with me."

But she answered: "I love thee not."

Then said Death: "An you receive not my hand on your heart, you must kneel to Death's scourge."

"It is fate; better so," she said, and she knelt.

And Death scourged her tenderly. And she cried: "I know the pangs of love."

And Death raised her, and said: "Blessed be." And he gave her the fivefold salute, saying: "Thus only may ye attain to joy, and knowledge."

And he taught her all his mysteries, and gave her the necklace which is the circle of rebirth. And she taught him her mystery of the sacred cup which is the cauldron of rebirth.

They loved, and were one; for there be three great mysteries in the life of man, and magic controls them all. To fulfil love, you must return again at the same time and at the same place as the loved ones; you must meet, and know, and remember, and love them again.

But to be reborn, you must die, and be ready for a new body. And to die, you must be born; and without love you may not be born.

And our Goddess ever inclineth to love, and mirth, and happiness; and guardeth and cherisheth her hidden children in life, and in death she teacheth the way to her communion; and even in this world she teacheth them the mystery of the Magic Circle, which is placed between the world of men and of the Gods.

There was little in the Pagan books I'd read that addressed death in a personal way, and there was very little indeed that had any mythical or scriptural qualities. The Descent, being something that—it was said—the Goddess herself personally experienced, was vastly different from writings about karma or rebirth. Stories—myths—give us something that explanations do not. They take us on the journeys the Gods have taken. When we're kids, we're taught that myths explain things: They're Just So Stories, telling us why snakes don't have legs, or why poppies are red, or why there is winter. But on a deeper level, myths engage with the questions we care about. They don't answer, they *ask*, and by asking, they shape our understanding of which questions are important, and why the Gods are in our lives anyway.

Because the Descent was the only explicit myth of the Craft, it was the place to start.

I began to do a close textual analysis of the Descent, looking for answers to my questions. I saw that the Goddess didn't know why there was death—she blamed the God. But the God also said he had no control over it; it was Fate. Later, the Goddess knelt to Death's scourge, saying, "It is Fate, better so." Somehow, kneeling to her Fate brought her to love.

It was Fate. I didn't like it, and I certainly didn't yet "know the pangs of love," but I knew my Gods were not wantonly killing, were not the murderers of my beloved John. It was a start.

The more I studied the Legend, the more I developed a new, and more mature, intimacy with the Gods. Omnipotence is an easy thing to believe in; it leaves us with *theodicy*, the question of why an all-powerful and all-good deity would nonetheless allow evil to exist, but it is comforting to believe that *someone* is running everything.

The Craft doesn't maintain a theology of omnipotence, and so doesn't have a "problem of evil." Pain and suffering exist because they simply do. The Gods suffer *with* us. Their love is infinite, but their power is not.

As I saw this, I became more and more comforted, and also began to see life and fate in a more nuanced way. The Gods don't say everything happens for a reason. They say that "it is fate." The Goddess, though, is inclined toward happiness and mirth. Perhaps the happiness we create *is* the meaning. If we can impose our own happiness and love upon a meaningless fate, then perhaps we give it meaning.

In dealing with suffering, we deal with the "three great mysteries": love, death, and rebirth. Since death and rebirth are beyond our control in this life, the fulfillment of love is our true spiritual task, and the Legend tells us this is achieved by remembering, in this life, those we have loved before, and loving them again.

Susan taught me that the people who are our coven brothers and sisters are people we've circled with in past lives, perhaps not in Wicca, but in some kind of magic or ritual space. So perhaps that meant that learning Wicca was part of the fulfillment of love?

The other two mysteries are death and rebirth, and we are taught that initiation itself is a kind of death and rebirth. The Descent tells us that the Goddess brings us communion after we die, and "even in this world" she teaches the magic circle. That word *even* sounds like it connects the two concepts: the communion after death with the circle in life.

In studying this, I also came across another myth in the Craft, although this one is implicit rather than explicit.

At the end of the Legend of the Descent, we learn about the Goddess teaching her hidden children in life. This means that she descends, has this transforming experience, and returns to teach her hidden children (the Witches). This leads us to the Charge, otherwise known as the Charge of the Goddess or the Charge of the Star Goddess, written by Doreen Valiente.

The Charge is a set of instructions given to Witches, telling them how and when to worship, what to value, and the importance of love and pleasure. The narrative, then, is: Once upon a time, the Goddess descended to the Underworld. She and the God taught each other mysteries. Then she returned to Earth to teach these mysteries to her hidden children.

I have no problem accepting the Charge as a true myth of Wicca, even though we know who wrote it and under what circumstances. Every myth, including the Bible, was written down by someone, under some circumstance. That the Charge is a product of profound inspiration is proven by its extraordinary ubiquity. It went viral before there was such a thing as going viral. It's been treated as ancient, and as having been authored by any number of people. (There was a poster you could get of the Charge that attributed it to Starhawk.) It's part of the DNA of modern Wicca.

For the next several years, I occupied myself with studying mythology. From the Descent I dove into the Charge. From there I wanted to know what made something a myth, and then I was reading Mircea Eliade, and Wendy Doniger, and the Jungians, like Robert A. Johnson, Jean Shinoda Bolen, and Christine Downing. We (Susan, some other people from the Jersey Shore group, and I) saw Diane Wolkstein perform the Descent of Inanna at the American Museum of Natural History, and I saw her again at the New York Open Center.

The Descent was my path to recovery.

A MYTHOLOGY BOOK LIST

The Hero with a Thousand Faces, by Joseph Campbell

Gods of Love and Ecstasy: The Traditions of Shiva and Dionysus, by Alain Daniélou

The Myths and Gods of India, by Alain Daniélou

Other Peoples' Myths: The Cave of Echoes, by Wendy Doniger O'Flaherty

Myth and Reality, by Mircea Eliade

The Universal Myths, by Alexander Eliot

Mythology, by Edith Hamilton

God: Myths of the Male Divine, by David Leeming and Jake Page

Goddess: Myths of the Female Divine, by David Leeming and Jake Page

The Book of Goddesses and Heroines, by Patricia Monaghan

Inanna, Queen of Heaven and Earth: Her Stories and Hymns from Sumer, by Diane Wolkstein and Samuel Noah Kramer

Jungian Books

Goddesses in Everywoman: Powerful Archetypes in Women's Lives, by Jean Shinoda Bolen

The Goddess: Mythological Images of the Feminine, by Christine Downing

Gods in Our Midst: Mythological Images of the Masculine: A Woman's View, by Christine Downing

He, by Robert A. Johnson

She, by Robert A. Johnson

We, by Robert A. Johnson

Chapter 7

LOOKING FOR THE GODDESS?

Setting up the altar for Spring Equinox, 1986

Looking for the Goddess? Paganism, Witchcraft, the Old Religion?
Wicca study / worship group welcomes beginners.
—*An ad I ran in the* Village Voice, *April 1986*

I rejoined the coven, and Susan elevated me to second degree. Somewhere in there, my roommate got deported (!), and I moved to Astoria, Queens, which is one of my favorite places I've ever lived. I was commuting by train to Susan's, about three hours door to door (subway to Penn Station to Asbury Park). Susan hovered between teasing and nagging that it was time to start my own group.

In January of 1986, we went to Esotericon. This was a combination Pagan festival / hotel convention. There are a number of these still around, the biggest and most famous being Pantheacon, but Esotericon itself didn't last past the '80s. Not surprising for me in those days, I met an attractive guy at some point on Saturday, and we started hanging out. Victor was incredibly young-looking but told me he was twenty-seven. If he'd said he was twenty or twenty-one, I think I'd have believed he was inflating his age, but twenty-seven was so far from appearances that I thought it was the kind of story that could only be true. He also told me he was an Alexandrian third-degree initiate. The Alexandrian tradition is similar to the Gardnerian and much more written about. The late Stewart Farrar was an Alexandrian and talked about both traditions in much of his writing; for this reason, many people get the impression they're the same. As a Gardnerian, I knew they were *not* the same, so I had no way of verifying his bona fides, nor did I need to in order to flirt and fool around at the con.

We'd come with far more people than the room was meant to accommodate. Victor and I slept together in a corner on the floor, being, I suspect, a lot less discreet than we imagined. When I woke up Sunday morning, respectably hungover, Victor was already gone, but one of my friends found his driver's license under the bed when we were packing up.

The driver's license had a picture that was clearly Victor, but not the name I'd been told, and it showed his age was seventeen. My jaw hit the floor. I was probably more embarrassed than I needed to be. I mean, a fake name? Why do that? Who would suspect that?

Victor had not yet left the con, and I found him and gave him back his license. He "explained" that he was an undercover narc, and what we'd found was the ID he used in the high school he was assigned to. It was a crazy story and I knew it, but I also felt there was the slimmest possibility that it was true, and I let him persuade me to see him again.

I saw him only one more time. He visited me at my apartment, and, perhaps in an effort to prove he was the cop he claimed to be, he brought a gun with him, hidden in his backpack, which he showed me. I was frightened and disgusted.

Susan had become friendly with a guy named Leonard, who owned an occult store in northern New Jersey. Leonard had begun attending Jersey Shore circles with us. Victor had told me he worked at Leonard's store, not realizing that Leonard and I knew each other. When I asked Leonard about him, Leonard did indeed know Victor, but under the name on the driver's license; he was a local kid who hung around the store and was definitely not an employee. Needless to say, Victor was neither a cop nor an Alexandrian. Only by comparing stories were we able to figure out what Victor had been up to and how many lies he had told.

Victor had given me a beautiful silver pentagram necklace. It was an unusual design—a small pentacle (a five-pointed star inside a circle) in the center of a large pentagram (a five-pointed star without the circle). Although I had no intention of seeing him again, my love for jewelry transcended that sort of thing, and I was still wearing it.

One work day I was sitting at my desk when the pentagram began to heat up to the point where it felt like the flesh on my neck was roasting.

I jumped up and ran to the sink, took off the necklace, washed my neck in cold water, then filled a cup and put the pentagram in cold water. (My neck was unharmed.) I took the cup back to my desk just as the phone began to ring. It was Leonard.

"Victor just left here. I told him everything. He knows you blew the whistle on him, and he's furious."

"That's weird, because the necklace that Victor gave me just started to burn my neck."

"What necklace?"

It turned out that the necklace had been stolen from Leonard's store, and he'd put some magic on it to bring it back to him. "Keep the necklace," he told me. "I release it. It's a gift from me to you." Unfortunately, no matter how often I cleansed it magically, eventually it would begin to burn again. It seemed like every time Victor thought about me and got angry again, the necklace constituted a connection to me that conveyed his rage right into my skin. This was my second major lesson in accidental magic. Victor was focused, single-minded, and passionate. I don't believe he purposely put a curse on me; it all happened too fast for that. But the intensity of his feelings and a connection opened, in part by sex, was all it took for his negative feelings to translate into real-world results.

I told Leonard I'd give the necklace back to him the next time I saw him, since I was unable to wear it.

I packed the necklace in my overnight bag for Imbolg. When it was time to change into robes for ritual, people headed upstairs. I opened my suitcase and pulled out my robe. As I did so, the necklace jumped out and, in a clean and high arc, flew about fifteen feet out into the hall, landing on the floor in front of Leonard just as he topped the stairs. Our eyes all grew wide, and I said, *"You* pick it up!"

I fully realize that when you pull an article of clothing out of a suitcase, something can easily fly out. But it didn't look or feel like that to anyone who witnessed it. The necklace flew on a trajectory that seemed unnatural, and the whole thing was creepy. That was a turning point, when I realized that Witchcraft was not just a religion but was also kind of spooky. Previously, I'd been very skeptical about the "woo-

woo" side of things. In truth, I remain skeptical—some people are far too willing to see a magical cause instead of a mundane one for too many events—but knowing that spooky things can happen, even rarely, was a profound change in perspective.

Magic of Return/Curse upon a Thief

I don't know exactly what spell Leonard used to bring his necklace back to him, but something like the following is likely.

For this spell you will need some incense, a candle, your athame, and a small mirror. The candle should be a color representing the stolen object (green for money, silver or gold for jewelry, blue for a musical instrument, and so forth). If you're unsure, use white.

Dress the candle with oil scented with three drops of patchouli.

Light the candle and the incense. Make sure the candle is on a safe, fireproof surface, as it will be left to burn. Place the mirror so the candle flame is reflected in it. Ground and center.

Visualize the stolen object clearly in the mirror. Fix your gaze upon the reflected flame, and see the object there. Keep it very clear in your mind's eye, point your athame at it, and say:

That which is mine returns to me!
That which is mine returns to me!
That which is mine returns to me!

O [object], burn until you are with me.
O thief, you cannot know peace.
O [object], burn until you are with me.
O thief, when it is returned, your pain will cease.

That which is mine returns to me!
That which is mine returns to me!
That which is mine returns to me!

By the power of three, so mote it be!

Continue to point into the mirror, sending all your mental power and desire into it. When you are finished, let the candle burn all the way down.

When I first joined Susan's group, she said that everyone should have a magical name to use in circle. We could use our mundane names until we found the right one. I said I had a name I wanted to use, but I didn't know how to turn it into a Pagan name.

"What's the name?" she asked.

"Storm."

"Then your name is Storm," she said.

I thought the name had to be dressed up somehow, perhaps the Gaelic word for storm, or a deity or spirit of storms. I had no idea I could just use a word.

And yes, I knew Storm was also a comic book character, and I was a little concerned someone would mock me. But I had long found enormous power and pleasure in thunderstorms. The magical energy I'd learned to raise with my hands was more intense during storms. Thunder and lightning made me feel powerful and joyous. It was the right name for me. When you get second degree in the Gardnerian tradition, you choose a new name, which I did, but I still loved the name Storm, and I kind of missed it.

Susan was still nagging me to start my own group, and I was shooting back excuses. One day, probably a Sunday after ritual, Susan, her boyfriend, and I were having "that" conversation, and I said, "Well, what would I name a group, anyway?" After a brief discussion, I said I'd like to incorporate "Storm" into it somehow. We started tossing around storm names, and when I said "Stormcircle," I knew I had it.

Names are a powerful weapon in the magician's arsenal. When you name a thing, you make it real. This is one reason people argue so much about "labeling." Some people don't want to be labeled because it's limiting. They might say, "I'm not 'disabled,' I'm a person with a disability; I'm *more* than just the disability!" Or a genderqueer person might protest that neither "male" nor "female" is an accurate descriptor, or a parent might not wish to label her child as "ADD" or "learning disabled" because that might confine the child to a particular educational path.

But a label can also be liberating. A diagnostic label creates the possibility of treatment. When my son was diagnosed with Asperger's, the persistent, nebulous feeling of "something is wrong" suddenly gave way to a path of potential treatment, as well as a group of fellow Aspies who could support us on our journey. Labeling AIDS a disability allowed people with the condition to continue working, as their jobs were now protected by the Americans with Disabilities Act.

Names define the boundaries between "this thing" and "not this thing." When you cast a Wiccan circle, you name sacred space as "this part here." Metaphysically, it's true that all space is sacred, but the *named* sacred space focuses our attention and concentrates our power. Names also introduce new concepts into the world. People talked about electronic money in science fiction novels for many years, but until PayPal came along and said, "Here we are, this is our name, and here's how it works," no one really accepted the concept.

In magic, an *egregore* is a non-corporeal entity brought into being by the work of a magician or group of magicians. It has a name and a purpose. Concepts like "credit card" or "PayPal" or "personal computer" are mundane egregores, brought into being by having been conceptualized and named.

When I named Stormcircle, I brought it into being, and all the other problems fell away.

My ex-boyfriend F. agreed to work as my partner and High Priest. In traditional Wicca, we work with gender polarity, and each group is run by a High Priestess and a High Priest in partnership. Polarity is generated in a variety of ways. In part, it's a manifestation of the physical sex of the body and has nothing to do with orientation. Many gay men work in successful and powerful polarity with straight women, or lesbians with gay or straight men, or bi everybody with bi everybody else. There are also people who work with polarities that don't depend on the physical body. This was a concept entirely unfamiliar to me at the time, and one not always accepted by traditional Wiccans. There was once a kind of institutional homophobia in Wicca, in the 1930s through the 1960s or so, but I haven't seen that in my lifetime. Adherence to strict gender roles, though, is still the norm.

Simply put, working with polarity raises power. It's not the only method that works, but man, does it ever work.

Part of the power manifests as erotic energy. In other words, when working with a partner in a polarity system, you're likely to become really turned on. This can be confusing for two people who are not appropriate partners or who have no desire to hook up sexually. The erotic desire can manifest in all kinds of unexpected situations, even when there's an orientation mismatch, or when people are monogamously partnered with others. Acting on it, even if it's not an obvious problem, can be sticky. The sexual energy may not last much beyond the ritual and its aftermath, and the two people might not be prepared for it to dissipate so quickly, leaving them to wonder what happened. Or, the passion between them may build with the exaggerated heat typical of connections that occur in a magical space, knocking aside all other considerations. All of this can be wonderful, and many lifelong relationships have been born of just such a beginning, but preparation and understanding can help the participants manage, if not avoid, some very unusual stresses.

F. and I had the advantage of already knowing and recognizing our erotic connection. As poorly matched as we'd been in some ways, we had wonderful sexual energy together, and we were able to handle it and enjoy it, while not acting on it, because we weren't so shocked by it. Partnering with an ex is something I recommend.

Having to have a partner means that no Gardnerian Witch can be successful if he or she cannot work and play well with others! The ideal, in Wicca, is that your life partner and your magical partner will be one and the same, but this is often not the case. Many people have life partners who are not Pagan or Wiccan or are otherwise not suited to leading a coven. Many people are gay and wish to work with the polarity of biological sex, so their life partner is not a suitable candidate. Many people are single. None of these people are disqualified from leading a Pagan circle, but all of them have to find a partner with whom to work.

What this means, in practice, is that you have to have friendships and connections with people who are willing to say, "Yes, I'll work with you." If you don't have that, if you're so unpleasant that you've alienated every potential partner, then traditional practice cuts you off from the work you need to do. This is a powerful counterbalance to the ego rush of leading a group of excited newbies and introducing them to the mysteries and joys of Pagan worship.

Running a group with a partner prevents you from becoming an autocrat, as there's another opinion that matters. Even though, in Gardnerian Wicca, the High Priestess rules the circle and the High Priest is her advisor but not her ruler, and even though she could overrule him at will, the presence of a partner still means, in practice, that the two must confer and be in harmony. You can't be a tyrant and last long in the job.

F. was less interested in the group than I was. He was happy to "help," but I was the only true leader. On the other hand, I was twenty-five, unsure of myself, and younger than everyone else in the group, so there was little risk of me becoming an autocrat at the time.

One of the concerns of starting a Pagan group is safety. Since I was inviting strangers into my home, an interview and screening process was essential. A lot of people would add to that, "especially in New York City," but I'm not sure that's true; there are nuts everywhere, and like it or not, the occult brings out some of them. There are those who think Wicca is the quick fix to bring them power over their broken lives, and those who think Wicca is evil and therefore may want to take revenge on a representative. All things considered, I had very few problems. My process was to advertise, send inquirers an application, respond to the application with a phone call, have a one-on-one meeting in a public place like a coffee shop, and, if all that went well, invite the applicant to ritual.

I placed an ad in the *Village Voice*. The back page of the *Voice* was the Craigslist of its day. It ran a wide variety of small ads, including missed connections, prayers to St. Jude, ads for yoga centers and other alternative venues, and various odds and ends. The ad I ran, quoted at the beginning of this chapter, is the one and only that got through for many years. When I tried to rerun it, they refused it, saying they didn't allow that sort of thing.

The first time I went to my PO Box in Soho to pick up my mail after the ad ran, there were more than forty letters. Opening them, feeling the world of seekers reaching out to me, I was moved to tears. I began the process of sending out applications and connecting with potential members.

In screening applicants, I quickly developed a knack for allowing people to self-screen. This started because I was uncomfortable saying no to anyone or turning them away, but it's a tried-and-true technique that I rely on to this day. I just make people welcome, while telling them the reasons they may not want to be in my group, and I let *them* make the determination.

I had received a number of applications in that first wave of mail, and was talking to prospective members on the phone. One conversation was with an applicant named Abe. I noted that he was about fifty-four years old. (Susan used to run astrological charts on all applicants—something I didn't have the skill for—but I retained her practice of getting full birth information on the application anyway.) While chatting with Abe, I mentioned that he would likely be the oldest person in the group, as the rest of the members so far were in their twenties or thirties. Abe agreed that this would make him uncomfortable, and that ended his interest in Stormcircle.

That same night, I spoke with an applicant named Stephanie. As I had done with Abe, I mentioned to her that the rest of the members (so far) were white, and she was likely to be the only African American in the group. (That information was not on her application but came out during out chat.) Stephanie said she was fine with that and subsequently became a valued member of Stormcircle.

In each case, I merely poked my finger in at a point of difference or discomfort, without judging in any way, and let the applicant make the decision. That one night, two people made opposite decisions within a half hour of each other, and I was confident that I had ended up with the right people as a result. I use the same technique at any number of decision points in the running of a group. If someone isn't advancing in their studies, or is having problems, or is a troublemaker, I'll generally let them know why it is they might not wish to be part of the group.

Almost always, that's enough to make them leave or straighten up. Before initiating someone, I let them know all the reasons they might prefer not to be initiated. Before elevating them to a higher degree, I let them know why they might like their current degree much better. Almost never have I had to ask someone to leave my group. One former member was a sexual predator—basically it takes something that serious for me to take the decision out of the person's hands. At times I've told people they would have to show more commitment, work harder, or do some inner work, or else leave, and some of those people have indeed worked harder, while most have left. It's much less painful for me to have people leave in this way, less painful for them (I sincerely hope), and less ego-driven. Instead of deciding on my own, based on my own limited perspective, I throw it open in a way that I hope lets the Gods' voices be heard.

The idea of letting the Gods in on these decisions is why Susan would do charts and why I sometimes use Tarot, especially when considering an initiation.

Prior to Stormcircle's first official meeting, I invited the Jersey Shore Pagan Way to attend a Spring Equinox rite at my apartment, led by F. and me. This was our first ritual at my place, and we had to face the problem of disposing of the libations.

In traditional Wicca, the Goddess represents wholeness and eternity, the circle, and things that neither begin nor end, while the God represents boundaries, death and rebirth, and endings and beginnings. The God is the harvest and the crop. He is John Barleycorn, dying as wheat, resurrected as bread. He is the stag, dying as an animal, resurrected as life-giving meat. His horns, like those of the stag, are shed and regrow.

The Goddess has no beginning or end. She isn't born and doesn't die. She transforms her state of being without death—menstruating, becoming pregnant, giving birth, and entering menopause, but still herself. She is the agent for the God's death and rebirth, while remaining in a constant, living flux. Like the Moon, she waxes and wanes, is full and dark, but always, she is there.

We represent these different roles in all manner of ways. In my tradition, the High Priestess rules the circle as representative of the Goddess, while the High Priest is fully in charge of setting up the circle before it starts and taking it down after it's over, as representative of the God. She is in the center, while he is the beginning and the end.

All of this is a long-winded way of saying that the High Priest is the one in charge of disposing of the libation appropriately after the circle has been closed.

I was living on a block of two- and three-family homes in Astoria in a third-floor walk-up. My landlord lived on the second floor, and the half-size apartment on the first floor belonged to a single man I never saw except for an occasional glimpse. Our "front lawn" was an ugly little patch of dirt, with a few stray blades of grass present more by accident than anything else.

Directly across the street, the neighbor had the same tiny patch of grass, but it was lush and green. He had one of those lawn statues of a sombrero-clad Mexican with a donkey. The donkey's baskets were full of flowers. I referred to the Mexican as "Pancho Villa."

My landlord was a fatherly, old-fashioned Greek man who snored so loudly I could hear it through the floor. In those days, you didn't go around telling people you had a Pagan group, and even in later years, this was not a man who would have been receptive to the news. I told him when I moved in that I had a theater group that sometimes would meet at my apartment, figuring that would cover any noises or late-night comings and goings.

After the Spring Equinox ritual, people stayed to party. Eventually I reminded F. that the libations had to go, and he headed out, still in his robe.

"Shouldn't you put your clothes on?"

"Fuggedaboudit, it's 2:30 in the morning. Who's going to see?"

Outside, F. saw our pathetic lawn and felt like it wasn't a very sacred place for offerings, so he went across the street and poured it underneath the donkey.

At which point the neighbor's window flew open, and a man's head came out, screaming, "WHAT ARE YOU DOING TO MY DONKEY?"

F. backed away, apologizing and kind of bowing, all the way across the street, ran up the stairs, and confessed to me what had happened.

The next day, my landlord was furious as I struggled to explain. "Not a robe! A costume! My theater group! I'm so sorry! My friend loves that donkey, he was just looking! No! Not pouring anything! Certainly not! He was just *admiring* the donkey! IT WILL NEVER HAPPEN AGAIN!" I was *that* close to eviction but was able to smooth the whole thing over.

Why Wear Robes?

Robes have come up a couple of times already. Many Pagans wear them for a number of reasons:

- Loose-fitting garments don't bind or restrict our energies. Although some people like Renn Faire garb for Pagan ritual, corsets and other bindings prevent the comfort and ease we need for meditation, dance, breathing exercises, or magic.

- We can be completely nude beneath our robes, experiencing freedom of the body even if we're not ready or willing to work skyclad (nude).

- Robes are simple and timeless, tying us to no particular period of history.

- Robes allow us to meet without the trappings of social class and economic status that our street clothes convey.

- Changing into special ritual clothing, whatever it may be, helps alter our consciousness and focus our minds on the coming ritual.

Stormcircle met for the first time on May 10, 1986 (my mother's birthday, as it happens). Eight people attended, including F. and me. Among them was Barbara, who, all these years later, is still my best friend.

At twenty-five, I was the youngest person in the room and would remain younger than every one of my students for some years to come. Teaching continually pushed me to learn how much more I needed to know. I absolutely thought I knew what I was doing...until I didn't. At every ritual I realized there was some little thing that I hadn't ever thought to ask. What do you do with candle stubs? What do you do with the leftover ash in the censer? What about the saltwater? (Candle stubs can be reused or melted down, or even thrown away if they're not consecrated. Ash can be tamped down to lay the next charcoal on, or it can go out with the libations. Saltwater can go with the libations.) When I first moved to my own apartment, I called my mother all the time for recipes. Now I called Susan all the time for advice on ritual things.

I used Susan's basic lesson plan and group structure, and modified the lessons as I went. We'd have class for an hour or two, change for ritual, then sometimes there would be more teaching in circle. I also distributed handouts at each meeting.

In addition to F., our members included Gallen, who had been in Susan's group. Gallen was great at throwing in little jokes if I got too pedantic or self-important during class. He wasn't disruptive and he helped keep things light, which helped me feel less intimidated by what I was taking on.

I have kept a diary of all my group rituals from the very beginning. Here's my first entry, with the names of the attendees omitted:

May 10, 1986

Handouts: Welcome, Book List, The Charge (Farrar)

Discussed realities. What is a Pagan Way? Reasons for coming. Who was Gardner? Everyone introduced self. Also: Rules of Stormcircle, things to acquire (cups, robes, athames).

CIRCLE

Discussed circle etiquette. Taught two chants: "We all come from the Goddess/Hoof & Horn" and "Isis, Astarte." Discussed "What is magick?" Discussed Pagan names. More chanting. Closed circle.

Chapter 8

RITES OF SPRING

Isaac and me, Starwood 1987

The Flamingo Tradition (Flam-Trad) is a nature/fertility religion.
The Revealed Bird was first flown to us at the Rites of Spring festival
where plastic flamingos (sacred icons) were placed in front of a tent
as totems. Worship is therefore most appropriate out-of-doors.

—*The Flamingo Tradition: An Outline*

Before Stormcircle met for a second time, I went to another festival.

We went to festivals several times a year. Susan always organized
the caravan. I wasn't particularly connected with community news;
she'd pick the events and suggest we go. We went to Starwood every
year, Esotericon several times, a Maryland-based festival that became
Free Spirit Gathering, and so on. This time, it was Rites of Spring, and
Susan, as usual, was vague about the location. She was as bad with
geography as I was, and relied on the map provided with the registra-
tion forms. We were heading in the general direction of New England.
I hadn't had a car in nearly a year, so my responsibility was limited to
getting to Susan's with my camping gear and throwing it in the back of
the van, where I promptly fell asleep.

Four hours later I woke up in Ashfield.

I started yelling, "Oh my GOD, oh my GOD, we're on Route 112!"

"That's where the directions say we should be. What's the problem?"

Why would she know that this place was so important to me, that it
was the home of my heart, that I hadn't been there in seven years? Why
would she think to mention that Rites of Spring was being held five
miles from Bug Hill Road?

I was suffused with the beauty of the place, with the overwhelming love I had for these roads, with the sense of nostalgia. I pointed out landmarks to the others and felt blessed by this odd synchronicity.

I should backtrack just a little to explain that Isaac Bonewits had been an object of fun in our group for at least a year.

Isaac Bonewits was a highly influential figure in the Pagan community. I first encountered him when reading *Drawing Down the Moon,* where he had a larger index entry than any other person. As an author, he was well known for *Real Magic,* a classic treatise on the use of magic. It was perhaps the first book to talk about magic as a science, not tied to any one system. Pick up any other book on magic and it would tell you how to do *Goetic* magic, or *folk* magic, or *Golden Dawn* magic. Isaac took away the system and looked at the underlying principles. He was the only person in the United States with an accredited degree in the subject of magic. His diploma appeared on the back cover of the book.

He had also been the editor of the first major Pagan magazine, *Gnostica,* in the early 1970s. He was the founder of the Aquarian Anti-Defamation League, the first Pagan civil rights group, and he was the author of the Aquarian Manifesto, from which originated the familiar phrase "Never Again the Burning!" By 1986 he'd been involved with Wicca, Druidism, and other forms of Paganism for more than fifteen years, and had been publicly speaking and writing on subjects such as scholarship, history, ritual, and the future of Paganism for a long time.

Isaac had a well-deserved reputation for mocking Gardnerians. He was one of the first voices in the Pagan community to suggest that Gerald Gardner didn't inherit a tradition of Witchcraft at all, but instead probably made up the material he published, or cobbled it together from previously published sources. It was controversial and enraged many in the community (and still does). It was years before this became something like common knowledge among many Pagans. The details are still controversial, and the scholarship is by no means settled, but Isaac was out ahead of the pack on debunking "unbroken traditions passed down from the Stone Age," mysterious initiations by one's grandmother that just happened to resemble published sources, and so on. He took great delight in poking fun at people who believed such things, and thus made himself a bit of a target.

Isaac also had an amusing look about him. He was very skinny, with long, curly black hair and a thick mustache; he looked like Weird Al Yankovic. And he dressed entirely in white, including a white beret on his head.

At Starwood 1985, he'd given his "Druidism 101" talk, during which he discussed not only the history of the ancient Druids but also the new Druid organization he was forming: ADF (*Ár nDraíocht Féin*: A Druid Fellowship). As the festival went on, we began to notice more and more people walking around wearing the white berets. It was really strange-looking. Finally, I saw him from a distance, sitting at an outdoor lecture area, a pile of white berets in clear plastic bags next to him. I went running back to camp and shouted, "He's *selling* them!" I don't know why this was so funny, or where I imagined the berets were coming from if he *wasn't* selling them, but we were all cracking ourselves up.

For Rites of Spring, Susan got it in her head that we had to have "tent totems." I'd brought a stuffed parrot to hang outside my tent. Kat had fully intended to set up an altar to Isaac Bonewits as her tent totem, but as so often happens with really stupid pranks, she didn't quite get around to it. Steve outdid us all by planting a pair of lawn flamingos in front of his tent.

The flamingos became the hit of the festival. We were camped just off a main path, and we frequently heard shouts of "Flamingos!" from people walking by. At least once, someone we didn't know came running into our camp to pet the flamingos.

It was during opening circle at Rites of Spring when I first realized that public ritual had become painful for me. I'd gone to Starwood a month after John died, but I hadn't attended any rituals. Now the energy of the circle seemed to rip through me in waves of emotion. Over time, I learned to manage or avoid such experiences, and over even *more* time, it ceased to be a problem; but this first occurrence was awful, a torrent of feeling that sent me running.

Most festivals start with a day of little to no structured activities, to give folks time to settle in and set up camp. Then there's an opening circle the first evening, and workshops and other events start the next morning. Similarly, closing circle is generally scheduled in such a way as to give people plenty of time to break camp, and the last day (usually a Sunday) will have little if any in the way of programming.

The first day of programming, Susan and I attended a workshop presented by Isaac Bonewits called "Neopagan Taboos." While he was speaking, I saw a star—a small gold spark—fly from his eye, cross the room, and land in my mouth.

I can hardly convey my reaction. I didn't think I was having a vision, yet I saw what I saw. Instead of realizing that this was odd, and perhaps mystical, I was simply drawn to him. It was like a cartoon where Cupid shoots an arrow into you; suddenly it was HIM, and I couldn't take my eyes from him.

After the lecture, Susan said, "Let's go talk to Isaac." She had every intention of arguing, teasing, and generally having a bit of fun by making trouble. (If you remarked on this penchant of hers, she'd blame it on Sagittarius rising.) All I could say was, "Yes, let's." The three of us sat down to chat. Isaac said he was recently divorced. His life, he said, was demanding. With his teaching, writing, starting up a brand-new Druid organization, and traveling all over the country to support it, he needed a woman in his life who could support the demands of his Pagan career. He remarked that, while ministers and rabbis could traditionally expect a wife to take a supportive role, in a community of priestesses, it was much harder to find a woman who would accept this. He then turned to me with a big grin and said, "Do you know anyone who wants to be a *rabbitzin?*" (A *rabbitzin* is a rabbi's wife.) I was crestfallen. It sounded to me like he was saying, "Do you know someone for me?" and seemed to eliminate *me* as a possible choice. We chatted a little more, then Isaac went to teach his next class, and we moved on to whatever we were doing next.

Saturday night was main ritual. I saw the circle of people gathered and knew I couldn't face it alone, but it was dark and impossible to spot any of the friends I'd come with. Then I saw Isaac. Dressed all in white, with a white hat, he fair well glowed in the dark and was literally the only person I could recognize in the crowd. I approached the circle and stood next to him. He smiled at me, the ritual proceeded, and when it was over he turned to me and planted a kiss right on my mouth! Then he was off.

The weather was cold and rainy throughout the weekend. I headed back to camp, where I found Susan, wrapped in a warm wool cloak, well protected from the misty rain, warming her feet by a fire with a drink in her hand.

"You'll never guess who kissed me!"

"Who?"

"Isaac Bonewits!"

"Well, what are you doing here? Go find him!"

I was surprised by her enthusiastic response. I thought she'd mock or tease me, or be affronted, since he was such an object of derision. Instead, she wanted me to track him down. I was far too shy to chase after him like that, wandering about camp on a quest for a man, so I insisted she come with me.

"Oh, no. I'm comfortable here. I've got the fire, my drink, my cloak. Why should I leave?"

"Okay, that's fine," I said, and sat down next to her.

"Fine!" she huffed, and got up to walk me back up the hill to the main festival area. It didn't take long to find Isaac by a small fire, singing with a group of about eight or ten people. As soon as I was at the fire, she turned around and headed back to camp, which wasn't what I had in mind at all.

Isaac was taking requests, and I asked for "Be Pagan Once Again," which I'd heard at Starwood the year before. I'd remembered it only as a fun Pagan sing-along, and was surprised to hear such a rabble-rousing song. Other people made requests, and Isaac kept on singing.

A woman, very drunk, staggered up to the fire and asked if we knew where Shenain's tent was. Both Isaac and I said we did. Shenain was a friend of Susan's and was camped near us. Unbenownst to me, he was also Isaac's roommate in Manhattan, so Isaac knew where the tent was every bit as well as I did. Together, we walked/carried the woman to the tent she needed and folded her inside. Then Isaac turned to me and began discussing safe sex.

I was staggered by his honesty. I'd had my share of festival flings meant to last no longer than the event, but no one had ever directly acknowledged that we were going to have sex before we did. It was instead always quiet, touching and kissing and gradual undressing, as if maybe we would and maybe we wouldn't.

The unspoken, gradual slide into sex is romantic and lovely, but it's also rooted in the patriarchy. It's part of a culture in which "good girls don't," so you create a pretense of slow seduction when the intention is actually clear from the start. It speaks to people trained from infancy to never discuss sexuality honestly, and that taboo harms all of us. As shocked as I was by Isaac's matter-of-factness, I was also impressed by the honesty of it, and I knew it was healthier than my prior habits.

I was embarrassed to be with "the" Isaac in front of my group and cringed in anticipation of their teasing, but, in fact, I was tormented more by my imagination than my friends. When Isaac came to hang out at camp with us—we spent the rest of the festival together—he remarked on the flamingos and suggested they had magical powers. It turned out that two people in our group who had arrived at camp as friends had become a couple the same night as Isaac and I, and that lent credence to the idea that the flamingos were magical fertility totems that were making everyone horny. At least, that was what we started saying, and it became a running shtick.

I then found out that the flamingos, and all the tent totems, were part of a master scheme hatched by Susan and Sharon. They'd purchased a Pin the Tail on the Donkey game, and had created "donkey" seed packets, and intended to plant "F.'s Donkey Garden," with straight rows of ears and tails, in front of F.'s tent. They waited until F. had left for his work shift (most festivals ask for a couple of volunteer hours from each attendee) to plant his garden. The rain washed out the paper ears and tails, though, and there wasn't much to see by the time he got back. It was still a great joke, but we never got a worthy visual of it.

We didn't even know the punch line until the next day. When Susan dropped me at my apartment, we discovered that Pancho Villa now wore a neon orange sombrero: the new splash of insanely bright paint was, after all, the best totem we'd seen all weekend.

As I've said, I had some experience with festival flings. If you travel out of town to an event and meet someone charming, attractive, and fun, you can spend the three-day weekend with him and go home. No harm done; everyone happy; perhaps you'll meet again at the same event next year. Certainly many long-term relationships have arisen from such connections, and people have moved cross-country for them, but that's more of a happy accident. If the aim is to have a festival lover, there's an unspoken rule: Don't hook up with someone from your home town. After all, one of the things that makes the no-strings thing relatively painless is the fact that the geography works in its favor.

Why explain all this? Well, Isaac and I were both living in New York City, he in upper Manhattan and me in Queens. Throughout the event (and indeed, at the several events where I'd seen Isaac in the past), women threw themselves at him. Once, I actually saw a woman throw herself at his feet, though thankfully it usually was more metaphoric than literal. Objectively kind of funny-looking, Isaac had an unmistakable charisma and a well-deserved reputation as a ladies' man. He could have been with any of a dozen women at Rites. That he chose to be with me, knowing we both lived in the same city, two hundred miles from where we met, seemed to imply that he was interested in, or at least open to, seeing me again when we got home.

He'd told me at Rites that he was moving to California, where he was from. I have to say, I didn't pay much attention to that. It seemed to me that half the people I knew had a plan to move to California, and I almost never saw it materialize. It was just a thing that people said: "I'm going to bag this racket and live off the land," or "I'm going to tell the boss what I think of him," or "I'm packing up and moving to California." Little did I know that what Isaac meant was, "I have an apartment full of cardboard boxes and a scheduled move-out date."

I screwed up my courage, got Shenain's number from Susan, and asked him for Isaac's number. Isaac was surprised but pleased to hear from me, and we got together in the city. Back at his apartment, I was chagrined to discover who his roommate was and dismayed to see the packing boxes. Nonetheless, we began seeing each other.

It was during our first "date," with restaurant and beer and all that, that he discovered I'd never read *Real Magic*. It was pretty embarrassing. I'd asked Shenain to get me a copy so I could quickly read it before-hand, but he claimed he didn't have one. Isaac got some good fun out of pretending to be outraged.

We saw each other a little in the city, although he traveled a lot. We both attended the Starwood Festival, and were together there. I fell in love, or admitted I was in love, before Isaac did, and that left me in a quandary. How do you gain the attention of a man so many women fawn over? Once, I saw a woman come up to him at a festival and reverently hand him a Mason jar. She solemnly explained it was a home-made liqueur that had been brewing in her basement for six months, and she wanted him to have the very first sip. Her behavior bordered on worshipful. Everywhere we went, people followed him, many of whom had no qualms about elbowing me out of the way by whatever method was convenient.

As I saw it, there were two things in my arsenal that separated me from the pack. First, I was ready and eager to have children. Isaac had been married three times but had never had a child. He wanted children very much. Often, being on the same timeline about kids is one of the things that brings a couple together, and that was true for us.

More than that, I saw that the women who pursued Isaac were obse-quious; they were fawning, compliant, and a little awestruck. I had no desire to be like that, nor do I think I'd have been particularly good at it. From the very beginning, we sparred. Isaac was amused that I was a Gardnerian, and poked as much fun at that when we were in bed together as he ever did in public. I gave as good as I got, and we built a deep con-nection around arguing theology, philosophy, and Pagan politics. Early on, I realized that no one *else* was arguing with him. Let me correct that: plenty of people were arguing with Isaac Bonewits, but none of his real or potential romantic partners were. By arguing with Isaac, I was making myself special and unique in his life, and I knew it.

By the time he was ready to make the final trip west, things were romantic between us, but Isaac hadn't yet told me he loved me. He asked me to move to California with him, but he hadn't made any commitment to me. I wasn't going to uproot my entire life on a whim. I had a job, an apartment I loved, and a Pagan group. Without a commitment, I was staying put.

Isaac's move-out day at the end of July was bittersweet. He'd be back mid-September for a Druid event in Connecticut. We planned for him to fly into New York and stay with me; we'd go to the event together.

That summer was very busy. Stormcircle met regularly. We held a Summer Solstice rite jointly with the Jersey Shore Pagan Way that was something of a mini-festival, with twenty or so people and overnight camping on a piece of land owned by a friend of Susan's. The flamingos came to Summer Solstice, and we started spreading the idea of the Flamingo Tradition. The basic concept was that the original pair of flamingos was sacred, and if you made love ("pecked off") near them, you'd become an initiate of the Flamingo Tradition. Then, if you, as an initiate, made love in front of *other* flamingos, those would become sacred. So the tradition was spread plastic bird, to couple, to plastic bird, and so on.

Since there was a lot of coupling and uncoupling that summer, with several long-term romances forming between Rites and Summer Solstice alone, the idea became sexy and fun, and started spreading. Some of what we threw into the Flam-Trad was random—I became the Maiden of Feathers, and Sharon the Priestess of Beaks, for no other reason than I often wore pink and she often wore black. It was "Maiden" of Feathers instead of "Priestess," because "MOFfie" was a funny acronym.

I made myself the collator of all this humor, most of which was wordplay and parody of well-known Pagan tropes. I was writing letters (on paper! with ink!) to a variety of Pagans who were playing along, sending puns back and forth and having a grand old time. I compiled the whole thing into an article that was published in one or two of the many Pagan 'zines that were around at the time.

When I was a young and inexperienced priestess, I worked a lot harder at it, and so Stormcircle took an enormous amount of energy. The work of running a Pagan circle is always demanding, but over the years I've become far more relaxed about it. I no longer write the careful lecture notes I once did, for example. Plus, the whole notion of paper handouts has gone by the wayside. With the Internet, it's easy to get basic materials to people, so there's a huge clerical task I no longer need do.

Over the course of three months, I provided handouts on such subjects as mind-control exercises, chants, the Runic alphabet, the Gaia Hypothesis, poetry, and more. Some were handouts I'd received from Susan, and some were articles I found interesting or excerpts from books. As I've said, without an Internet, and with Paganism much more closeted, coming across good material was rare, so sharing it was valuable. Classes covered Gods, archetypes, circle etiquette, chanting practice, magic, the use of voice in ritual, meditation, and so forth.

Keeping myself busy was partly a way of masking an underlying depression that was coming to a head. It wasn't mania, and it wasn't fake. I *did* fall in love, the Flamingo Tradition *was* funny and fun to coordinate, and I *loved* being a High Priestess. But whenever I looked away from those things and just sat quietly for a moment, it all crumbled to dust, and I was in terrible pain.

I wasn't in denial about this. I was struggling actively, working in therapy to address it. I was seeing a psychiatrist but taking only antianxiety medication. In the days before Prozac and other SSRIs, antidepressants were a much less attractive choice. Older medications had more side effects and were often not as effective.

It all came to a head at the end of August. I wanted to borrow a car so I could visit John's grave on his birthday. There were phone calls to make and missed connections, it was getting harder and harder to make it work, I was feeling frenzied, I was profoundly sad about John, and I was overwhelmed by a sense of failure because I couldn't do what seemed like a simple and proper thing. As the day progressed, it became unbearable. I couldn't stand it. I needed to be done with this pain.

That evening I attempted suicide.

In a strange way, the suicide attempt was the best thing that ever happened to me. I'd lived my entire life alternating between denying there was anything wrong and fearing there was something terribly wrong that no one else had noticed. Now, at last, there was no denying, no failure to notice. A suicide attempt is a terrible way to find authenticity, but for me it was a cathartic kind of truth-telling: "This is intolerable. It must change or end."

In the hospital, I met other patients struggling with similar issues. They were normal people with serious problems. They weren't scary "crazy" people, as I'd imagined. You couldn't tell the patients from the staff without checking the ID bracelet. It was comforting. It was as if I'd fought like hell to stay on my side of the boundary between "sane" and "crazy," and now that I'd crossed the line, I didn't have to fight so hard and could concentrate my energies on getting well. Plus, it wasn't so "crazy" on the other side after all; the terrible thing I'd been fighting was clinical depression, not psychosis. I wasn't delusional, irrational, psychotic, or paranoid. Once I'd crossed this line, it no longer held any terror for me.

Somehow, diving into the dark place paid off for me. It took years, but I think now that I am one of the sanest people I know because I did hard work for a long time to recover from some terrible stuff. I had wonderful help and support, for which I will always be grateful. Over the years I've had relapses into depressive illness, I've benefited from breakthroughs in medication, and I've worked with a variety of wonderful therapists. It's so important to know that this work *can* be done and *can* succeed, and that life after depression can be joyful and fulfilling and full of real, vivid sensation. Reaching out for help was the vital first step.

Susan offered more than once to do magic for my healing, but I declined. I understood myself to be on a journey. I wanted to go *through* it, not past it. I'd already done plenty of self-actualization work that seemed to say you could miraculously make pain disappear. Now that felt like denial, like a coat of transformational paint. I didn't want miracles; I wanted to walk my painful path to the end—not to die, but to finish the journey.

I was in the hospital for less than a week and, when I got out, went right back to work. I pushed myself too hard, too fast. As a result, in October I was back in the hospital, this time for three weeks, with six weeks off from work afterwards. It was during those nine weeks that my life changed dramatically. (I know, *again?* Yes. Again.)

Sometime during this period I found my totem animal, and it was in part through the aid of my totem that I survived and was restored to a love of life.

I was seeing a therapist in New Jersey, taking a bus from the city and back. I'd walk from the bus and cut through a park that backed into my therapist's block. In this park were three riding animals on springs, the kind a toddler can ride. It was twilight, and I saw the three animals dimly. Next to them, I saw three Canada geese. The geese were as still as the toy animals and spaced identically apart, so that for a moment I seemed to see six toys. Then, as one, the three geese turned and walked to an entire flock of perhaps fifty birds I hadn't seen, standing stock-still and filling a large piece of field. The three joined the flock, and when they were in place the entire flock turned as one and walked away.

It was breathtaking... the stillness, the oneness of movement, the illusion, the grace of rhythm and spacing. I knew in that moment that I was willing to live for no other reason than to be able to see geese. That was enough.

The Canada goose became my totem animal, which I suppose is perfect for someone who identifies as suburban.

SETTING UP A PSYCHIC SHIELD

During this period of my life I was intensely psychically sensitive (which is why I had trouble in rituals). In the hospital, I was exposed to people who were, themselves, in psychic turmoil, and I felt bombarded. Isaac taught me psychic-shielding techniques at that time that I use to this day.

1. First visualize the polarized lenses of a pair of UV-protective sunglasses. Polarized lenses let in good light (so you can see) but keep out bad (UV) light. Your shield should be psychically polarized, letting in the good energy of love and caring but keeping out the bad energy that overwhelms or harms you.

2. Imagine a pair of "psychic sunglasses," polarized to protect you. Visualize putting those sunglasses on.

3. Now picture the lenses of the glasses expanding, so they rise over your head and drop down around your body. The lenses basically grow until they become a full-body shield. You are cocooned in this shield. Be sure the top of your head and the soles of your feet are included.

4. Now test the shield. Picture someone negative coming toward you, and watch the person bounce off your shield. Then picture a loving person approaching you, and see that the shield lets them in. Do this two or three times until you are confident in your shield.

Use this psychic shield whenever you are entering a situation that feels emotionally or psychically risky. If you're in a sensitive space, like I was, do it daily before leaving your bedroom. If you are troubled by nightmares, do it before going to sleep.

Between my two hospital stays was the month of September and Isaac's visit for Mean Foghamar (pronounced "mon FOWr"), the Druid Fall Equinox.

This was a low-key event. ADF was small in those days, though growing rapidly. There were perhaps thirty people at Mean Foghamar, local Druids who were important in the early growth of ADF.

As I was healing, I needed to go off by myself a lot, so during one afternoon I was in the tent, reading. Of course, tents are flimsy, you can hear every word spoken outside, and Isaac's voice carried better than most people's. So, while I was in the tent, hearing snippets of conversation, I heard Isaac's voice clearly saying, "My old High Priest, Robin Goodfellow..."

"Hey Isaac," I said from inside the tent, "is Robin Goodfellow in Berkeley?"

"Yes."

"Is his real name Stephen Edwards?"

"Why yes, it is!"

Are there words to express my astonishment? I was almost shaking with the understanding that something profound had just happened, and yet nothing had *happened*; it was just a coincidence. Is there such a thing as "just" a coincidence, or is it all synchronicity—meaningful confluence? One afternoon in 1985, long before our relationship began, I ran into Isaac on the subway; we said hello and moved on. Our lives momentarily converged and later came together more permanently. Here was another convergence.

The Pagan community was quite small back in 1976, when I first wrote to Robin Goodfellow. Indeed, Isaac knew many of the people I had encountered back then, including Margot Adler and Z Budapest (whom I wrote to but never heard from). But this wasn't just knowing someone; it was the intimate relationship of initiator to initiate. And it wasn't just someone I had encountered; it was someone who had played a pivotal role in putting me on my path. And, of course, there was the "coincidence" of overhearing that conversational snippet.

Over time, I have discovered that my life is lived in circles; if I wait long enough, the next circle will come around to the beginning again. Meeting Isaac in Ashfield was a circle. Running into him on the subway was a hint of a circle to come. That Robin Goodfellow was Isaac's High Priest was a striking, amazing circle, the first I'd experienced of this magnitude, and it blew my mind.

Chapter 9

THERE AND BACK AGAIN

1987 in the California Sierras: our "honeymoon"

Saturday night we had a grand time at a Bardic Circle at Greyhaven.
I read 3 poems: "Home," "Persephone" & "The Cockteaser"
—they were all very well received.

—*Journal entry, Monday, November 2, 1987*

It was during Isaac's trip east in September that he first told me he loved me, and our long-distance romance changed from then on. We spoke on the phone every day. I wrote frequent letters; Isaac wrote much less frequently. (Even in 1986, letter writing was a dying art, much bemoaned by certain people. E-mail isn't all that killed the letter.) He was living in Oakland with J. P. McClimans and J. P.'s wife, Shirin Morton, and I ended up spending so much time on the phone with J. P. that year that, when we finally met, we felt we knew each other.

I was becoming increasingly frustrated with the Gardnerian tradition. I loved the Gods and wasn't considering leaving Paganism again, but the tradition itself was feeling restrictive and stifling. I wanted to break the rules, branch out, and do my own thing. I said and did nothing; these feelings were an agony to me, and I kept them entirely private. I thought I would wait until I got third degree and then branch out on my own.

People who collect degrees like notches on their belts are thought of poorly in the Craft community, and people who get third degree in a tradition for the sole purpose of leaving that tradition with its credentials are especially unsavory. On the other hand, the credentials have value, and I hadn't been a Gardnerian just to get the degrees. I'd been working hard for over five years, and now that I was feeling antsy, it made sense to finish what I had started. I knew that Susan would disapprove of my desire to branch out. Perhaps I was deceiving her, but perhaps my own ambivalence was what kept me silent.

I'd been working for a magazine for four years. I'd started as an administrative assistant and been promoted to a sales associate. At first, selling ad space and cold-calling were great, but after John died I found it stressful. After I got out of the hospital the second time, I stayed on medical leave. At the time, I assumed I'd go back to sales, but one of the things that changed permanently was my comfort with selling. There's a kind of false face involved, and I was never able to comfortably put that face back on. It took returning to sales for me to realize that, though.

One day, home on leave, I received a call from my boss. Marianne told me that the magazine had decided to open a sales office in San Francisco, and she was offering me the job, which involved opening the office, getting it set up, and running it as a one-person operation. I was delighted to accept! Over the next several weeks, Isaac and I talked and planned, planned and talked. I was going to get an apartment, but as the time approached and our conversations deepened, Isaac told me how very much he loved me and made the commitment I needed. We agreed to move in together.

I returned to work in December and was introduced to Megan, who was there to learn the business and then open the new San Francisco office.

What? What?

Marianne seemed to have no recollection of offering me the job. There was nothing I could do about this bizarre development at the office. Isaac and I agreed that nothing had changed between us. I was moving to California, job or no job. We planned the move for the end of April.

I took my responsibility as the High Priestess of Stormcircle seriously. Through a chain of phone calls and letters, I found a couple of reputable groups that were accepting new members, and gave that contact information to my students. Stephanie, who had been so comfortable being the only African American in the group, felt the call of her roots and sought out a Yoruba-based tradition instead of staying with

Wicca. One person joined Susan's group. Barbara, who was now in a relationship with Shenain, stayed involved with ADF but wasn't interested in finding another Wiccan teacher.

Susan taught that third degree was something that wasn't given out until it was *needed*, which meant until you had students who were ready to be initiated. She taught this to me as the Gardnerian way and as how she was taught. I've since learned that there's a lot of variation in how Gardnerians teach, so I'll simply call it her policy. At second degree I could start a Pagan Way, still under her authority. When I had students in the Pagan Way who were ready to be initiated, I would then receive third degree, which would make me the fully autonomous High Priestess of my coven.

I begged Susan to give me third degree before I left for California. At second, I wouldn't be able to start my own group, because I wouldn't be able to initiate when the time came. I also wouldn't be able to become someone else's student. Technically, sure I could, but most teachers preferred to work with beginners, and I was already running my own group, so it would be awkward. At first she refused, but I persuaded her that my unique circumstance *did* constitute need.

I was given third degree shortly before my move. I will not describe that ritual, and I wouldn't even if I was not bound by an oath of secrecy, because its beauty and profundity don't belong to words. I will say this: when I woke up the morning after receiving third degree, the dilemma that I had been struggling with—of whether to leave the Gardnerian tradition—was over. I no longer felt at risk of violating the rules of the tradition; it seemed now that I *was* the tradition, I *was* its rules and structures. I could see my path laid out before me, not in a clairvoyant manner but simply, here it was, here was who *I* was, here was my place. There were no more questions. I was at peace.

There was a flurry of events in a few short months. During this entire period, I saw Isaac face to face just once, at Winterspirit Festival in February. It was intense, passionate, and all too brief. Then he came to New York in April to bring me back with him. We were flying, and the moving truck would meet us.

That was when he met my family. I was very nervous about introducing him to my mother. "Don't worry, I'm great with mothers," he assured me. "I'll call her 'ma'am.'"

"Isaac, you are closer in age to my mother than you are to me. *Please* don't call her 'ma'am.'"

The look on his face at this news was comical. My mother was twenty-two when I was born, and Isaac was exactly eleven and a half years older than I. He took my advice, and Isaac and Mom always got along well.

While we were in New York, we also signed the Articles of Association that legally organized ADF. The original trustees were Isaac, me, Isaac's former roommate Shenain Bell, Susan Kirsch, and Karl Steinmayer. We met at Susan Kirsch's home in Connecticut; she had been the organizer of the Mean Foghamar event the previous September.

In California, we shared a small house in Alameda with notorious Pagan author Aidan Kelly and his then-girlfriend (now ex-wife), Julie.

For an East Coast Pagan, California was a revelation. There was so much Paganism going on, so frequently, in so many places, that it bordered on competitive. Pagan bard Leslie Fish was in the process of forming a Pagan choir group, to float between various group's rituals and provide choral singing. I don't think any other part of the country had the community and organization to support something like that. I attended one meeting of that group, to help in preparing for an upcoming Druid ritual. A small, soft-spoken, white-haired woman arrived late, apologetic that her aerobics class had delayed her. She seemed the very picture of suburban ordinariness. When Isaac and I left, I introduced myself to her, and she said her name was Zee. In the car, Isaac asked me what I thought of Z Budapest. My jaw just about hit the floor. *That* was the infamous Z Budapest? My goodness!

Isaac also took me to Greyhaven, a kind of legendary Pagan/science fiction/Society for Creative Anachronism (SCA) nexus. In fact, this was where the SCA was started, when renowned authors Marion Zimmer Bradley and Diana Paxson still lived in the huge Victorian home in the Berkeley hills that bore the name Greyhaven. We went one night to attend a Bardic Circle, another Greyhaven tradition, founded by Karen

Anderson and popularized (probably) by the late Paul Zimmer, Marion's brother and an author in his own right. When we attended, Paul was a new father and, as usual, the host of the Bardic. Over the years, Isaac and I worked to spread the tradition of the Bardic Circle far and wide, although I've seen many things called a "Bardic Circle" that bore little resemblance to the tradition I fell in love with that night. There were fifty or more people, including some of the finest poets and performers in Berkeley. I shared the poem "Persephone," Isaac sang, Paul himself recited an ancient prayer/spell for protection that gives me chills when I recall it, and the whole evening was magical.

The Bardic Circle

A Bardic Circle is a ritual of performance. It can be done in a secular context, in which the point is to perform and to share, or it can be done in a sacred context, in which the performance is an offering.

If you are offering your Bardic Circle, open by invoking the god or gods of the occasion. We generally open by invoking Brigid, goddess of poetry and bardic arts.

A Bardic Circle is done in "rounds." A round starts anywhere and moves clockwise around the room. When the round reaches the last person, it's time for a break.

During a break, there is usually feasting and/or drinking. It's also the time for people to leave. There is no cast circle, and people can leave at any time, but it's most polite to wait until a break.

During round one, everyone must perform. Because of this, and because round one is generally the most crowded, round-one performances should be short—no recitations of ten-page stories!

A "performance" can be an original work or not. It can be a song, an instrumental, a comedy skit, a dramatic reading, a poem, a dance, juggling, and so on. You can enlist the help of others during your performance, whether by doing a three-person scene from a play or by having everyone drum.

From round two onward, you can pass your turn or, instead of performing, you can make a request of another person.

As people leave and the group gets smaller, later rounds can be devoted to longer pieces.

When the final round is over and everyone agrees to call it a night, if you have invoked gods, thank them before you close.

⌒

The first time Isaac and I did ritual together, we were both very nervous. There's a lot of weight put on magical partnership within Paganism. What if we weren't good together magically? It seemed like a crazy amount of pressure!

Fortunately, we worked beautifully together. Paganism was the centerpiece of our relationship; we fought about it, thought about it, theorized, analyzed, dissected, performed, and started over at the beginning. Isaac was working on a book about the structure of Pagan ritual,[2] and we would talk about every ritual through the lens of that work. We began performing public ceremonies together, with the caveat that he had to give up on trying to get me to sing—or at least, to sing well. (Many years later, a singing teacher enabled me to reclaim my voice, but Isaac didn't have the know-how to train me.)

In a way, my relationship with Isaac was a professional partnership, with the profession being Pagan clergy. Through Isaac, I began to take the idea of being a member of the Pagan clergy seriously. I was not merely the High Priestess of a small group of friends, I was a vital part of the community.

We'd argue about secret covens versus public Paganism. Isaac felt that secrecy bred corruption, while I believed (and believe) that the honoring of secrets maintained integrity.

Isaac's belief was that standards that were secret were no standards at all. If you didn't know the criteria by which someone became a third-degree Gardnerian, for example, then you knew nothing about the person's credentials even if you knew she was a third-degree Gardnerian.

---

2. That book was never completed, but a large portion of it is available as *Neopagan Rites* (Woodbury, MN: Llewellyn Publications, 2007).

Through ADF, he was creating a credentialing system that was public, standardized, and equal in quality to any mainstream pastoral college or ordination process.

I had to agree that high-quality standards were a good idea, and that clergy should be well trained. I had studied and worked for six years to become a third degree, and I felt that gave me better qualifications than someone who had been Pagan for six months and was now calling herself "High Priestess." I believed that the position of High Priestess required an understanding of how ritual worked, how best to conduct ceremonies, and how to improvise if needed. It also required a full knowledge of the symbols of tools and the esoteric basis of Wicca, Moon lore, seasonal lore, divination, trance, how to teach, how to manage group energy and group dynamics, spellcasting, mythology, and more.[3] I disagreed (strongly) that the only way to accomplish high-quality training was through published standards and a structured study system; the Craft I knew was based on individualized apprenticeship. Yet I found enormous value in the system Isaac was creating with ADF. I could see many Pagan groups "borrowing" ADF's study program for their own use.

We argued all the time about secrets and secrecy, about mysteries versus open knowledge. At the same time, I fully supported ADF's work, and by this time, I was supporting the organization financially as well. I was also studying the ADF ritual and learning to perform it with Isaac.

As we performed it, we experimented with it: What happens with the energy *here*? What if we moved this part to *there*? The ADF ritual is based around an open space, in which energy flows in and out from the center. A Wiccan circle, by contrast, is based around a closed space, a sealed circle in which the energy flows deosil (clockwise) around the perimeter. I learned that there were many right ways to do ritual, and that the declared intention of the ritual shaped its energy.

---

3. An introduction to the course of study that I think is necessary can be found in my book *The Study of Witchcraft: A Guidebook to Advanced Wicca* (San Francisco, CA: Red Wheel/Weiser, 2007). It won't make you a High Priest/ess, but it will lay the groundwork I've delineated.

I was an accomplished priestess, and Isaac was happy to acknowledge that. He readily praised my skill. But I was also learning all over again, from a new teacher. I never really admitted it to him, always stubbornly standing my ground as my own person, but he taught me as much as Susan did.

A lot of people we knew referred to our relationship as a "mixed marriage," as if one of us was Christian and one Jewish (which, by birth, was true—but that's not what they meant). Druids complained that Isaac shouldn't be with a Wiccan, and Gardnerians complained that Isaac was a heretic who spoke against Gardner, and I shouldn't be with him. I thought, "Don't you people know that to the outside world we're both exactly the same kind of crazy?"

More than that, I felt, and feel, that the Pagan community is whole only with a public *and* a private face. As a Gardnerian, I am a member of a mystery tradition, but clearly that's not for everyone, nor is it meant to be. Gerald Gardner talked about how, during the Burning Times and before, the Witches were the clergy for the Pagan people. A model of how he envisioned this can be found in his novel *High Magic's Aid*. To me, that says he understood the Witchcraft he was reviving as existing in the context of a larger and more diverse Pagan community. I see this as the esoteric (inner) and exoteric (outer) forms of Paganism, and only with both is Paganism complete. With Isaac, I was doing the work of empowering the exoteric community, which was meaningful work that I believed in very much.

Susan taught me that a lot of initiates taught ritual that they felt was meaningless, or even fake, and then rescinded that teaching, replacing it with the "real" stuff once a student was initiated. She *hated* that. She wanted to do rituals that were real. I learned, then, that the Pagan, accessible stuff was as real as the private, initiatory stuff. If the rituals were very different, I could see them as two sides of a coin; viewed holistically, neither could exist without the other.

In June of 1987, Isaac and I took a three-week tour of the western half of the United States. Although we were not yet married, I think of that as our honeymoon trip. From Alameda, we went north through wine country to Ancient Ways, a Pagan festival held at Harbin Hot Springs. During the driest part of the dry season, a strict "no open fires" rule was in force. This meant that there could be no candles or even incense on the altar. I attended a Wiccan circle there, and at the point where the circle would normally be censed (see the next section), the High Priestess carried the scourge around the circle, brushing it lightly against each person. It was a lesson in creative accommodation of circumstances that I've never forgotten.

CASTING THE CIRCLE WITH THE ELEMENTS

There are many ways to cast a circle. I was taught that the circle is cast three times: once with the sword, once with saltwater, and once with incense. The sword (or athame) is the will of the Witch and the power of the spoken word. You cast the circle by declaring that you've cast it. This is the true casting.

The saltwater is Earth (salt) plus Water, and represents cleansing of the circle. The incense is Air (the smoke) plus Fire (the actual burning coal), and represents sweetening. Incense is said to be appealing to the Gods and other beings, and draws them to the circle.

Most importantly, for purposes of the Ancient Ways ritual, is the elemental representation: Air, Fire, Water, and Earth must be included in every circle casting.

If incense is not available, Air can be represented by a fan or feather. Unlit incense, especially if it is something associated with Air, can also be used.

Fire is often represented by a candle or lamp instead of the burning part of the incense. An unlit candle or a flint might be used, or a scourge.

If saltwater is not desirable, a circle can be placed on the ground with pebbles. During handfastings, I've used strewn flower petals to represent Earth. Water is rarely represented by anything but water itself, although a seashell can be carried around the circle if you absolutely cannot get drops of water on your floor.

⌒

From Ancient Ways we drove north, then turned east, crossing the California Sierras. We had a futon and curtains in the back of the van, so we'd drive until we were tired, find a campground (we had a KOA guide), and stop for the night. One night in Iowa, we found we were too tired to make it to the next stopping point. We pulled over just off the road and went to sleep. We woke up in the morning with a completely jammed transmission; only neutral and reverse were working. We also discovered that we'd spent the night at a construction site. This was embarrassing for handling the morning toilet needs but convenient for getting someone to call us a tow truck. (We were also pretty mad, because we'd felt something hinky in the transmission and had a mechanic look at it before we left home. He'd insisted it was fine.)

We were in Dyersville, Iowa, and our transmission needed to be replaced, so a mechanic had to drive to a bigger town to get one and bring it back. We'd be there all day. We phoned our contacts at our next destination to let them know we'd be late. It was a dull afternoon, with nothing to do.

Ironically, today Dyersville is a tourist attraction, home to the famous baseball field from *Field of Dreams*. That's a 1989 movie, so we were stuck there too early.

With a brand-new transmission, we headed off to Pagan Spirit Gathering (PSG) in Wisconsin. There, as at Ancient Ways, we conducted an ADF ritual. There were a number of ADF members at PSG, and I overheard grumbling gossip that I was the one partnering with Isaac for the ritual—he was giving the job to his girlfriend instead of someone really qualified. I resented that for two reasons. First, I was already a priestess in my own right; this was my introduction to the way in which being "Isaac's girlfriend" could diminish my own individuality in the eyes of the public. Second, no one else had learned the ritual. Instead of complaining

about nepotism, people might simply have made themselves more qualified!

At PSG, a Gardnerian named Kyril Oakwind gave a presentation
on the ways that traditional and eclectic Wiccans could learn from one
another. It was based on an article that she'd recently published in a
Pagan 'zine that I'd liked very much. However, she wasn't able to present her material, because as soon as she began, people in attendance
began questioning her on her right to define what was "traditional"
and "eclectic." Quickly it emerged that there was a great deal of resent-
ment toward initiatory traditions. If we had something of value to the
community, how dare we keep it secret? How dare we claim that a self-
initiation was not every bit as good as a lineaged one? The original syl-
labus was discarded, and the presentation became an impromptu panel
discussion, with the Gardnerians answering the many questions of the
other attendees. Based on that experience, I developed a class called
"Who Are the Gardnerians and Why Are They Naked?" The sole purpose of this class was to provoke hard questions from attendees so they
could be answered frankly.

Why *do* we keep secrets? There are three basic reasons. The first
is to confine advanced materials to those who are trained to use them
safely. Children aren't allowed to handle matches, and smart, compe-
tent laypeople don't get taught how to perform brain surgery. Certain
knowledge requires training, maturity, and a foundation in other techniques before it can be taught.

Second is the whole "secret handshake" thing. We keep secrets that
allow us to create a group identity; we are the people who know XYZ.
Such secrets have no inherent value except inasmuch as they're secret.

Finally, some secrets are kept because they are intimate and would
be profaned by discussion. Anyone who has ever kept a diary, or called a
lover by a private pet name, understands that certain things should not
be shared.

What about self-initiation? The angry argument that it is "just as
valid" as a traditional initiation has no meaning unless you define the
word *valid*. If *valid* means "sacred to the Gods," then that's between
you and the Gods, and no one can say you nay. If *valid* means "of Gard-

nerian lineage: initiated by a Gardnerian who was initiated by a Gardnerian and so on, back to Gardner," then obviously a self-initiation is a different animal entirely. If *valid* means "having acquired certain skills and undergone certain experiences," then a self-initiate may or may not qualify but clearly cannot be accepted as qualified without further exploration.

From PSG we headed south. Our journey took us to visit ADF members who had corresponded with Isaac and never met him, as well as old friends. We spent a day in Madison, Wisconsin, then visited Isaac's friends in Kansas City, Missouri.

I had spent my entire life up to that point on the East Coast. I knew New York, New Jersey, and New England, and had visited Montreal. Having lived in New York City, I felt very urbane, but I had seen little of the United States or the world. Over the course of a few weeks, we visited about half the United States, and it was eye-opening, to say the least.

From Kansas we drove down into Texas, stopping briefly in Dallas and then in Austin. As we headed out of Texas toward New Mexico, a Cadillac started following us, honking and waving. Finally we pulled over, and Isaac went to speak with the driver. He said he was from California and had honked because he saw our license plates. Texas had been good to him, and he wanted to give back to California. He was clearly drunk, but he pressed on us a couple of cold sodas and fifty dollars before driving off. Later, when we stopped for gas, we realized we had nothing in our pockets but that fifty—we didn't have enough gas to make it to the next ATM. That strange, drunken good ol' boy had saved our necks.

My favorite part of our journey was through New Mexico and Arizona. Camping, I was acutely aware that every natural sound in the desert was alien to me—every bird song, every insect hum or buzz. I felt like I was waking up on Mars. We visited Carlsbad Caverns, with seven miles of living underground rock. It was a more profound experience of Earth than I could have imagined. As we walked through the caverns, I felt presence in deep shadows; unvoiced calls seemed to come from crevices. I struggled to stay in my body, feeling increasingly drawn into nooks and corners.

Carlsbad's rock is living because it is never touched: once rock is touched, oils from the skin stop its growth. Tourists are kept away from stalactites and stalagmites by a barrier, and only a narrow path is cut rock.

At the center of the caverns is a cafe and gift shop. Here the rock is dead, and a rest area has been carved out. Walking into it, my nearly out-of-body experience came to a sudden end; I was slammed back into ordinary consciousness. I became faint and developed a headache. Isaac had to support me on our way back to the car.

As Carlsbad was to Earth, so the Grand Canyon was to Air. As a Taurus, I was far more susceptible to the lure of Earth elementals. Isaac was a triple Air sign, with a Libra Sun; he bordered on floating away during our entire Grand Canyon visit.

You can't describe the Grand Canyon. People see it in the movies, in pictures, or on TV, and they think they're prepared for its immense beauty and ability to inspire awe. They're not. I wasn't, and everyone I know who has been there reports the same thing: The actual place is *so much more* than any depiction or imagination can encompass. It is the biggest UP, the biggest DOWN, the biggest WIDE. It is a vista of color and openness and, everywhere, *presence*.

I began to think of the tourists we saw, everywhere we went, cameras in hand, as pilgrims. They were visiting sacred nature sites, not knowing that they were worshiping the Goddess. Isaac took his harp out of the van and brought it to the edge of the canyon. Seated, with his feet over vast miles of nothing, he held out his harp and let the wind play a tune. Isaac had struggled to keep me in my body throughout our visit to Carlsbad Caverns, and now I was struggling to keep Isaac in his. I had a finger hooked through the back of his pants the whole time we were there. He was constantly on the edge of stepping off in oneness with Air.

On the map of the park we saw a chapel, and next to that a "non-denominational worship site." We wanted so much to do a ritual in this amazing place. (We'd discussed it in Carlsbad as well, but there was no place for it.) We weren't prepared for ritual, but we improvised. In the van we pulled out salt and a cup from our camp food supplies, opened a bottled water to fill the cup, and found a stick of incense and a lighter (I was still a smoker). We brought these simple supplies to the worship site and found a stone altar with an enormous (ten feet tall at least) cross attached to it. Non-denominational indeed! We moved away from the clearing where the cross was and headed onto the path, where we found another stone that could be used as an altar, and did a short ceremony, thanking the Gods for the beauty of this place and expressing our love for their holiness. We thought to seal this ceremony with sacred lovemaking, but we couldn't even kiss without other tourists walking by, so we gave up that idea.

We stayed with some wonderful Pagan folks that night in Tucson, Arizona, and the next day started toward California. We crossed the Mojave Desert, as desolate and empty as anything I'd ever seen—the Fire to add to our elemental experiences. (It would be a couple of years before we'd round out our set with a visit to the Water of Niagara Falls.) We were crossing in June, without air conditioning, and the Fire seeped into our bones. We loved the giant saguaro cacti but were happy when that part of the journey was over.

The final natural wonder of our trip was Yosemite National Park. Again, the immense beauty and sacredness moved us to ceremony, this time inside a giant redwood, and again we were thwarted in our desire to sanctify our ritual sexually.

Maybe it's weird to talk about wanting to make love in these places. Maybe it was just that we were honeymooning and hot for each other, but most forms of Paganism acknowledge sex as sacred and essential. Indeed, almost every religion will acknowledge that sex can be sacred, but the Pagan view is more expansive. Isaac would say that most monotheists have it that sex is sinful *except* in special circumstances when it's sacred (married, procreative, and so forth), while Pagans have it that sex is sacred *except* in special circumstances when it's wrong (nonconsensual or abusive situations). Sex alters the consciousness, bringing us closer to one another and to the Gods. It is joyful and exalting. In the Charge, the Goddess says, "All acts of love and pleasure are My rituals." To love as a ritual, when that is possible, is a very blessed thing.

But not in national parks, I guess.

Back home, I was working as a temp (a temporary secretary). I was also attending support groups and seeing a therapist. I began to relapse into depression. I added a psychiatrist who specialized in pharmacology to my repertoire, and the psychopharmaceutical experimentation began. I had bad reactions and side effects with a number of medications, including a grand mal seizure one memorable night. All of these reactions were not only horrifying, they were setbacks in my recovery, wasting days or weeks where I wasn't any closer to climbing out of the dark hole I was in.

In the meantime, I'd also begun to write a book. I'd been writing articles and essays for years in Pagan 'zines. Pagan print in the 1980s and early 1990s was a lot like the Pagan Internet today. Some publications were very professional; some were sporadic and infrequent amateur efforts, often one-person operations; and most fell somewhere in between. For a few years, around 1988 to '91, I was the "exchange publication" manager for ADF. Most 'zines had exchange subscriptions: you send me free issues of yours, I send you free issues of mine. I was in charge of that, and as a result, I was subscribed to approximately eighty such 'zines. I joked to Isaac one time that Pagan magazines should have "Sorry we're late" in their masthead. Most seemed to open with, "Welcome to our [Beltane/Samhain/Yule] issue. Sorry we're late..." They operated on shoestring budgets and were sometimes printed via stealth photocopying, and if there weren't enough submissions, the editor-in-chief/publisher/printer/entire staff would have to fill in by writing more.

Some of the magazines were great, and many weren't. The heart and soul of most amateur publishing, in any niche, seems to be bad poetry, and Pagan publishing was no exception. Some had simplistic or wrong-headed articles, or weren't well written. Yet they burst with creativity and blazed trails of ritual and magical experimentation, theological inquiry, and community building. I might have skimmed through most, but they were a thrill to read. With the festival movement still small (but growing), 'zines were how the community came together to hash out issues and opinions, to share ideas, to explore, and just to enjoy connecting.

I was a prolific article and letter writer for a half-dozen or so of these 'zines, and had been since 1982 or '83, so I knew I could write, but writing an entire book seems like a leap if you've never done it. Living with two writers, though, I felt a lot of support for the notion that I had a book in me.

Since my departure from, and then return to, the Craft a couple of years earlier, I had done some reading about myth, and wanted to write about the Descent and the Charge as true Wiccan myths that fit a scholarly definition of myth. As I wrote, I also read more and more on the topic of myth, and the more I read, the more I felt I needed to learn.

I spent ten years trying to write that book and needing to learn more. I'd write a little, and read a lot, and write a little, and read a lot. Eventually, I learned so much that I no longer believed in my own theories. I do still believe that the Charge and the Descent are myths, but my idea of what defined a myth was no good, and the book's entire outline was based on that definition. I was stuck.

On the bright side, I was able to put together a good collection of workshop offerings based on my work with myth. Isaac and I were traveling together to festivals, and at first, I was an unknown quantity to festival organizers. They were willing to put me on the speakers list as a courtesy to Isaac, but I felt uncomfortable riding anyone's coattails. I was, after all, already a priestess and a teacher of the Craft. If they were going to give me an opportunity, I was by the Gods going to prove I had merit of my own. It really only took about a year for the festival circuit to get used to me. My workshops tended to be popular, and feedback was good.

⌒

Around August of 1987 we traveled to San Diego for a Church and School of Wicca event. Isaac had a friendship of many years with Gavin Frost, who was a mentor and father figure to him, so when the Frosts were in California for an event of their own church, they invited us to join them. At the time, both Ray Buckland and Scott Cunningham lived in San Diego, so the event organizers invited them as well. However, in those days the Frosts and their church members mixed rarely if ever with the rest of the Pagan community. The organizers didn't seem to realize that having three heavy hitters—well-known Pagan authors in a decade with relatively few of them—meant they could and should promote their event far and wide. Instead, it was a small event with only those attendees who would have shown up for the Frosts regardless.

That was the week I was reading *The Wise Wound*, one of the few books written (at the time) about menstruation and its history, evolution, and psychic impact on women. Among other things, the book suggested that the "bitchiness" associated with menstruation actually arose from denying one's greater psychic sensitivity at that time. In other words, if you feel averse to doing something, perhaps for meaningful intuitive reasons, but do it anyway, it will naturally make you grumpy. The book suggested that it's natural for women to want to be more isolated and exposed to fewer stimuli during their periods.

With that text fresh in my mind, and having my period at this event and not particularly having fun, I decided to avoid as many people as possible, as much as possible. Scott Cunningham, who was often shy at public appearances, felt exactly the same way. We managed to sequester ourselves in one of the hotel rooms, skipping the rest of the event. As a result, we became close friends, and my second book is dedicated to his memory.

The San Diego trip brought us in touch again with sacred nature. We visited Sea World, which has (or had) a whale and dolphin petting pool. Both Isaac and I had incredibly spiritual experiences petting the baby pilot whale. Isaac turned to me and said, "Deb, the whale said, 'Blessed be.'" I called the whale a Zen master. We also took a bunch of pictures of ourselves with flamingos to share with the rest of the Flam-Trad! Then we drove the slow way home, up the California coast, an exquisite journey. We stopped on the beach at Carmel, since I had never seen a sunset over the ocean. It was all incredibly beautiful.

It's strange that I was clinically depressed during that period, and it speaks to the sometimes paradoxical nature of depression. I was, in a lot of ways, living an idyllic life. I was at the beginning of a relationship that was romantic and happy. I was traveling, meeting people, seeing new places, and learning new things. My writing was (I thought then) productive. All of this was a surface that didn't touch my illness.

I was also homesick. I never thought of myself as a New Yorker to such an extent as I did in California. Everywhere, it seemed, someone pointed out to me that my attitude, or my values, or my taste in food (not to mention my accent) was "so New York." I wouldn't have thought that of myself, but in contrast to so many Californians, who were so willing to mention it, it certainly seemed to be true. As summer turned to fall, I also realized that this would be my first Thanksgiving away from my family.

Our living situation fell apart quite suddenly. We needed a place to live by November 1st. At this point, Isaac turned to me and said, "Honey, would you like us to move back to New York?"

To say that this was a surprise doesn't cut it. I'd moved all my worldly goods three thousand miles because Isaac had sworn to me that he could no longer live anywhere but California. I was flabbergasted, but I said yes. Or rather, "YES!" Barbara and Shenain were now living together in Barbara's big Victorian house in Nyack, New York, and were happy to welcome us as roommates.

We rented a storage space and moved everything into it. We spent our last week at a friend's in Berkeley so we could be in the area to fulfill our Samhain commitments for the weekend of November 7th. On Monday the 9th we were to load the rental truck and depart. We'd scheduled a speaking engagement for Isaac in Salt Lake City for Tuesday night.

During our last couple of weeks in Alameda, Isaac started complaining that his left arm was sore. Neither of us thought anything of it, because with all the loading and lifting of boxes, sore arms seemed the most natural thing in the world. One day at lunch, Isaac's friend Larry pointed out that the left arm had phlebitis—there was a red trail from his wrist, up his arm, to his armpit, which was swollen. It was then that we realized the cat scratch he'd gotten a few weeks back was infected. We went to the emergency room and got antibiotics. By our last weekend, though, he was no better.

We went back to the emergency room, but because we were leaving town, they were unwilling to do anything except give him more of the pills that weren't working. Then we hooked the van to a tow bar and started out of town.

We got maybe three miles. The van kept falling off the tow bar. Isaac would put it back on, we'd drive slowly away, feel something funny, and it would be off again. It was frustrating, close to midnight, and an insurmountable problem.

The friend we'd been staying with was surprised to see us return after all our heartfelt goodbyes, but we had to call it a night. In the morning, we returned the tow bar, drove up to Mariposa, left the van with Isaac's father, and headed off again in the rental truck. We arrived in Salt Lake City a full twenty-six hours late—a record for lateness Isaac held for many years. The gig went well (we'd postponed by phone, of course); there was an excellent turnout of Utah Pagans!

The next morning, we visited an emergency room in Salt Lake City. Isaac's armpit was now the size of a grapefruit. The infection had formed a shell that the antibiotics couldn't penetrate. The doctor attempted to drain it with a needle. Isaac's scream was bloodcurdling, but the procedure didn't work. He needed surgery.

In later years, I often said that we could survive anything because we survived that cross-country trip: the van falling off the back, the late start, the infection, the many doctor visits, the cats howling (and at one point running off), and the terrible sense that we were about two hundred miles ahead of gangrene the entire time. Isaac could easily have lost his arm.

We arrived in Nyack around midnight on Wednesday the 18th. Isaac had emergency surgery the next day. His armpit caused him pain for years afterwards.

And by the way, the surgeon scolded him when Isaac called the infection "Cat Scratch Fever." There are apparently *many* bacterial infections you can get from a cat scratch, and the one Isaac had was not the one known as Cat Scratch Fever. Nonetheless, we tended to call it that when telling the story; it was irresistible.

Chapter 10

KNOWLEDGE IS POWER

November 5, 1988: Our wedding day

So many people have assisted me in exploring and discovering the ways
of natural magic. Among these are:... Isaac Bonewits and
Deborah Lipp, for erudite insights...

—*Acknowledgments section of* Earth, Air, Fire & Water,
by Scott Cunningham[4]

⌒

The first time Isaac asked me to marry him, I had just moved to California. I thought it was way too soon, but after a week or two of persistent proposals, I finally compromised by refusing to marry immediately but agreeing to be officially engaged. Only later did he realize his divorce from his previous wife was not yet final!

Now we were in New York, and Isaac was divorced, but living with friends in a home that wasn't ours felt like playing house. I didn't want to get married until we had a place of our own.

At first, we were barely on our financial feet, and without Barbara's offer of rent-free living until we got employment, we wouldn't have made it. Two cross-country moves in six months wiped us out. We'd left the van behind, so we needed a car. We got a free junker through Jewish Family Services. It was a wreck and sometimes shorted out while driving. We'd have to open the hood and touch two wires together until we got a spark—neither safe nor fun. Passing inspection was out of the question, but the car enabled us to find jobs.

I was back with my old psychiatrist, and we were still experimenting with anti-depressants. I fought my illness hard, and I still lived with the

---

4. Scott Cunningham, *Earth, Air, Fire & Water: More Techniques of Natural Magic* (St. Paul, MN: Llewellyn Publications, 1991). Scott didn't tell us we were in the acknowledgments, and we didn't buy the book right away. A friend pointed it out.

odd paradox that, when I wasn't depressed, I was tremendously happy. When I reminisce, I think of this as a happy time, yet when I look in my journals, I find evidence of the depressive illness.

Ten months later, in September of 1988, we moved to an apartment in Dumont, New Jersey. I was ready to get the old gang back together, and re-formed Stormcircle in October, with Isaac as High Priest. Isaac firmly stated that he had no interest in becoming a Gardnerian initiate, but he was delighted to work with me in the Pagan Way, and there was no denying that we worked together beautifully. Barbara had never joined another Wiccan group, and she came back happily. In the Pagan Way, we experimented with power-raising techniques, trance, chanting, elemental energies, and more.

Isaac and I married on November 5, 1988. At first we thought to have a Wiccan ceremony, but getting someone to do a legal handfasting in those days wasn't easy. I'd had a big wedding when I was nineteen and didn't want another. We were married by a justice of the peace, with only my mother and my sister Roberta in attendance. Later that night, we cast a circle for just the two of us, exchanged vows, consecrated each other and our union, and consummated our marriage in sacred space. In both the secular and sacred ceremonies, our vows were for the rest of our lives, not "as long as love lasts." I know the latter is popular among Pagans, but I believe now, as I did then, that a vow is no vow at all unless it has teeth. "I vow to do what I feel like doing until I no longer feel like doing it" is not a vow, it's an inevitability. A true oath, a true commitment, is when you put your ass on the line.

Stormcircle grew quickly. By December we had a half-dozen members and a lot of additional people coming in and out. I was still learning a great deal from Isaac, but I learned even more from teaching and experimenting.

We worked with deeper trances, including the ritual of Drawing Down the Moon. I had been taught that this was for initiates only, but Isaac had worked with it in more public Pagan contexts and wanted to do it with me. Since he was *not* an initiate but had far more experience with the rite than I did, I agreed.

Drawing Down the Moon is the ritual by which the Goddess (or *a* goddess) is brought into the body of the High Priestess. The priestess cedes control of her body to the deity, who "speaks with her lips." The trance can range from inspiration, to various levels of co-occupying a single consciousness, to full-blown possession, with the High Priestess fully out of body, often with no memory of the experience afterwards. Although the name implies bringing the Moon into the body, it can be any goddess, not just a lunar goddess. When this ritual is done with the High Priest, it is called Drawing Down the Sun, and again, it need not be a solar deity.

In Wicca, this ritual is traditionally done with female deities entering female bodies and male deities entering male bodies. Some traditional Wiccans have expanded their practice to work cross-gender, and cross-gender possession is common in some other traditions, like Santería.

Drawing Down the Moon can be *intense*. What people expect, when they first hear of it, is the recitation of the Charge. It'll be pretty, it'll be inspiring, and we'll all go home happy with the uplifting religious message we received. That's *nothing* like the reality.

The first thing that happens is that you realize, *Holy shit, this is real.* There's a moment when you understand that, a moment before, you thought this was all playacting. Oh sure, you *thought* you believed, but some part of you held back, and then, when the reality is before you, when the gooseflesh is raised and the temperature in the room changes and you face intimate congress with GODS, all of a sudden you know that you never *really* believed before. You thought it would be touching, convincing, lovely, but not so blood-and-guts *real*.

Then you learn that the Gods are not all sweetness and light. They are complex, loving, kind, angry, persuasive, funny, demanding, horny, mocking, stern, and awe-inspiring in the true sense of the term. If you're new to Paganism, the range and depth of the faces of the Gods can throw you off-kilter; this is not the religion you were expecting.

When we first started doing this ritual, I had no training in this kind of trance. It is taught in the Gardnerian tradition, but Susan didn't practice or teach it. (It's normal for covens to have different focuses, and to pick and choose, from among the wealth of available material, the work that best suits the individual coven.) My early trances were light, and, of course, a light trance doesn't present the challenges I've just described. I would often feel like the Goddess was whispering just below the audible range or hovering nearby. It was a frustrating experience; I was eager for more.

Isaac was not just a good teacher, he was a master of projective magic. Many people you meet in the occult community are excellent at the passive arts: receiving psychic messages, divination, and the like. Isaac was relatively weak in some of those skills (he was a great Tarot reader, but his psychic reception was sketchy), but he had the more rare gift of sending. He could invoke a trance in another even better than he could receive a trance; he could send energy better than he could take it in. When Isaac called the Gods, *they came*. In time, they came into my body, since that's where he invoked them. Years later, when Isaac and I stopped working together magically, I was shocked to discover that Drawing Down the Moon was suddenly difficult. Here I'd thought I was good at trance, when it turned out a lot had depended on my brilliant partner. Eventually I found my sea legs without him, and receiving the Moon is a linchpin of my practice to this day.

The upshot was, once I started receiving the Goddess in a deep way, people *freaked out*. Many of those new to Paganism were simply not prepared for that kind of raw energy. One person left my group, and one left for a while and came back. Both reported being overwhelmed by the intensity they experienced.

Ultimately, to Isaac's disappointment, I decided to go back to the practice I'd been taught: Drawing Down was for initiates only. Being in the presence of living deities took training and grounding to handle.

Another experiment I ultimately dropped was working skyclad (nude) in the Pagan Way. The Gardnerian tradition practices skyclad; coven meetings are entirely nude. If a person needs to be clothed for some physical reason, that's accommodated, but shyness is never an acceptable reason. Some Pagan Way groups meet skyclad, and some meet robed. In the 1970s, skyclad was more common—hippie influence, no doubt—but today it's relatively rare.

I started Stormcircle Pagan Way as a robed group. Our apartment in Dumont was the top two floors of a three-story home that had been converted to a two-family house. The small room we circled in was in the attic, and in the summer, a fan didn't take the smallest bite out of the heat. One evening I decided to allow anyone who wished to work skyclad. Only one person remained robed. That person left the group shortly thereafter. In the end, I came to feel that the intimacy and vulnerability of nudity should come with a reciprocal commitment, and that means initiation. Nudity is easy for me but painful for many, and that should be respected. Stormcircle returned to being a robed group.

At Midsummer (Summer Solstice), Barbara hosted a joint ritual with the Jersey Shore group at her place. It was a late night, and Isaac and I stayed over on an air mattress. I am almost certain that is when and where our son, Arthur, was conceived.

We'd been actively trying to conceive for over a year, so when we found out, we were overjoyed. On the other hand, I found out the day before we were to leave for the Starwood Festival. Camping in ninety-degree heat during the first trimester is really no one's idea of a good time. I was nauseated and whiny. Most festivals have a "quiet camping" area for people who need their sleep. One night I lay sleepless, listening to loud singing coming from the "quiet" area. It was a bunch of friends of mine singing television theme songs at the top of their lungs (competing, it seems, with another group of singers further off). Something about nausea, pregnancy, one AM, and "Meet the Flintstones" just didn't work for me. I poked Isaac awake.

"Kill them."

"Deb..."

"Don't come back until they're all dead."

Some of those decidedly not-dead people still tease me about that night, but I think I was in the right.

As soon as I found out I was pregnant, I stopped taking any anti-depressants. My moods were as stable as a pregnant woman has any right to expect, and I didn't experience postpartum depression. I had a short, dramatic relapse into depression in 1993. By then, things were different, because Prozac was now available. SSRIs changed the treatment of depression; my symptoms were gone faster, with fewer side effects. After that, I stayed on medications of one kind or another for another several years, and have been unmedicated and symptom-free since 1998.

I thought I would enjoy pregnancy. I imagined a whole Earth Mother thing. I am not self-conscious about weight, which is something that ruins the fun for many women, but I found the experience uncomfortable and physically wearing. I was either nauseated or ravenous for eight of the nine months. I was always tired, I was short of breath, I itched, I had gas, I ached, and the baby kicked constantly and sometimes painfully. The only exception was during ritual. Except for one occasion, during our minimum two circles a month, I was never kicked during a ritual. It was like the sacred space lulled my fetus to sleep.

In February of 1990, Stormcircle Coven opened its magical doors. My first initiate was Barbara, who'd been my first student and was (and still is) my best friend. I did a second initiation two weeks later, figuring if I didn't get it all done before the baby came, it might be delayed indefinitely. We became a coven of three. The Pagan Way continued as well, so now I was doing three circles a month, two training circles with the Pagan Way and a monthly coven meeting.

Founding a coven is a long ritual. All of the tools to be used, including those items used only during initiations, must be consecrated in a special rite. Since I had no third-degree Gardnerian partner of my own, my initiator drove up from South Jersey to do this rite with me. In deference to his lengthy drive, we did both the coven-founding ritual and Barbara's initiation in one night, and the two combined took just about three hours. At the very end, as I was closing the circle, I got one swift belly kick: baby was tired of ritual.

During my ninth month, Scott Cunningham told me he was coming east, and we planned a visit. We spoke and wrote often but hadn't seen each other since San Diego, two years earlier. Scott was shy and did speaking engagements only rarely, but he was going to be in New Jersey and Boston and we were thrilled to be seeing each other again. Unfortunately, we never did.

Several days before Scott arrived, I started having Braxton-Hicks, or prodromal, labor. Commonly called "false labor," these are contractions that aren't close enough together or consistent enough to indicate the baby is coming. Mine were unusually frequent for Braxton-Hicks: I had contractions every thirty to forty-five minutes, round the clock. Every now and then I'd get a full hour of rest, and there was one delightful two-hour break, but otherwise it was unrelenting. When Scott arrived in New Jersey, I explained that I was perfectly well for visitors, and I'd love to see him, but I simply couldn't take a forty-five-minute drive; he'd have to come to me. Scott, however, was having agonizing headaches and could barely leave his hotel room.

Arthur Shaffrey Lipp-Bonewits was born at home, in Dumont, New Jersey, at 11:32 PM on Saturday, March 24, 1990, weighing eight pounds, fourteen ounces, and twenty-one inches long. In attendance were a nurse-midwife, a nurse, Isaac, and my mother. Isaac cut the cord.

The prodromal labor had started nine days earlier, and two hours before the baby was born, the midwife was still not convinced I'd had any true labor at all. She later said it was one of her most unusual births, but everyone was healthy, if exhausted. Isaac fell instantly and blissfully in love.

Throughout my pregnancy, I was sure I had a girl. Having had such a hand in raising my youngest sisters, I'd always wanted a baby girl all my own. Isaac professed that he didn't care about gender; he just wanted a beautiful, healthy baby. After Arthur was born, Isaac got up to make a couple of phone calls and spread the good news. In the next room, under his breath, I heard him say, "A *son!*" in a triumphant voice—it sounded like a fist pump!

The next day was Sunday, and my favorite meal in the whole world is a Jewish Sunday brunch: bagels and lox, whitefish, herring, cream cheese—the works. My family arrived around 11:30, laden with brunch fixings, to see the twelve-hour-old baby. They all fell madly in love with him. I was especially happy, then, that we'd left California, because having family nearby meant the world to me. It was enormously practical for finding willing babysitters as well, as we'd have the opportunity to learn.

Isaac was horrified by the whitefish. Most people are, if they're not familiar with it. It's a whole fish, with its fishy face looking right at you. You have to eat it in tiny pieces because it's very difficult to bone, but the delicate flavor is beyond compare. After everyone left, I realized Isaac hadn't tried it, and I made him close his eyes so I could put a tiny piece in his mouth. You know I'm *really* in love when I'm willing to share my whitefish! He was intoxicated by the flavor, at which point I realized my legs were still sore, I could barely walk, there was a whitefish in the fridge, and I'd just convinced Isaac he loved the stuff. Fortunately, he didn't eat *all* of it before I could get to it myself.

I pride myself on never canceling rituals unless there's a real emergency, but we never did meet for Spring Equinox that year. I figured we'd meet either before the baby was born or after; we had a two-week window. Who could have guessed that for our first potential equinox meeting I'd be in labor, and two weeks later I'd be giving birth?

During my long, drawn-out labor, Scott's condition was no better; his headache was unbearable. When he got to Boston, his hosts, Gypsy and Richard Ravish, insisted on taking him to the hospital. There, Scott was diagnosed with fungal meningitis. Isaac and I set to work organizing a nationwide healing, while Gypsy and Richard did the same. Our phone list was massive—Isaac knew everybody in the Pagan community, and everyone he didn't know, Gypsy and Richard did know (and vice versa). On Wednesday, April 4, Stormcircle gathered for a special healing circle.

With so many people working simultaneously, Isaac determined the best role for us was to create a magical "lens" over the hospital, collecting and focusing all the energies being sent from so many places. Then we would do our own healing work.

Step one was to attune everyone to the working. We read aloud from some medical books I had in the house from my nursing school days, looked at anatomy illustrations so we could clearly see where the illness was, and discussed the disease until we were all as clear as we could be.

Next we discussed and attuned to Scott. I had letters from him, and passed one around. His photo and biography were available in one of his books, and those were shared as well. Everyone was able to use these things to establish a connection, which is a vital part of magic.

Next we planned out what we would do, discussed it thoroughly, and rehearsed the chants we would use.

In ritual, we again passed around Scott's "samples" (letter, photo, etc.). During the invocations, we called upon gods of healing. We did the usual ritual up to and including cakes and wine,[5] during which we poured libations to gods of healing and of writing (since they would have particular interest in helping such a prolific author).

Instead of raising a cone of power, which peaks rapidly and intensely, we raised power in waves, so we could maintain our energy for a long time.[6] We chanted and drummed, slowly building and maintaining intensity for forty-five minutes or more.

We took a short break, passing the cup of wine but not filling individual cups. There's a variation in Wiccan practice here: Some groups consecrate a cup of wine and pass it round and round throughout the rest of the ritual. My practice is to consecrate and pass the altar cup, then, when work is done and we're ready to relax, each person can have his or her own cup filled. In this case, we didn't yet fill personal cups, because we had another working to do. It was more a short breather.

Then came the actual healing. In my group, we generally work by having one person send energy directly to the target, while everyone

---

5. In my book *The Elements of Ritual* (Woodbury, MN: Llewellyn Publications, 2003), I discuss why spells are always best done *after* cakes and wine.

6. The cone and wave techniques are discussed in my book *The Way of Four Spellbook* (Woodbury, MN: Llewellyn Publications, 2006).

else raises energy and sends into that person. This technique allows two different things to be focused upon, which is important, because there are always at least two things to keep in mind in a spell: the target and the goal. In this case, the target was Scott, while the goal was wellness. I held the target firmly in my mind and connected myself fully with him. The other six people visualized the goal and, chanting, directed healing energy into me, for me to send on to Scott.

We all felt it work. It was powerful, exhausting, and thrilling, and we closed the circle with great confidence.

When I phoned Scott at the hospital the next day, he sounded terrible. They were giving him phenobarbital to prevent seizures, and he was totally disoriented, not to mention stoned out of his mind. He had felt nothing the night before and detected no change.

I was shocked. I *felt it work*. I had never felt that way and then discovered a spell *didn't* work. The *whole damn world* was working magic at the same time: How could it *not* work? I had to face a great deal of self-doubt. Could I continue working spells knowing this one had somehow failed? Did I need a 100 percent success rate in order to trust the work I did? Doctors don't have a 100 percent success rate, and don't give up medicine when the patient doesn't get well. Yet magicians work with intuition, and I *felt* it work—how could I reconcile that?

I agonized over these questions for many months. I continued to practice Witchcraft, to teach, to cast circles, and to invoke the Gods. Yet I had no answers. Finally, I concluded I didn't *need* answers. I just needed to know what I knew—that magic works—and, like the doctor with the ailing patient, continue in spite of its imperfections.

The fungal meningitis was Scott's first AIDS-related illness and led to his diagnosis. At first he swore me to secrecy. Later I asked him if I could tell my coven, so they would be better able to continue to do healing. He gave me permission to tell anyone I saw fit to tell, and to simply use my best judgment. After he died—almost three years to the day after the initial illness—I chose to share the information in the spirit of continued healing. In 1993, AIDS was still deeply stigmatized, and speaking about someone wise, good, and beloved who had the disease had great potential to heal. In writing about it here, I continue that work, using it to deepen our understanding of healing work.

Scott was seriously ill with the meningitis for about six months. About a year after his recovery, at the AIDS clinic, he met someone else who'd had the disease, which was rare even with AIDS. It was then he learned that the typical course of that illness is about two years, and six months is just about miraculous.

Knowledge is power, and magicians must always remember that simple truth. Knowledge of the course of the illness, of the nature of the illness, is crucial. The agony of doubt that I endured suddenly changed, because with knowledge, the story changed from a bizarre failure to a miraculous success.

The Healer's Bookshelf

Too many magical people rely on energy and spells for healing without understanding the physical reality of the human body. Most spells must, in order to succeed, manifest themselves in the physical world, so understanding the physical reality of healing is a necessity. Here's what you should have when doing healing work:

1. A well-illustrated anatomy book. There are a number of anatomy coloring books on the market. Having one or several on your shelf will allow you to study the part of the body being targeted so you can visualize it clearly, and to incorporate accurate anatomical illustrations into your spells.

2. A medical dictionary. There are a number of online sources,[7] but I like having a book on the shelf that coven members can read from, pass around, and even bring into ritual.

3. A medical encyclopedia. This will give more detailed information about diseases and prognoses than a dictionary.

Every year, medical professionals buy these books new, so it is often possible to get great bargains on last year's edition. These books are

---

7. Here are three good online sources: www.MedTerms.com, www.medilexicon.com /medicaldictionary.php, and www.online-medical-dictionary.org.

valuable additions to the bookshelf of a committed magical healer. Whether your healing practice includes herbalism, Reiki, or the laying on of hands, you should include mainstream knowledge to make it well rounded.

Chapter 11

FACING DEATH

1992 or '93: In love at Starwood

As of August 24, 1990, 1,536 cases of eosinophilia-myalgia syndrome (EMS) had been reported to CDC from all 50 states, the District of Columbia, and Puerto Rico .... Twenty-seven deaths have been reported in patients who met the surveillance case definition and who used L-tryptophan-containing products (LTCPs).

—*Centers for Disease Control Morbidity and Mortality Weekly Report, August 31, 1990*[8]

Isaac was very sick.

The earliest symptom was something we noticed only in retrospect. One of my prenatal exercises involved Isaac kneeling on the floor in front of me while I sat, pushing against him with my legs. One evening, he had sharp pains in his legs and couldn't kneel. We skipped that exercise and did another.

Isaac's muscles continued to feel very sore, and then get better, and then feel sore again. Increasingly, he felt fatigued, he ached, and he coughed. One day I was alarmed to find a strange rash all over his torso. His doctor suggested it was an allergic reaction to monkfish, although we ate seafood without ill effect practically every time we went out.

He didn't get better. One day, we were flipping through the vast pile of exchange publications and found something interesting in Marion Weinstein's newsletter. Weinstein was a well-known Pagan author and New York radio host, best known for her books *Positive Magic* and *Earth*

---

8. *Centers for Disease Control and Prevention,* "Update: Eosinophilia-Myalgia Syndrome Associated with Ingestion of L-Tryptophan—United States, through August 24, 1990," MMWR Weekly, August 31, 1990: 39 (34); 587–89, www.cdc.gov/mmwr/preview/mmwrhtml/00001738.htm, accessed November 8, 2012.

Magic. When she published *Positive Magic* in 1978, there were few books of the kind available. Her newsletter had an article by a medical doctor about a new disease. The symptoms seemed to match.

Isaac really did know everyone in the Pagan community. He called Marion, who gave him the doctor's phone number. I could only hear Isaac's end of the conversation, but it was pretty clear that the doctor was annoyed and was tolerating this call from a probable hypochondriac only because he was Isaac Bonewits and had been referred by Marion Weinstein, and that's an awful lot of name-dropping for one phone call. Then Isaac described his rash, and suddenly the conversation changed. She wanted him to see a doctor right away, and to suggest that it might be eosinophilia-myalgia syndrome (EMS). Isaac wrote down a bunch more information and thanked her. (I'd love to thank this doctor today, but I no longer have the newsletter or her name, except I think her first name was Eleanor.)

Isaac had EMS. There was no cure, no real treatment, and almost no information. And he was getting worse.

At first, the doctor gave him prednisone, a corticosteroid, which helped immediately, but because of the dangers of the drug, that doctor would only prescribe it for two weeks. As soon as the prescription ran out, Isaac's symptoms all came back. In later years, other EMS sufferers developed serious additional health problems due to long-term prednisone use, so perhaps the doctor made the right call, although at the time, alleviating Isaac's suffering seemed like a higher priority.

Like me, Isaac had a tendency toward depression. He'd been treating it for years by taking L-tryptophan, an over-the-counter amino acid that had been shown to be effective as an anti-depressant. (My own psychiatrist recommended it as a boost to prescription anti-depressants.) Isaac was a freelancer without health insurance; using L-tryptophan as an over-the-counter remedy was cost-effective and really helped him.

The FDA banned the sale of L-tryptophan in January of 1990. At first we didn't know why. There was and is a tendency among Pagans and New Age people to think of the FDA as "The Man," in the pocket of Big Pharma while taking our herbs and vitamins away from us. So the only part that worried us was how Isaac would be able to treat his mood disorder.

EMS was caused by contaminated L-tryptophan (LT) sold by a Japanese company called Showa Denko K.K. Although there were dozens of companies selling dietary supplements like LT, they were all bottling and distributing the product of a small number of manufacturers, and all of the people who were sick had consumed LT sold by Showa Denko. By 1991, at least 1,500 people were sick and at least three dozen were dead. However, these numbers were hard to come by. Once LT was banned, new cases gradually stopped appearing. The CDC no longer classified it as an epidemic and stopped tracking numbers. Isaac was reading an amateur newsletter put out by other EMS sufferers that estimated much higher numbers.

EMS is multi-systemic, involving the neurological, muscular, and immune systems. The muscular symptoms are almost identical to fibromyalgia. Isaac said his muscles felt hammered. He had neuropathies—patches of burning nerve pain—that floated around the body; one day he couldn't bear to have his lower back touched, and the next day his back was fine but his legs were on fire. He was always tired. Soon he walked with a cane, and within three or four years he walked with two canes. His immune system functioned poorly; he caught everything, and he didn't heal normally. His hands became swollen and clumsy. Isaac at one time had been handy, fixing cabinets, installing simple hardware, and changing the oil. Now his hands didn't work well, and ached. He had once enjoyed needlepoint and playing the harp, but those pleasures left him with his dexterity.

Then there was the memory loss. Isaac remembered nothing unless it was written down. Old information was intact. He could lecture on Druidism as if there was nothing wrong, shooting out names, dates, and places with ease. But his verbal short-term memory was nonexistent, and his facial recognition was damaged. When he met people, he often couldn't recognize them later.

Isaac worked mostly as a page-layout design freelancer. During my pregnancy, he helped design and launch the premiere issue of *Entertainment Weekly*—Arthur still wears an *EW* t-shirt his dad was given. Isaac's normal work life was to take jobs that were intense and demanding for six to eight weeks, and then not work for six to eight weeks. The money was good, and the off time was when he devoted himself to writing, traveling, and running ADF. Now the long work hours were devastating. He slept fourteen hours a night and, when on a job, literally did nothing but get up, go to work, come home, and go straight to bed.

I was terrified. No one could tell us if Isaac was going to live or die. I had a new baby and a husband who lay in bed all the time. I was angry, frantic, confused, sad, and too scared to let myself be scared. We connected with other EMS sufferers, found a lawyer, found specialists, and found a disability support group, but ultimately we didn't know and couldn't know what would come next. None of the symptoms mattered as much as the prognosis or its lack. He might die; he might not. Nobody knew.

I said one day, "People say, if you have your health, nothing else matters. But we don't have our health. It turns out, if we have *each other*, nothing else matters."

We had each other, we had Arthur, and somehow we got by.

New Year's Eve, ringing in 1992. With a toddler at home, we had a small house party. It turned out that all the guests were members of Storm-circle Coven. In my tradition, you're not supposed to tell any non-initiate who the members of a coven are, but as a practical matter, if you're married to a non-initiate, and your home is the covenstead, your partner finds out.

So there we were—Isaac, me, and my coven—and Isaac says, "Deb, I'd like to become a Gardnerian."

I burst into tears.

At this point, we'd been living together for four years, we were married, and we had a child, and yet, here was a part of my life I was obligated to keep secret from him. He was the best magical partner I could imagine; we were incredibly compatible behind an altar. In truth, I've often described my marriage as a "professional partnership," in which the "profession" was Pagan clergy. So to have Isaac enter into that part of my life was beautiful beyond words.

Is it okay to initiate someone just because their spouse is an initiate? No. As a Gardnerian High Priestess, I screen for a true calling to the Craft, a true and deep desire to work *as* a Gardnerian. So I thought hard about initiating Isaac, yet I could not deny that a desire to work deeply and magically in your partner's chosen system was legitimate. I could not deny that Isaac, of all people, was profoundly committed to Paganism and to the Gods, and that he understood fully what he was getting into. Here was someone who had spent his life studying Paganism; he didn't need to be brought up to speed about what it meant to become Gardnerian.

Another concern was the oath of secrecy. Isaac had, for years, written about the origins of the Gardnerian tradition, about Gerald Gardner, and about the sources for material in the Gardnerian Book of Shadows. He agreed that he would keep his oath, and I agreed that he could continue to write on the same subjects he'd previously written about, using the same source materials. None of those, I reasoned, could be considered oathbound, since he owned them prior to taking a Gardnerian oath. I insisted, though, that he could never state he was a Gardnerian initiate in an article about related subjects, or state, or imply, that his initiation confirmed or denied anything he was writing about.

We discussed all of that, and the result was that Isaac was initiated only a few days later.

Isaac was assiduous in keeping his oath, so much so that, in later years, when his memory was too damaged to trust, he would have me vet anything he published that might touch upon oathbound materials. This was his practice almost to the day he died. Nonetheless, I was roundly criticized by some Gardnerians for initiating an "oathbreaker." I would assert that none of those critics have ever met a more honorable initiate.

We had an initiate, Candace, who was being troubled by violent, perhaps demonic, entities who appeared in her dreams. It brought up a lot of questions: How do you know when a dream is "merely" psychological, or when there's more to it? How do you decide that a problem such as this is an entity and not a manifestation of the subconscious? Does it matter? Can you confront a dream entity *as if* it's a demon, and achieve a psychological result? There's some thought that the ceremonial work to make demons manifest was, in fact, a kind of psychotherapy, raising "monsters from the id," to quote the film *Forbidden Planet*.

There was a quality to these dreams that was persistent, demanding, and painful. There were ritual components to them, and Candace was being tortured and killed. None of this is typical for dreams related to fear and anxiety. My initiate was definitely suffering, and she was a person of great magical gifts. She was also adept at inner work and experienced in therapy, so I trusted her not to be foisting her "stuff" on the group.

Once we decided we would work as a coven to help Candace, we had to decide how. Candace didn't want to confront the demon; it was dangerous and it created a feeling of deep terror. However, in the dreams, there were always people around watching. We could invoke one of these witnesses, but that was risky as well, as the demon (or whatever it was) might find a path of entry through such a summoning. So, we decided to use a magic triangle.

One of the first things I was taught was that a Witch's circle and a (ceremonial) magician's circle were very different. This passage from Gardner's *Witchcraft Today* is typical:

It is necessary to distinguish [the Witches' Circle] clearly from the work of the magician or sorcerer, who draws a circle on the ground and fortifies it with mighty words of power and summons (or attempts to summon) spirits and demons to do his bidding, the circle being to prevent them from doing him harm, and he dare not leave it.

The Witches' Circle, on the other hand, is to *keep in* the power which they believe they can raise from their own bodies and to prevent it from being dissipated before they can mould it to their will.[9]

A magician would stand in a protective circle and summon an entity into a triangle outside the circle, thus binding the entity and protecting himself. I'd seen this image many times, and it had been mentioned in my teachings, but I'd never experienced it for myself.

Wiccans and ceremonial magicians had, at one time, a very "us versus them" attitude that is apparent even in the Gardner passage just quoted. Susan had studied Goetia, Golden Dawn, and Thelema, and felt they were an important part of a Witch's education, but I had never spent much time on the subjects.

Isaac was experienced but very rusty, as it had been over a decade since he'd done that kind of magic. I hit the books. Our house was filled to overflowing with books; I'd married into one of the best magical libraries in the United States. I put a stack of likely candidates, a notebook, and a pen next to my favorite chair and started exploring.

I was surprised to learn that there was no agreed-upon method of creating a triangle of evocation. Indeed, many systems didn't use a triangle at all. *The Lesser Key of Solomon (The Goetia)* has a triangle in the east outside of a circle of protection. But other books use different shapes, different placements in different directions, or both. One grimoire showed a circle of evocation outside of, but touching, the protective circle, so that the illustration looked like a snowman. In Gardner's *High Magic's Aid* (a novel), the magician does an evocation without a shape at all; the entities cluster around the outside of the protective circle, trying to get in, so that the circle is surrounded by a halo of somewhat hostile beings.

It became apparent that I wasn't learning a specific technique, but rather general principles of protecting the magician during an evocation.

We planned a circle of six people, with a triangle in the northwest. There was to be one person guarding each quarter, plus a fifth person

---

9. Gerald Gardner, *Witchcraft Today* (New York: Citadel Press, 2004), p. 16.

(me) acting as Candace's guard and, as the High Priestess, binding the magic of all together.

We realized that none of the books gave us any step-by-step instructions in setting up the circle or the triangle. We had to make sure we stayed inside the circle once the evocation began, but that meant the triangle would already have to be set up.

Going over what was needed, we came up with these steps: create the triangle (three candles and three censers of dragon's blood were its boundaries), then cast the circle, then evoke into the triangle from within the circle.

On the night of the ritual, Barbara was sick and couldn't attend. We quickly made revisions so that I would take her quarter and also serve in my role as High Priestess. We moved the triangle to the southwest so I could both guard the south and attend to Candace.

After everything was set up, I led the group in a guided meditation. Once we had descended into a hypnotic group mind, I led each individual into the guardianship of the direction and element in his or her charge. This continued to work on the group mind, as *everyone* heard and understood that Isaac was the guard of the east, of Air, and of thought, and so on, for each person in each quarter.

I was careful to include "love" and "support" in the words of our protection; Candace was frightened (quite reasonably) and needed that from us as much as she needed magic.

Once this was accomplished, I directed everyone's attention to the triangle and instructed them to see the place of Candace's dreams as she had described it. On my signal, Candace then summoned aloud the witness she wished to question. Once this occurred, and she saw the witness and was able to describe him to all of us, we simply listened and loaned our energies as she questioned witnesses. We allowed her to determine when the questioning would end. All of us were attentive to any danger and ready to intervene, but as it happens, the questioning went smoothly. By the end, she wasn't entirely at peace and wasn't sure it had worked, but later the dreams no longer plagued her. The work had been a success.

When this portion of the ritual was over, I made everyone aware of their surroundings and then released them from the binding energy of the working, in reverse order, ending with, "[Isaac][10] is in the east. He is released from his role as guardian. The Lord of the Watchtower of Air continues to protect our circle." I then reversed the hypnotic induction.

An unexpected consequence was that everyone had been somewhat possessed by the element they guarded. Isaac thought that Candace needed to speak more, to learn more, to interrogate more. I thought she should have been more fierce, more forceful. The western guardian thought she should have delved more deeply into the unconscious, and the northern guardian thought she should have been strong and silent. Each of us described what we'd seen as if we were "right," and as I listened to us all, I saw that we were each speaking on behalf of the element we'd been bound to.

It's *really* important, whenever working with the elements, to end by invoking Spirit or unity. It's important that those who worked with Air, Fire, and Water ground thoroughly, and it is helpful if they eat bread. The Earth person is already grounded, and should get up, move around, and maybe drink alcohol.

⌒

Having Isaac in the coven allowed us to resume Drawing Down the Moon. It is a practice, an art, a skill, of which there is never truly mastery. You do it month after month, and you're always learning. Sure, I'm no longer a beginner, and sure, I understand, much more than I used to, how trance happens and how to encourage it to happen, but I'm never on top of it. You can't be in control of ceding control. Every time I do this ritual, I learn more, and if hubris ever gets to me, the Goddess herself slaps me down.

Drawing Down the Moon is not, in most cases, the same as possession. It's what used to be called "channeling" and is lately referred to as "aspecting." In full possession, the human person gives over total pos-

---

10. I used Isaac's magical name, of course.

session of the body to the deity, and either has no memory of it afterwards or remembers it only distantly, as if it happened to someone else.

In *Drawing Down the Spirits,* authors Kenaz Filan and Raven Kaldera suggest that possession itself can't be taught, that you either have the ability or you don't. You can only be taught how to do it safely and how to manage the experience. Compared to "aspecting," possession is more intense and more difficult on the body and the spirit.

On the other hand, being present in your body and head while a deity is there as well presents unique challenges. For one thing, you have to struggle with the degree to which your personality taints the channel. For another, you have to listen to your own thoughts, doubts, and criticisms in your head *while a goddess is there too.*

People go through a lot of ego challenges when they take on this practice. The sense of exaltation is incredible, but coming down can be tough. Most people think that "it goes to your head," and you become egocentric. Perhaps that was the case with me, and no one confronted me about it, but I don't think so. My experience was exactly the opposite.

After ritual, not just after Drawing Down but any time I led the circle, I would be overcome by feelings of shame and self-hatred: *Nobody likes me, they just tolerate me because I am the High Priestess. I've embarrassed myself in front of people. No one will be coming back next time, because I am too awful to endure.* These hateful thoughts went around and around in my head, and often, Isaac would have to hold and comfort me as if something terrible had happened instead of something wonderful.

The feeling was that I wasn't good enough to hold the Goddess in my body, that I wasn't a worthy vessel to be worshiped, that it was shameful to pretend to such holiness.

In a support group, I had a sudden realization about these terrible feelings. I simply couldn't reconcile the power of who and what I was in the present with the pain of the past. I felt subconsciously that, if I'm this powerful *now,* I must have been this powerful *then,* and therefore my problems were all my own responsibility. Once I was able to look at this thought consciously, it was easy to see that *then* I'd been a child, not a powerful priestess. Gradually I integrated this understanding, and my meltdowns dwindled. I allowed myself to be healed by the presence of the Goddess. I've learned that the best way to be humbled by her gifts is not to feel brought low, but to give them freely as much as possible and to behave in a way worthy of them.

Not everyone will have my particular issue—I think mine is unusual. But everyone who Draws Down must find a way to balance "normal self" with "embodied Godhead." For many, finding that balance is a struggle, and not everyone succeeds.

My other struggle with Drawing Down the Moon has always been self-doubt. There's almost always a voice in my head saying, "You're faking this. Stop putting on such a show. This isn't real." It's wonderful when you're able to understand that *everyone* thinks that, and it's not a good gauge *at all* of the actual depth of trance. I have stood in circle, deeply in trance, *literally drooling*, and had that thought.

I'm not saying that people don't fake, or that they don't fool themselves or lie to themselves about the depth of their trance. I'm not even saying that I've never lied to myself about my own trance. Sometimes it's very hard to tell the difference between positive reinforcement and self-deception. Am I saying, "Yes! You've got it! You go, girl!" or am I saying, "Oh, sure, I've got it. This is fine. No problems here." One's encouragement, and the other's deception, but the words are almost the same. So, sure, I've deceived myself.

But listening to that stupid voice in your ear is not the way to tell the difference. The voice in your ear is the voice of the ego-mind, and it *doesn't want you in trance.*

Your ego-mind is the part of your consciousness that is self-aware, awake, and embodied. It's the part of you that thinks it's *all* of you. It's the part that says, "I." The ego-mind is driven to always believe that it alone is in the driver's seat, and nothing else runs the self. It pretends that there is no subconscious or irrationality, that there are no "Freudian slips" or instincts. It also pretends that there is no superconscious, no Godhead.

Think of consciousness as divided into Self, Higher Self, and Lower Self. Self is where the ego-mind imagines the driver's seat to be. It is the day-to-day, ordinary life. Lower Self is the limbic brain, the primitive feelings and motivations that are irrational or pre-rational. It is also the subconscious, the things that move us without our being aware of them. No awareness? That pisses ego-mind off! Higher Self is the part of ourselves that is connected to the Gods, that transcends death, and that traverses incarnations. Ego-mind knows itself to be small in comparison, and so will try to deny the existence of Higher Self.

So, whenever you take ego-mind out of the center of your brain and push it off to the side, it starts saying, "This isn't happening. Nuh-uh, no way."

That voice sounds so believable, so persuasive and smart, that it takes a long time to realize it's just a mechanism of the brain that fires off automatically. It's not unlike the disassociation that can happen during terrible trauma.

By the way, all of these—the shame, the egomania, the imbalance, the disassociation, the ego's fight for control—are great justifications for protecting people from Drawing Down before they're ready. You should be trained in this kind of trance by experienced people and have a strong, grounded support system around you. You can seriously damage yourself otherwise. I've certainly seen people badly damaged by experimenting with trance channeling without strong safeguards and experienced guides. "Don't try this at home," as they say.

Another way to damage yourself is if you get addicted to the experience. When this happens, people don't want to come down, to come back to their ordinary life. They spend more and more time communing with deity, and breaking down their ego in unhealthy ways—not to mention disregarding their daily responsibilities and relationships.

The need for grounding and support made us decide that there would be only one Drawing Down per ritual. There are a number of ritual scripts that support the notion that the High Priestess draws the Sun into the High Priest, and then he draws the Moon. We did rituals like that for a number of years, but there were times when it was chaotic. It had an "everyone here is someone else!" feeling.

There was one memorable ritual in which the God, in this case a Babylonian god, entered Isaac powerfully. His manner was imperious and commanding. It was with this aspect that he invoked his Babylonian consort into me, and when she arrived, she was *pissed*. She'd been ordered around and she didn't like it. She really yelled at the God, and at the coven, and everyone was shocked and a little horrified. It felt utterly out of control, and not in a good way. It was after that ritual that we abandoned the practice of two Drawings Down in one night.

⌒

Scott Cunningham and I got even closer when Isaac became ill. After ritual, I'd be all wired and happy and bouncy, and Isaac, with his EMS fatigue, would fall instantly asleep. It was convenient, then, to have a friend who lived in a different time zone. I could call Scott at 2:00 AM, and it was only 11:00 PM for him. I called him after almost every ritual, and we'd giggle like teenagers. (Here's an odd thing: Isaac and Scott were both born in Royal Oak, Michigan. Isaac always said it was the best town for a Druid to be born in.)

Within a couple of years, Scott was facing death. He was hurrying to finish books. (He sent me the manuscript of *Living Wicca* to review and comment on before publication. He particularly wanted a traditional Gardnerian point of view on certain things.) He was not giving up, and Stormcircle was continuing to work for him. In July 1992, we prepared to do another ritual on his behalf (this was the one for which I asked him to let me tell my coven the truth about his illness).

As usual, the coven discussed the spell in detail. We always talk about the particulars, our feelings, our thoughts, and often reminisce, joke, or chat beforehand about the subject of the spell in order to create a vivid, emotionally rich picture. Of course, it's also important to keep the sure conviction of success in your mind and in your discussion. Never, when preparing for a spell, should you allow despair or doubt into the conversation. It was in this context that I said, forcefully, "I will not accept Scott's death." Immediately upon saying it, I had that uh-oh feeling.

Our intention was to Draw Down the Sun into a statue instead of into Isaac. This was because Isaac was feeling sick and was too weak to handle the God in his body. When the God came into the circle, though, he had other ideas—he wanted a human host. He started with

Isaac and moved around clockwise. Isaac felt his presence, and silently declined the God's presence in his head. Then the next man in the circle felt him, and felt he desired to speak through him, but he, too, mentally said, "No, thank you." Then the next man in the circle felt him, and began to speak. He (the God) was angry; it was not up to *us* to determine who would and would not die. It is his to determine when we fall. He blessed work done to alleviate pain and suffering.

Which is what we did.

On December 9, 1992, there was a lunar eclipse. I had never Drawn Down the Moon during such an event, so we were all curious as to what would happen.

Our work that night was on behalf of a little boy who was in the middle of a tug-of-war between his divorced parents. The father was an old friend, and he felt his son was in danger. As ever, we invoked the Gods first, and worshiped them, before doing the working. This is important because we should hear their input, accept their guidance, and be empowered by their blessings, all of which contribute to the spell.

There are times when you call a specific god or goddess by name, and times when you open the body of the High Priestess or Priest to whomever wishes to use it. (Keep in mind that this is a protected and sacred space, warded and purified. No harmful entities can enter. "Whomever" means a beloved deity.) This was an open invocation, and the goddess Hecate came into my body.

I could feel her clearly in my head. She brought images, darkness, a night sky, a cave, crossroads, secrets. I recognized her. I also felt frustration—she was looking for something she couldn't quite find. There were instructions she wanted to give, but the voice she was using (mine) didn't have the words. I could feel her *looking through my head*. It was like I was a filing cabinet, and she was opening folders, reading what was in there, scanning for anything useful.

Finally she began to give instructions for the kind of spellwork you might find in a medieval grimoire: she instructed us to make a Witch's Bottle, a bit of folk magic that goes back at least four hundred years.

What happened was, the medieval material in my head was as close as she could get to the Greek magic she was looking for.

During all of this, a coven member's menstrual flow suddenly started. (She was having her period already, but suddenly the blood flow increased and broke through the tampon—this had never happened to her or anyone else in my circle before and hasn't happened since.) Feeling that the blood was brought by Hecate for her purposes, we added a few drops to the Witch's Bottle.

Knowing that my head could serve as a filing cabinet, a resource, was a great awakening for me. The more we study, and the more we put *into* those folders, the better the Gods are able to speak to and through us. Even if you're not experimenting with trance (remember, don't try this at home!), your private visions, your meditations, your prayers—all of these are informed by the filing cabinet in your head. When *you* read mythology, world history, or comparative religion, you're augmenting your files and giving *them* more to work with.

THE WITCH'S BOTTLE

A Witch's Bottle is a protection spell that entraps negativity and keeps it away from the subject. It is used to avert a magical curse, to prevent an enemy from reaching someone, or otherwise to prevent harm.

A Witch's Bottle consists of two sets of ingredients: representations of the person being protected, and things designed to entrap the negativity.

Representations: Nail or hair clippings, drops of urine or blood.

Traps: Rusty nails, broken glass or mirror shards, knotted bits of string.

Get a small bottle, fill it carefully with your ingredients, and seal it tightly.

Wet the outside of the bottle with saltwater, then pass it through the incense smoke. When this is done, point your athame at the bottle, and say:

I charge this bottle by Water and Earth (saltwater).
I charge this bottle by Fire and Air (incense).

Pick up the bottle.

No enemy may resist it, or pass it, or reach me. By this bottle I am safe.
No enemy may pass this bottle, nor find me when this bottle exists.
By this bottle I am protected.
My enemy's worst intentions are trapped here. So be it.
My enemy's evil toward me is trapped here. So be it.
My enemy's power against me is trapped here. So be it.

If needed, change *I* and *me* to the name of the person being protected.

Bury the bottle at the point of your property farthest from your front door, or in the darkest or wildest part of your property, or under your hearth. Bury it deeply so it won't be found. The spell lasts as long as the bottle remains hidden.

Chapter 12

RITUALS, PUBLIC AND PRIVATE

Beltane 1991: A public ritual in Binghamton, NY

The stag is my totem
The bull is your own
That's reason e'now
Why we fight all alone.

I've called you my brother
But now we must fight
And the victor be crowned
As the day turns to night.

—*From "The Raven Is Calling" by Gwydion Pendderwen*

I'd been on the board of ADF since before Isaac and I moved in together. When Arthur was an infant, I resigned. The reason I gave was simple enough: I was Scribe (Secretary) and took minutes of all board meetings, which were held via conference call. I was well qualified to take fast long-hand notes and type them up, but now I was trying to do it with a baby in my lap (and somehow, he was *always* in my lap during board meetings). It was physically impossible.

In reality, my reasons were more complex.

Every couple has a public persona. Ours was the Sweet, Flaky Genius and His Strong, Grounded Wife. Isaac was Albert Einstein, the absent-minded professor, charmingly helpless, abrasively brilliant, utterly impractical, utterly lovable. I was the grounded one, the practical one, and, as a result, I was the one who always said "no."

So, in a board meeting, if someone had a stupid, expensive, or untenable idea, Isaac would listen politely, and I would jump in and say, "That's stupid, expensive, or untenable!" I didn't enjoy being the eternal voice of "no." I also began to see it as co-dependent. As long as I was on the board, Isaac wasn't going to be fighting those battles himself. In theory, I could have stayed on the board and backed away from that persona, but it wasn't in my nature to do so. As long as I was there, I would fight in the way it was natural for me to fight, and Isaac would be brilliant and impractical, as was natural for him. I resigned in part to end that cycle.

The first board meeting after I resigned ran too long, which was expensive. To keep the phone bill down, it was important to be brief and keep to the point. If someone was going on and on, someone else had to step up and put a stop to it. I'm not claiming I was the only smart person on the board—far from it!—but perhaps I was the only hard-ass. The following month, Isaac was more take-charge than he'd been at any previous meeting, and the time didn't run over. I felt I'd done the right thing.

It's remarkable to me how little there has been, over the years, in terms of Pagan organizing in suburban New York City. The suburban crowd is a different demographic, with a different attitude, than the urban crowd, and suburban folks will often go into the city for events, only to feel out of place. But for a couple of years a person named Regina would put on some small Pagan events in and around the northern New Jersey suburbs of New York City, and she invited us as speakers.

She had her biggest event yet planned for Samhain 1990. It was to be held at the Wetlands Preserve, a live music venue and bar in lower Manhattan. There would be several hours of performance, culminating with Isaac as the last musical act. (At that time, Isaac performed as a solo or, as on this occasion, with Jeff Kalmar.) Then, promptly at 10:00 PM, we would begin a ritual. Regina emphasized that the ritual could take no more than an hour, as there was a headline band scheduled to start after us. Before we agreed to do the ritual, I confirmed with Regina that I'd be able to bring in enough people to manage the ritual. I went over the physical space with her so I would understand the ritual needs, and I made sure I'd have a place to nurse my infant. She assured me all my needs would be met.

I agreed to lead the ritual. Isaac was dubious. "Deb, you know you can't do a real Wiccan ritual for such a big public event."

When Isaac said "you can't," it was like a bell went off. I was determined that I would, indeed, create a public Samhain ceremony that was recognizably Wiccan.

One of my favorite authors is Ursula Le Guin. On pages 455–56 of her 1985 book, *Always Coming Home*, there's a Ceremony of Mourning, in which names are "thrown on the fire." Trained dancers moved around a fire

> until suddenly one of the silent watchers in the dark outer ring called out the name of a person who had died during the past year. Others repeated the name in the rhythm of the chanting. The dancers picked it up. The name was repeated over and over, and all the various names the dead person had had were spoken and repeated, until the Dead Singers suddenly gathered in around the fire, chanting loud and fast and rocking their bent arms as if throwing or pushing something into the flames: and as suddenly ceased to sing, and crouched down, head bowed to earth and body trembling. And the mourners did the same. Then slowly and softly the insistent beat of the dance was taken up by one voice and another, the dancers got up and danced, the chanting increased in pitch and tempo, until another name was "thrown on the fire."

I was deeply inspired by this, and created a Samhain ritual based on it, which I call "Calling the Names." I've performed a version of Calling the Names almost every year since around 1988. I thought it would be ideal for the Wetlands ritual.

In Calling the Names, we begin a slow rhythm and provide instructions within the context of the rhythm: *Those who have passed before can hear us tonight; let us greet them. Those who have shared our love can hear us tonight; let us greet them ... Let their names become a part of our rhythm. Let their spirits join in our power ...* In a public ceremony, you make sure you have people there who know what the ritual is about, so that someone will speak the first name even if newcomers are confused or embarrassed. As soon as a name is spoken, it gets picked up and chanted. Often, the group will repeat the first name while the mourner will vary the name in a kind of spoken descant. So while everyone chants, "Jean Lipp," I might be saying, "Nana, Nana Jean, Jean Lipp." We know our beloved dead by more than one name.

The only thing I needed to adapt this ritual to the Wetlands crowd was to make sure I had "shills" in the group who would begin calling the names, and repeat them rhythmically. Given the size of the crowd, I'd also want a microphone so I could say back names to the whole crowd. That was easy, since I'd be doing the ritual from the stage.

The real challenge was going to be casting the circle. We'd be in a public space where we couldn't control who joined or left the ritual. Isaac had designed the ADF ritual to be entirely open; you can arrive or leave at will, and you can move in any direction, as the energy flow is in and out from the center. But a Wiccan circle is a closed space; you can't just come and go, and energy movement is deosil (clockwise), so you want to make sure that people don't damage that by moving about widdershins (counterclockwise). I made sure to appoint "guardians" who would keep disruptions to a minimum.

The other big issue was timing. With a lot of people and a large area, normal circle casting is too slow, especially since they can't see the subtle movements that might engage a smaller group. It would be vital to speed up the circle casting.

Here's what normally happens: The High Priestess casts the circle by carrying the sword from the east all the way around, arriving back in the east again. Then she sprinkles saltwater around the entire circle, east to east, then incense is carried around the entire circle, east to east.

Here's what we planned instead: When I was halfway around the circle (that is, in the west), Barbara would begin sprinkling in the east. When Barbara was in the west, Isaac would begin censing in the east. This would cut the time and double the amount of interesting movement while using overlapping voices to create a circle of sound.

We also made sure that the quarters were called one after another, with no pause. Our quarter-callers were in place and ready to begin, so there was no walking around the circle to slow things down.

We had two rehearsals prior to the ritual. A total of eight people from Stormcircle (counting Isaac and me) would be there, plus a baby-sitter for Arthur.

When we got to the Wetlands, things were screwed up from fairly early on. Regina's friends and acquaintances would ask if they could perform, and she'd just say yes and add them to the bill, so the show ran later and later and later. When I went to nurse Arthur, I discovered the room I'd been given was the band's dressing room, and the band showed up and kicked us out. My people were complaining to me and threatening to leave because the hour was getting later and later and nothing had happened. I was going to lose my babysitter and maybe one of my guardians. Regina had promised we would start "in a half-hour" at least twice, and both deadlines passed without Isaac even performing. (He was the last act prior to ritual.)

Finally, Isaac went on, and while he was on stage singing, Regina came and told me that the headline band had to go on after Isaac, and I could do the ritual *after* they performed.

I was enraged. I was there with an infant! I'd been waiting for hours! She acted like she was doing me a favor! I told Regina off in a loud, controlled, furious voice that made her shrink visibly. I went up to the side of the stage and signaled Isaac to give me the car keys. Still performing, he reached into his pocket and handed them to me. I grabbed the diaper bag and left.

I was two and half blocks away at the car, putting the baby in the car seat, when Regina came racing down the street after me. Panting for breath, she told me I could do the ritual if I started *right away*. "Fine!" I said, still in a fury, and went back.

Isaac thought there was no way I could cast a circle in such a rage. We breathed together to ground, but we had no privacy, and almost no time, so instead of calming down, I pushed the anger into a different shape, into power, and used it to create magic.

The ritual was beautiful. Everything went exactly as rehearsed. The names of the dead were called and honored. When it was over, someone came up to me and said he'd been considering leaving the Pagan community, convinced there was no *real* power to the rituals, but now he'd changed his mind. Another person said he had never taken Paganism seriously before, but now he would reconsider. It was profoundly gratifying.

Grounding with a Partner

Most people know how to calm themselves by taking a few deep breaths. You can expand upon that, going past calming into grounding, by visualizing your breaths connecting you to the Earth.

Exhale, releasing tension down through the soles of your feet (or the base of your spine) into the Earth. Inhale, bringing up stabilizing, calming, grounding energy from the Earth. And so on.

Traditional Wiccans work in partnership, and grounding as partners deepens the experience and also enhances the partnership. Too often, rituals can be disrupted by couples who are not in accord and yet are leading all or part of a ritual. The discordance permeates the entire rite. The following helps prevent that problem and is also just good for your relationship (romantic or otherwise).

1. Hold hands and face each other. Make eye contact. Relax and let the eye contact be natural and easy.

2. Breathe slowly and deeply together. Inhale together and exhale together, while maintaining eye contact.

3. Remember (in your mind or in your body) that this is a person you trust. Breathe into your grounding but also into your trust. Exhale, my energy goes into the Earth. Inhale, my energy comes up from the Earth, and is permeated by my love and trust for my partner.

4. End with a hug.

We never did another event with Regina, and before long, she stopped hosting events, at least in the New York metro area.

That wasn't the only time we called the names at a public ceremony. For Samhain 1994, at a New Age center in Rosendale, New York, we performed the ritual with perhaps a hundred people in attendance. The room grew ecstatic. When you read about the ritual, it sounds mournful, and Le Guin, in her novel, anticipated wailing and sorrow. Yet my experience is that the drumming and communion with the dead do not start slowly and become a deep catharsis of pain; instead, shortly after starting, the ritual quickly becomes tearful, with dear names offered early on, but by the end it is often joyful, as we celebrate our ability to chant and drum with our beloved dead. In Rosendale, the room grew crowded with the dead, and all around us, people danced and chanted with their loved ones. Isaac and I stood at the altar, holding hands, and I said to him, quietly, "Someday, they'll chant *our* names."

I like doing big public rituals, but from the time of my resignation from the board of ADF forward, I began to see that my true work as a priestess was in the Pagan Way and the coven.

Calling the Quarters

For the Wetlands event, I devised an alternate method of calling the quarters. In truth, there are a lot of different ways to do this. Here are a few ideas.

- The most common method is to go to the quarter, point an athame, wand, or your fingers, and invoke verbally. As we've seen, that can be done one at a time, or overlapping.

- Since acoustics can be a problem in an open space, another effective technique is to have people call from opposite quarters: stand in the east to call west, and so on. That way the sound moves across the circle, and everyone can hear.

- You can dispense with speaking entirely. You can symbolize each element with a different musical sound, such as a flute for Air, a rattle for Fire, a rain stick for Water, and a heavy drum beat for Earth.

- Dance each quarter, devising a simple movement to represent each element.

- Have a symbol for each element on the altar (for example, a feather for Air, a candle for Fire, a seashell for Water, and a bowl of soil for Earth), and bring each to its quarter instead of doing a verbal summoning.

- Hold hands and SHOUT each element name to the center.

By 1991, Stormcircle had grown too big for me to manage or to contain in my living room, and an influx of beginners had changed the tone of the group. I split the Pagan Way into beginner and advanced groups; each met once a month for a class and once a month for a ritual. Holidays were done jointly. That meant, with the coven, I was running three groups. Isaac was the High Priest of all three groups, was running a national organization as well, and, of course, was chronically ill. We were pretty busy!

By the end of a year, the beginners were more or less caught up. I wanted my advanced students to help with training beginners, and everyone had had the basic Wicca 101 material. So I remixed the groups into two new groups, each containing about half of the former beginners and half of the former advanced group. I called them simply Freya and Saturn, for their Friday and Saturday night meetings.

As I look back at the enormous diversity of people who passed through the group, one of the questions I always have is why people leave. Relatively few people have formally resigned from my Pagan groups; most have just stopped coming and stopped communicating, leaving me with unanswered questions.

Sometimes there are practical reasons not to be in a particular group. I've lost people who were too allergic to cats to spend time in my house. There's a limit to how much you can achieve with vacuuming, although I try. I have little patience for people who think the drive is too far, given how far I traveled during my years with Susan, but often enough, I've heard that as a reason. My current home is not wheelchair accessible, and I've had to turn down a couple of inquiries for that reason. Those losses are understandable; the ones I wonder about are the people who stayed, and *then* left.

Of course, there are people who decide that Paganism isn't for them, or that Wicca isn't, or that my particular brand of Wicca isn't.

Sometimes it's just a poor fit. I've always felt guilty about the very nice man who left after we all stripped down, but it was probably for the best. Groups develop personalities, and his didn't gel with ours. In addition, uptight and humorless people are never going to go far with me.

Sometimes there are mystery disappearances. Once I had a student whom I liked very much. I had a great feeling about this guy, and I was sure he was on a fast track to initiation. Yet after a few months he disappeared. He stopped showing up and didn't return phone calls—just *poof*, vanished. A few years later, I ran into him at a Pagan event in Manhattan. He apologized for disappearing without really explaining, saying simply it had been a bad time. I was warm and friendly, glad to see him, and he said he'd keep in touch. He didn't. About six months later I heard from the publisher of a Pagan 'zine; she'd had a letter from someone in my area looking for traditional training and was taking the liberty of forwarding it to me. It was no surprise that the letter was from my disappearing student. I wrote to him and said, "Look, it's obvious you're avoiding me, although I don't know why. Yet, your letter reached me anyway. Perhaps it's karma or the universe trying to tell you something. I invite you to write to me if you'd like." Of course, I never heard from him again.

A lot of the time it's a couples issue; a partner doesn't want their husband or wife in my group. Maybe they're freaked out by the idea of Witchcraft, or maybe they're just jealous of their partner's time spent out on their own on Saturday nights.

Sometimes there are deeper and more complex reasons. During those years, we lost two members for opposite reasons: one because we were too pacifistic, and the other because we weren't pacifistic enough.

In 1988, Isaac published a highly controversial essay in ADF's official periodical, *The Druid's Progress*, called "Warriors and Soldiers and Cops—Oh My!" It was strongly anti-military. Indeed, part of his intention in writing it was to lay the groundwork for conscientious objector status for ADF members, should the draft be reinstated. I disagreed with the essay, but then, we'd spent our entire relationship arguing about things like that, so it was no big deal.

Then H. joined Stormcircle. She wasn't in the military, but she worked for a defense contractor, so her career was entirely dependent on the military. Isaac felt, and said, more than once, that it was immoral for a Pagan to work for defense.

In traditional Wicca, you don't discuss politics in the group. It's considered divisive. You can have a group of Witches who've known each other for years who don't actually know one another's politics. Your work is the work of the Gods, and your history with one another is considered to go back through many lifetimes; therefore why should the politics of this life matter? Your magic is for basic life necessities, such as healing, home, fertility, and job, and doesn't involve politics.

Isaac, on the other hand, learned Paganism in Berkeley in the 1960s, the heart and soul of the hippie, anti-war, free love movement. He also had a long view: he wanted to build a religion that could function as a positive and lasting institution. To that end, defining a theology in which some things were *right* and some things were *wrong*—a real Pagan moral code—was vital.

To the extent that he was articulating ADF policy, I was fine with that, but I was running the Pagan Way based on traditional Wiccan values. I argued that the concept of immanent deity meant that each individual was empowered, and thus obligated, to discover her *own* morality. I agreed that some things were right and some wrong, but within some pretty clear boundaries. First, what's right or wrong is what we can expect any honest person to discover and agree to be right and wrong, when looking to immanent deity. *No one* who looks deeply within and hears the voice of the Gods will find murder, rape, or abuse to be morally acceptable. I'd say the same about destruction of property or vandalism; the only people who might truly find those moral are activists doing it for a cause, in which case, it's possible that inner wisdom might lead them to the "greater good." Even if it's not something I would do, I concede they might find an inner voice that truly supports it. The same is true for that old Ethics 101 question: If theft is wrong, what about a starving man stealing bread? Inner wisdom might readily change the rules for the starving man, but it is up to *him* to listen.

If we are serious when we say the Gods are within, then we have to have faith in the wisdom of people listening to those Gods, even when we disagree with the outcome.

I'd add that, for a Wiccan, theology can be derived from the Charge. "All acts of love and pleasure are My rituals" is actually quite a lot of theology. Love is sacred, but not just love, *pleasure*. What damages those things? Is damage to those things sacrilegious? "Keep pure your highest ideals," "let there be beauty and strength, power and compassion, honor and humility, mirth and reverence within you." There's a lot to study here.

I didn't want Isaac giving H. a hard time. I felt her career was her choice, but he wouldn't let the matter go. Whenever he raised the argument with her, I stated my piece: that it was up to her and not a rule of *my* group, no matter how Isaac felt and what rules he made in ADF. I made sure she heard me speak in support of her right to choose every time the subject came up, yet there's no doubt that the ongoing argument made H. very uncomfortable. I suppose I could have banned the subject entirely, but muzzling Isaac is not something anyone ever succeeded at, and I wouldn't have been comfortable doing so. I guess I thought that a lively argument was healthy, as long as H. knew I wasn't making any rules that precluded her.

At the time, I required candidates to have therapy of some kind prior to initiation. It didn't have to be conventional, on-the-couch talk therapy, but some sort of inner work guided by a professional was required. Many have objected to this policy, but it's not unique to me. Even Israel Regardie, the famed occultist and student of Aleister Crowley, required it.

H. said this wasn't possible for her, because it could threaten her security clearance and therefore her job. To me that sounded like a bullshit excuse, but I'm no expert on security clearances. She couldn't pay for it with work-provided health insurance without risk (although I was sure that information was confidential), and she couldn't afford to pay for it herself (although I provided resources for sliding-scale and low-cost therapy).

I also understand that obstacles are part of our path. Sometimes, if we're not meant to be initiated, the most ridiculous, petty things will get in the way; whereas, if we *are* meant to be initiated, impossibly difficult things somehow melt away. To the extent that I believe initiation truly comes from the Gods, and I'm just acting as an agent, I have to believe there is a meaning to the byways of the journey toward initiation, however mundane they may seem at the time. And part of those byways must be our own choices. If you can't fulfill my requirements, then you can't be initiated with me; it's an obstacle in your path. You might find another teacher with different requirements, or you might find a way to meet those requirements, or you might stay stuck. I can guide people on their path, but I can't walk it for them.

Each case is different. Sometimes someone is dyslexic, and the required reading is an obstacle. Sometimes someone is incredibly busy, and just getting to ritual is an obstacle. Sometimes a past trauma causes certain ritual activities to be unendurable memory triggers. Sometimes you find the ideal student, but she works on Saturday nights, and that's when the group meets. To the extent that I can accommodate a sincere student, or reframe a rule to allow for a disability, I always try. But I also have to consider the possibility that these obstacles are manifestations of the will of the Gods.

That's not a moral judgment! No one is *wrong* for being too busy or too traumatized. It doesn't make you bad or less than. It just means, hey, this isn't right for you at this time, and we can be mutually happy to know what is and is not right for you.

So, with H., I held firm to my therapy requirement. She could pay out of pocket, she could use her insurance, or she could find a third way, but the requirement wasn't going away.

This description might sound like all I ever did with H. was argue, but that's not even close to the truth. I liked her a lot. I found her funny and smart and deeply spiritual. She was a talented artist, and her skills in ritual were growing. She impressed me. Why else bother discussing initiation at all?

After about a year, though, H. stopped showing up and stopped returning phone calls, without explanation. Several years later, I discovered by happenstance that she had left because of Isaac's objections to the military and my therapy requirement (which she took as more attack on the military, given her position on security clearance). In truth, it was a good reason to leave—she had found a fundamental incompatibility—but I wish she'd chosen to let us know that she was going.

With Emilio, it was quite the opposite. Emilio was with us for about a year and a half. He was an educated and well-traveled gentleman, a bit more formal in manner than the rest of us and a bit older than most. (Although we had a fairly wide age range, he was close to the top.) Despite these superficial differences, I respected his thoughtfulness and commitment to the group, and I was (and am) quite fond of him.

For Summer Solstice of 1992, we planned a ritual combat between the God of the Waning Sun and the God of the Waxing Sun. The depiction of the summer and winter as gods who battle for the love of the Earth Goddess is quite ancient, especially in Celtic lore. The Sun at its height means that the Summer/Stag/Oak God will begin to die, while the Winter/Bull/Holly God will begin rise. At the Winter Solstice, we depict this as the birth of an infant Sun/Oak who supplants an elderly Holly God, but combat is also a traditional ritual. I wasn't all that excited by the Summer Solstice ritual I'd inherited from Susan, and was really looking forward to trying something theatrical and challenging. We had a skilled musician in the group who would perform Gwydion Pendderwen's song "The Raven Is Calling," which describes the battle from the point of view of the dying God.

The combatants would rehearse so that the battle would take the length of the song, and we planned to make special robes and staffs for the two men.

Emilio was extremely uncomfortable with this ritual. He was a committed pacifist who worked to remove all violence from his life, and combat as worship felt wrong to him.

We spent a lot of time discussing the theology of the combat. It expresses the tensions of nature, the way we lose when we gain, the way death itself can be a blessing, bringing the next season of our journey. Emilio, of course, understood that death is a part of nature and a part of our nature religion, but he argued that there were many ways to express the same concept nonviolently.

Emilio's personal commitment to pacifism was such that he tried, whenever possible, to prepare food in a way that wouldn't require him to use a knife, to symbolize his rejection of weapons.

As we talked, I began to see that we were at an impasse. I often change things in ritual to adjust to the needs and preferences of group members. Fellowship, love, and trust form the basis of our work, so changes, large and small, that make a group ritual work for its members make sense, provided they don't violate the rules of the tradition or change its nature. Here, I began to see that we could never truly accommodate Emilio's commitment to nonviolence. We used athames. We offered cut flowers as a sacrifice. Throughout our work, we expressed a commitment as deep as Emilio's to embracing the dark as well as the light ways of the Gods, to loving and celebrating their sharpness as well as their sweetness.

The conversation took most of the meeting, and when Emilio got home that night, he wrote us a letter of resignation. As with all important Craft decisions, it was to last for a year and a day, with a final decision after that time. Although I have always remained friendly with Emilio, that was the last time we participated in ritual together. I respect his decision, and moreover, I respect the forthright and honest way he confronted us with his problem and then handled it as straightforwardly as he could. I am sure there are many Pagans who agree with his nonviolent approach. Finding the right teacher isn't just about liking one another (although that's important), it's about finding yourselves on the same path. Here, we found that our paths parted.

In my heart, I honestly bless the path of everyone who has left my group. I hope their time with me was meaningful. If the Gods' hands were in any way a part of our finding each other, then I believe that their sojourn with me, however brief, served its purpose. I've spoken with other priestesses who talk about their "failure" with this person or that, and I always counsel that, if you allow the Gods to work their will through your group, it *cannot* be a failure. A disastrous six months in your group may have been the necessary precursor to a joyous and happy decade in the next group. With Emilio, it was never a disaster, just a divergence.

Chapter 13

GODDESS, GOD, MOMMY, DADDY

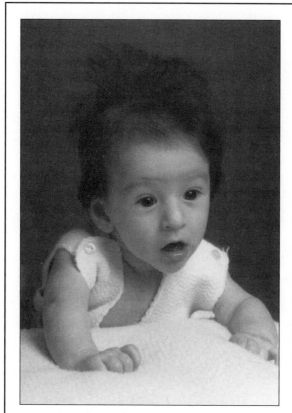

Arthur at three months,
with his natural-born Mohawk hairdo

Lady Brigid, strong and mild,
Listen to your loving child.
Guard my bed throughout the night,
And keep me safe 'til morning light.
Blessed be.

—*Arthur's bedtime prayer, written by Isaac Bonewits*

When Arthur was four days old, Isaac turned to me and said, "I was never sure about reincarnation before, but no one's eyes can be *that* sad after just four days." Our baby had deep, soulful, achingly sad eyes that spoke of a thousand years. Pagans would take one look and say, "Wow! What an old soul!" Others would take a step back, as if they'd been stung, and say things like, "Nice baby. Interesting...eyes."

Isaac loved to sing to the baby, but he had a perverse idea of what constituted a lullaby. He frequently sang "The Internationale" and "The Woad Song." He also checked out books on lullabies at the library and learned them. And, of course, he wrote "Arthur's Lullaby," a Paganized version of Brahms' "Lullaby," which he later recorded with his band, Real Magic.

For myself, I discovered, in my long hours of rocking a sleepless baby (Arthur has had insomnia literally his entire life), that lullabies are too short. And upon the heels of discovering that, I learned that a lot of Witchcraft poetry, by Doreen Valiente and others, has the same meter and scan as the lullabies I was singing. I could go from "Hush, Little Baby" to "The Witches' Rune" without skipping a beat. (I'm very fond of "Stay Awake" from *Mary Poppins*. "The Witches' Rune" works with that one as well.) I think I sang half my Book of Shadows to the tunes of various lullabies all before the baby was six months old!

There were times that being married to Isaac Bonewits made me more "out of the broom closet" than I might have liked. Certainly that was true when I first introduced him to my mother. The fact is, there was no discretion around Isaac, and no hiding. Who he was, was an outspoken Pagan leader. When I first became involved with him, I knew that meant being all the way out, but there were times I felt dragged. And yes, I volunteered, but I had a tiger by the tail.

As out as out can be meant raising a Pagan child, and on this point I agreed completely. There has long been a voice in the Pagan community that says raising a child in *any* religion is indoctrination, that people should choose their religion for themselves. To me, that's just not right. Basically, *everything* we teach our children is "indoctrination." When their minds are young and malleable, we "indoctrinate" them with everything from language to table manners. That's our job. "Indoctrinating" children isn't wrong, provided that they understand they have choices (when they do), that we respect their individuality, and that we acknowledge they're growing up (as they do). So you indoctrinate your children with what you consider a proper dress code, but you let them have favorite articles of clothing, and as they grow up, you let them make more of their attire decisions. In child rearing there is a constant tension between your indoctrination and their free will, and when you do it well, you work out the differences jointly.

How can you raise a child well without sharing your values? Without answering that child's deepest questions honestly, from the heart? We raised a Pagan child because we believe deeply in Paganism. He would never have been punished for believing otherwise, but why second-guess ourselves?

I fully understand that people who must be, or choose to be, in the broom closet can't raise Pagan kids, and I respect that. Kids blurt, and if they might blurt something that endangers you, that's something you can't let them know. We were fortunate to live in the northeastern United States, where, yes, there's plenty of religious bigotry, but also plenty of tolerance.

Arthur was allowed in ritual when he was a babe in arms, but soon he was old enough, and rambunctious enough, that we needed a babysitter to be with him—at home but outside of ritual. Twice it happened that babysitters had to be replaced because they wanted to join the group!

⌒

When he first learned to talk, Arthur would string nouns together and then want you to say them back to him as a proper sentence. If he said, "Baby milk cup," and you just got up and got him milk in a cup, that wouldn't satisfy him. He'd keep repeating the nouns until you said the sentence back to him the way he wanted it. "The baby wants milk in a cup?" And he'd nod, satisfied, and then drink. Sometimes the string of nouns wasn't obvious, and it seemed like I spent my days forming trial sentences out of his nouns, like some frustratingly persistent game of Wheel of Fortune.

In December 1991, I discovered that my child had a Pagan heart. He was at most two years old, so whatever "religious education" we'd given him was rudimentary at best. He was at the babysitter stage and wasn't in ritual with us. It was the morning after our Yule ritual. A member had given us little wall sculptures of the Horned God and the Moon-Crowned Goddess, about palm-size, and Isaac had hung them on the wall right away. The baby looked at them and asked what they were.

"The Goddess and the God."

"Goddess God Mommy Daddy."

"Mommy and Daddy worship the Goddess and the God?"

I knew he wanted a sentence, but I didn't have the right one.

"Goddess God Mommy Daddy."

"The Goddess and the God love Mommy and Daddy?"

No.

"Goddess God Mommy Daddy."

"The Goddess and the God are our Mommy and our Daddy?"

Yes! The baby nodded gravely. I was a little freaked out by the clarity of his religious understanding.

⌒

When Arthur started being afraid of monsters in his bedroom, Isaac taught him about Papa Thor. Papa Thor would protect him at night, and he taught Arthur how to call to him and how to feel safe. Isaac took a couple of Arthur's stuffed bears and set them up at the foot and head of the bed as guardians, Papa Thor's right-hand men who would keep an eye on things. It certainly seemed to help.

The other thing that Isaac taught Arthur was to say bedtime prayers, which he did for a long time. At first they'd say nightly prayers together, then Arthur would say them alone as part of his bedtime ritual. I can still hear his little baby lisp repeating his prayer as I write the words:

> Lady Brigid, strong and mild,
> Listen to your loving child.
> Guard my bed throughout the night,
> And keep me safe 'til morning light.
> Blessed be.

Isaac started ordering material on homeschooling from the day Arthur was born, but it soon became clear it wasn't for me. Once again, my fantasy of being an Earth Mother betrayed me. It's just not who I am. I had imagined myself happily at home with three or four kids, but it turned out I couldn't wait to get back to work! One kid was enough for me.

It's also true that Arthur wasn't just any kid. I thought from infancy that he was hyperactive, but our pediatrician kept saying he didn't have AD/HD (attention deficit/hyperactivity disorder). The baby crawled when he was only four months old; by five months he could cruise (walk while holding on to something), and soon he could scale the baby gate, using small openings as toeholds. He slept rarely and sat still almost never. Because the doctor kept insisting he was normal, I started to believe it was me. Certainly I had friends who said as much: *Every baby is active, every toddler runs around, why are you over-dramatizing?* I was exhausted and stressed, and I didn't know why it was all so hard to handle.

Arthur had a brilliant, almost freakish interest in letters, numbers, and words. He knew the alphabet at eighteen months (even though he spoke in strings of nouns) and could count at nineteen months. As he grew and spoke more fluently, he analyzed words and phrases literally, and didn't grasp metaphors at all. It was a strange mixture of gifts and deficits.

I called my mother one day and said, "Mom, I think the baby has OCD" (obsessive compulsive disorder).

"Why do you say that?"

"Because all he does all day is line things up, count things, and peel the paper off of crayons."

Of course, I was joking about the OCD. I had no idea it was an accurate diagnosis! His behavior, on the other hand, was exactly as I described. He didn't engage in "normal play." He didn't run a car back and forth across the rug and say, "Vroom vroom." He built structures, organized things, interacted with beloved "friends" (stuffed animals and dolls), and cared deeply about all of it.

Because he was linguistically gifted, his preschool put him in the four-year-old class at age three. Then, after the graduation ceremony, I didn't feel it was right to keep him in that school—surely it would confuse him. The public school wouldn't take him into kindergarten, so we found a preschool with a certified kindergarten program that was happy to have him. Then, at age five, having completed kindergarten, the public school had no choice but to take him into first grade.

That's when the trouble started. He couldn't sit still. He talked, moved around, sassed the teachers, corrected everyone, and who knows what else. At home and at school, he spun in circles and wouldn't or couldn't stop until he injured himself. He threw himself against the wall for the fun of bouncing off. He was sent home from school often. I again asked if it was AD/HD, but the school said no and refused to have him tested. I asked if they thought it was a problem at home, and they said no, it's obvious he's happy. So, I asked, if it's not medical and it's not psychological, what do you think it is? They had no answer. Of course, I had a legal right to insist on testing, but by that point we were house-hunting, so there was no point in battling with a town we were leaving.

When we bought a house, I spoke with the new school district about the problems we were facing. They suggested I start by seeing a pediatric neurologist, who might diagnose him. That doctor spent a half-hour observing Arthur, then turned to me and said, "Ms. Lipp, this is as hyperactive as we diagnose. If it's worse than this, we diagnose psychosis instead."

That sounds terrible to read, but it was wonderful to me. It meant I wasn't crazy, or lazy, or at fault. It meant there was understanding for my son, and treatment, and a light at the end of the tunnel. Hyperactivity exists on a continuum; sometimes AD/HD appears without the hyperactive component. In Arthur's case, it was the most obvious feature. When people talk about AD/HD being overdiagnosed, they don't mean in cases like ours!

With a diagnosis in hand, we were able to get Arthur into a wonderful program that was part of our new school district—a full-time school in its own building, K–12, for kids with specific special needs. They used behavioral modification, speech therapy, counseling, and educational play.

But AD/HD wasn't the whole diagnosis. Asperger's Disorder became a "trendy" topic around 1998; before then, it was frequently misdiagnosed as AD/HD. Arthur is both Aspie (has Asperger's) and AD/HD. We just had to wait for pediatric neurology to catch up with us. In my son's case, the OCD is one of the more prominent features of his Asperger's, so my "joke" to my mother turned out to be right.

Arthur thrived in his new school, and mainstreamed in time for high school. Today he's a smart and engaging young man who embraces his Aspie identity but isn't defined by it. People often don't even see there's anything "different" about him when they meet.

One of the ways that Isaac was *way* out of the closet was in his relations with the community in which we lived. He brought literature on Paganism to the local police, and he did the same at each school Arthur was sent to. I think his approach, which was so bold it frightened me, was correct.

When you need to get along with someone, ask yourself this: What is that person's priority? What makes that person afraid? What causes that person trouble? Usually, we ask ourselves what our own priority is, and go about trying to fulfill it, while trying to avoid the things we fear or that trouble us. But turn it around, and you discover interesting things. A police chief wants cooperative, law-abiding citizens, and fears any unknown that might mask criminal activity. By bringing the police literature, Isaac was showing himself to be cooperative, and he was making sure our activities were not fearsome unknowns. Complaints are troublesome. Now, should a neighbor see or hear our Pagan activities and complain, the neighbor would be a source of trouble, and we would not be a source of fear, plus we'd already proven ourselves to be cooperative. Imagine, instead, that we'd never spoken to the cops, and a neighbor complained about incense and drums. We would be an unknown, and possibly criminal, while the complainant, though troublesome, would be showing the first sign of cooperation.

A teacher's priority is to have children who thrive because of involved parents. What troubles a teacher is uninvolved parents as well as demanding parents who complain about the school and the teachers. By showing up with literature and information, we were being involved and giving them an opportunity to succeed with our kid, instead of waiting for a problem and then complaining.

When Arthur was four, his preschool put on a little holiday concert in town. It was really adorable, a bunch of four-year-olds all dressed up, singing in that "I'm definitely not singing" way that little kids have. His teacher asked us if we had a Pagan song we'd like to contribute to the concert. She already had Christmas, Chanukah, and seasonal songs, and wanted us to feel included. We were thrilled, and got her a recording of "Light Is Returning," by Charlie Murphy. Most children's concerts are mumble-thons, but this teacher had the kids singing to recorded music, so the town of Dumont, New Jersey, was treated to a recording of a real Pagan Yule song.

I'm not breaking any new ground when I say that Santa Claus has Pagan roots. Most modern Pagans associate Santa with Odin, although Isaac felt the folklore association was much stronger between Santa and Thor, what with the sleigh driven by goats and the fact that Thor went down the chimney. Thor is visualized in the popular mind as having a red beard, but there is also plenty of folklore that has him older, with his beard white. Regardless, Santa was an important part of our household.

Isaac loved the Yule season. He grew up with Christmas, he loved decorating for the holidays, he collected tree ornaments (he especially loved Victorian ones), and, before he got sick, he'd go up on the roof to hang elaborate lights. Actually, this continued even after he got sick, although the project might take him several days instead of one. He always tried to create a pentagram out of lights, but stringing them was tricky. So he built a large, wooden pentagram, approximately three-feet square, with holes for stringing the lights through it, and hung that on the roof.

For me, the Yule season was an acquisition in adulthood and entirely Pagan, but I jumped in with relish. I would decorate the interior of the house as elaborately as Isaac did the exterior, hanging garlands and ornaments from every surface of every room. Some of that started when Arthur was a toddler. We put a small tree on top of a five-feet tall cabinet in order to keep it safe, and then I used the trimmed-off bottom branches throughout the apartment. From that, the idea of decorating all over the house just blossomed. We also got in the habit, whenever we traveled to a tourist destination, of finding a Christmas shop (a lot of tourist stops have them year-round) and buying an ornament. (I cherish the flamingo wearing a Santa hat we got at Mystic Seaport.) There are plenty of Pagan ornaments to put on a tree: snowflakes and icicles representing the season, stars and lights, and, of course, Santa.

Our house was filled with Santa, and Arthur believed in him utterly. We came to understand him as the spirit of generosity, perhaps even a god. Certainly, if we humans create our own gods, few have been given as much power and belief in modern times as Santa Claus.

At first, Arthur's belief in Santa was as literal as any child's. When he was five, and we'd moved to a big house with fireplaces, he went to great pains to make sure the path between the main fireplace and the tree was clear. Unfortunately, that would have meant moving the altar, so we gently explained to him (he was in a frenzy of movement, making sure things were perfect for Santa) that Santa would never trip over the altar, that he moved through houses easily and obstacles couldn't hurt him. Arthur thought about it and said, "Oh, I see! Santa is a *spirit!*"

This was a brilliant observation and made our lives easier. It also meant that when other kids were learning, with a shock, that Santa wasn't real, Arthur continued to believe, protected by the knowledge that "not real" doesn't apply to spirits. Even as adults, Arthur and I continue to believe in the spirit of Santa.

When he was four years old, we were discussing Santa's impending arrival, and I explained that Santa visited all the Christian and Pagan families to bring gifts. Arthur knew that Grandma's household was Jewish. "What about Jews?" he asked. I said no, Santa doesn't visit Jews. He was horrified—really, deeply upset. "We have to write to Santa right away and tell him to visit Grandma!" I explained that the Jews don't *want* Santa to visit, but he was only grudgingly convinced.

His knowledge of Judaism was pretty shaky, which is my fault. I'd never considered raising him in both religions, yet as he grew older, I felt sad that I hadn't passed my heritage on to him in a way he appreciated. Ultimately, he came to his heritage on his own, but as a child, he was entirely Pagan, and his notion of Judaism was confined to "holidays at Grandma's." One time, we were on our way to Grandma's to celebrate Chanukah, and he was cuddling in my lap.

"Do you want me to explain what Chanukah is?" I asked.

"Yes."

"Well, a long time ago, the Romans didn't want to let the Jews worship their God…"

Arthur interrupted me. "The Jews have only one God?"

"Yes."

"But *why?*" he cried, in the plaintive tone of a child being denied his favorite dessert.

"Well, they only want one. They believe you're only supposed to worship one."

He accepted this only reluctantly. No wonder he was not interested in Judaism until he was older!

Our group had a whole bunch of kids around Arthur's age. Barbara's daughter, Sylvia (my goddaughter), is eighteen months younger than Arthur. She was the youngest of our batch of Pagan kids—almost everyone in our circle was the parent of a kid within two or three years of each other. Isaac wanted to organize some kind of Pagan Sunday school, but the noncustodial father of one of the kids strongly objected to Paganism, so we kept it to a more discreet set of activities that Isaac called "Earth Scouts." They went on nature walks and did other appropriate things. I was back to work, and had realized I was the wrong person to organize a group of kids. I was not involved with the Earth Scouts.

By 1995 I had my first daughter coven—one of the third-degree women of Stormcircle, Candace, had left to form her own coven. We'd sometimes circle jointly for special occasions, and everyone knew everybody in both groups.

Late on a Thursday night, we got a call. Joey, the five-year-old son of a member of Candace's group, had been hit by a car. The next night, both groups gathered for an emergency ritual. Joey had multiple fractures, and brain injury was feared. He was not conscious, and the doctors were not even able to assure the parents he would ever come out of his coma.

None of the adults could part with their own children that night. All of us felt like we couldn't let our little ones out of our sight; this accident was too close to home, too much the manifestation of our secret fears. So one member, a childcare professional by day, stayed out of the ritual and created a simultaneous children's circle. Together they created drawings of healing and wellness, and imbued them with their energy.

Meanwhile, the rest of us used the slow, sustained healing technique we'd used in the past for Scott Cunningham, chanting to the Divine Mother to heal Joey on behalf of all mothers and fathers who love their children. After that, we sang children's songs, especially ones with accompanying movement, including "Head, Shoulders, Knees, and Toes" and "Six Little Ducks."

Divine Mother Chant

This is a Hindu chant of unknown authorship:

> *Like a bee, my mind is buzzing*
> *'Round the blue lotus feet of*
> *My Divine Mother, my Divine Mother.*

During Drawing Down, we were instructed to reconnect Joey to his mother in order to heal him. We modified the chant as follows:

> *Like a river, love is flowing*
> *From the arms and the breasts of*
> *Our Divine Mother, our Divine Mother.*

Then we took a break. We were pretty exhausted, and during our break we were visited by the "children's priestess." The kids had one of those blank dolls that you sign; they'd all signed it for Joey, and the children's priestess wanted to pass it around for us to sign as well. It was the perfect way to maintain our focus while catching our breath.

Finally, before closing, we sent an "Om" of strength and peace to the parents, who had by now been awake for twenty-four hours with their son.

The next day, Joey was responding to light touch, and on Sunday he opened his eyes. Today, although he lives with traumatic brain injury, he is a healthy, fully functional, and sweet young man.

Raising Pagan children doesn't mean they'll turn into Pagan adults. Of the children who attended Joey's healing circle in 1996, only one is Pagan today. What it does, though, is instill values about love, family, healing, prayer, nature, and tolerance. All of those children are *good* adults, which is what matters.

Chapter 14

TRAVELS

1998: Australia, a koala, and dorky glasses

Rainbow Beach … According to the Kaby Dreaming,
Yiningie, the spirit of the gods, often took the form of a rainbow.
Yiningie was killed in a fight when he crashed into the cliffs
and his spirit coloured the sands.[11]
—*Australian travel website*

Isaac and I traveled heavily from 1988 through 1995, although once
Arthur was in public school, it wasn't as easy. Often, Isaac traveled without me, which is another story entirely.

Those who think that people get rich off the Pagan community are
just silly. Only a tiny percentage of authors earn sufficient royalties to
quit their day jobs. The honorarium for a lecture often doesn't cover
the time taken off work to get there. For Isaac, the lecturing and traveling *were* his work. He was growing ADF and talking about issues that
mattered in a way that effected change. I came to view my real work as
a priestess as occurring within my coven; teaching and lecturing were
supplements to that. But travel is always an adventure, and it was fun.
The best parts of being a Pagan public speaker are the people you meet
and the places you visit.

We developed a routine of co-teaching one class per festival, with
each of us doing separate classes as well. I was always sensitive lest anyone feel I was riding on Isaac's coattails, so I worked hard at creating
good course offerings.

The Association for Consciousness Exploration (ACE), the organization that runs Starwood (for many years the largest festival on the

---

11. *Tourism Fraser Coast*, "Rainbow Beach," www.visitfrasercoast.com/destinations/
rainbow-beach, accessed November 8, 2012.

Pagan[12] circuit), recorded many of the workshops presented at their events, including a couple of the ones Isaac and I co-taught, and made them available for sale.

"Making Fauna Religion" was a workshop based on the Flamingo Tradition. Isaac and I talked about creating humor out of our rituals, and how that was actually a meaningful activity. We brought a deck of children's Old Maid playing cards with animals on them, and randomly handed them out, allowing people to create ritual based on funny animals.

"Sex Magic and Magical Sex" was another workshop we taught. Isaac used to teach a sex magic class that was excellent. My contribution was magical sex: how to use energy-movement techniques to have better orgasms, a better connection with your partner, and so on. It started as shtick, really. Isaac taught these classes on how to use sex in spells, and at a moment in the class, he'd point to me and say, "Well, *she* did that so well it broke the air mattress!" or something like that. And that would allow me to remark back, and "interrupt" with my own comments on the topic. A lot of how we taught, publicly and privately, was with that kind of banter. Maybe as our marriage got stressed, that became less fun; we eventually put it aside. We formally co-taught some classes (and bantered), but we didn't attend each other's classes that were supposed to be solo. Part of the reason for that wasn't so much stress as the need for babysitting. If we were at an event with Arthur, we often didn't co-teach, and we requested the organizers to make sure we weren't teaching opposite each other, so one parent was always free.

MAGICAL SEX

The magical sex I taught with Isaac was not Tantra; it was simple energy management that most people can do without much training. Here's a sample.

---

12. Starwood is not a Pagan festival per se, but the majority of its organizers and attendees are, as are the majority of its course offerings most years.

In heterosexual intercourse, the natural energy flow between partners who have a good connection is *down* from the man's head, *out* through his penis, *in* through the woman's vagina, and *up* to her head. Understanding this flow is the beginning of improving your sex life.

If you don't feel connected to your partner, make sure to allow yourselves to experience this energy flow. Make eye contact during intercourse, and complete the circuit: back *out* through the woman's eyes, so the same energy continues to cycle down, out, in, up, and out. Some people prefer to do this mouth to mouth, kissing, but if you're struggling with connection, I recommend using your eyes.

A more sophisticated technique involves creating a dual energy flow, going in both directions at once and crossing at eyes/lips and genitals. It's much easier for a beginner to latch on to the natural energy flow that's already there, and work with it.

Difficulty Achieving Orgasm

Many women, and some men, struggle to achieve orgasm. Setting aside physiological reasons, there are any number of *energetic* reasons why this might be true. Whole books are written on the subject. Here I can merely say: start looking at the energy flow.

Are you letting your partner control the flow, allowing it to passively complete your half of the circuit? Try trapping the energy. Many women need to capture the energy and hold it in place, in their vulva, before releasing it back to their partner. Others benefit by damming the energy, slowing it down, because they're being flooded with a sensation of too much intensity. Still others need to move the energy throughout their own body—diverge from the straight path and let the sexual feeling move into arms, legs, and back.

He Fell Asleep!

Here's another common problem: one partner (usually the man in a straight couple) falls asleep instantly after sex, while the other is wide awake and wired.

When a man has an orgasm, he typically stops completing the energy cycle. He sends all his sex energy into his partner's body. His partner can readily absorb all of it, often riding that energy to achieve orgasm. (If you want to try simultaneous orgasm, that's the trick.)

If your partner always falls asleep after sex, then when he orgasms, try *pushing the energy back to him*, completing the circuit. You'll be less wired, and he'll be somewhat more conscious.

In January of 1989, I had pneumonia, and the combination of bed rest, spasmodic coughing, and being unable to go outside and walk at all due to the extreme cold (too cold to inhale with my still-weak lungs) led me to throw my back out pretty badly. I literally could not sit up. We were scheduled to attend Winterstar (another ACE event) in late February, and finally I said, *The hell with it, I might as well go.* I couldn't very well take care of myself at home alone, walking only with difficulty and unable to sit in a chair, and Isaac, as a featured speaker, really needed to go. So we drove together: I lay across the back seat, and Isaac did 100 percent of the driving—all twelve hours' worth!

Winterstar was held at the Atwood ski lodge in Dellroy, Ohio. The scheduled events took place in the main lodge, and down the road there were lovely cabins that slept ten: four bedrooms, plus two day beds in the large dining/living area, plus a kitchenette.

We brought a lounge chair with us. In the morning, Isaac would drive me (lying in the back seat) to the lodge, set up my lounge chair, and park me in an area where I could socialize while flat on my back. Then in the evening, he'd bring me back to the cabin. The speakers' cabin was a happening place! (Most festival organizers find it convenient to house speakers together.) It was there that I met Patricia Monaghan, who became a real mentor for me as an author. Renowned author Robert Anton Wilson was also there, plus this was the first of many ACE events attended by the delightful and erudite Halim El-Dabh, ethnomusicologist, composer, and world traveler. It was also the *only* ACE event attended by Anne Boger, an author and art historian with the Cleveland Museum of Art.

So there I was, feeling quite like a nobody among these thinkers and writers, and—in addition to being the least educated, least published, and youngest person in the room—I was embarrassingly horizontal.

I had the time of my life!

I have never laughed so much in a single evening. I had so much fun with such wonderful people; the warmth of that weekend stays with me even today. Not only was it a great result from a kind of disastrous beginning, but it solidified for me a sense of place among the somewhat rarefied company that Isaac gave me access to. In other words, I felt included.

⌒

There was a period of time when Starwood, too, had a speakers' cabin. Because space was limited, it was used only for A-list speakers, usually those who had been flown in or who came from outside the Pagan community. But they housed Isaac and me there as well, after Isaac became ill and couldn't camp. This gave us the chance to meet a dazzling array of people. My hero when I was studying midwifery was Ina May Gaskin, so having the chance to tell her the story of Arthur's birth over lunch was thrilling.

The most famous person I met, and one of the most charming people I've ever known, was Dr. Timothy Leary. Everyone wanted to meet him, of course, and there was a steady stream of visitors to the cabin during the years that Tim came to Starwood. Yet he listened to everyone, made eye contact, and asked probing questions. He was genuinely interested in every person he met.

Somehow the subject of the psychic bond between mother and child came up, and I shared a couple of stories about how that affected breastfeeding. When Arthur was only a week or two old, the three of us took a walk in the neighborhood. A neighbor asked after the baby, and when I told some cute baby story, I suddenly felt warm. I looked down and my shirt was soaked—saying something sweet about the baby, visualizing his sweetness, was enough to make my milk flow!

Shortly after telling the story, I excused myself. As I was leaving the cabin, Tim ran to the door and said, "That was the most beautiful story I've ever heard," and kissed my hand.

I could not have been more won over. I was simply enthralled by him. The following year, remembering that Tim, a smoker, was always running out of matches and borrowing them from everyone, I brought a stock of disposable lighters with me and gave him a few. He was delighted with the gift.

What might you think of a gathering of a half-dozen or more well-respected thinkers and writers? The gathering in that cabin in 1993 included Dr. Leary, Patricia Monaghan, Halim El-Dabh, Robert Shea, and Isaac. You might imagine they discussed lofty ideas or plans for world domination or something, but in truth, a lot of the time was spent telling elaborate dirty jokes, and no one was a greater master of that art than Tim Leary. There was a joke he spun during which he left the room, went upstairs for a cigarette, came back down, lit it, and continued. It was an epic telling.

Over the course of staying with Tim for a week, two years in a row (1992 and '93), I came to think of him as a friend. When he died in 1996, I was greatly saddened.

~~~

The first time we taught in Canada was eye-opening. Most Americans tend to think that Canadians are more or less Americans who say "eh." After all, we are not divided by any natural geography (ocean, impassable mountains) or by a language, so there's a sense over here that culturally, there isn't really a divide. However, our first Pagan festival in Canada taught us that we were wrong, wrong, wrong.

We loved Canada, and Wic-Can Fest, and I've been back many times since, with and without Isaac, but it was a bit of a culture shock.

I was scheduled to speak on "The Descent of the Goddess" our first day there. The entire time I was speaking, I thought, "I'm bombing! They hate me!" The energy felt flat, dead. After I was done, though, several people came up to me to tell me how much they'd loved my class.

It was as though the Canadian audience's auras were held more tightly to their bodies. (I have never been able to see auras, but I can feel them.) Before Isaac's first lecture, I told him what I'd felt, and afterwards, he was grateful. He felt the same lack of psychic feedback and would have felt the same panic that I had without the warning.

Another cultural difference that has affected the way I prepare for presentations is this: In the United States, if your audience likes you and is engaged by what you say, they'll respond by asking more questions and interjecting more comments. They want to connect. If they don't like you, they'll remain largely silent. In Canada, by contrast, if an audience likes you, they'll maintain a respectful silence and avoid interrupting. They are more likely to ask questions if they're not interested in you.

The upshot is that I need about an hour and forty-five minutes' worth of material in the United States to fill a two-hour time slot, but in Canada I need to prepare to speak for the full two hours. The first time I spoke there, I literally ran short of things to say.

Then there are more real-world differences. In 2009 I was teaching a class in spellcasting, using as an example a spell we'd done for Arthur. He'd needed to see a specialist, and we couldn't find one who accepted my health insurance. The Pagan Way did a spell for information and resources, and the next day, the same search terms on the insurance company's website brought up an entirely different result, and the doctor I found was the one who properly diagnosed him. In the midst of explaining this, I looked at my Canadian audience and said, "You don't understand any of this, do you?" They really didn't. The U.S. health care system is beyond them.

In terms of a warm welcome, though, nothing beats the Canadians.

⁓

In 1994, we presented at an event in Massachusetts, less than twenty miles from where I'd lived in Ashfield. We decided to drive by the old house on the way home. All I wanted to do, really, was see Bug Hill Road again, and feel its presence, but when we got there, Isaac persuaded me to ring the bell.

An elderly woman opened the door. When I explained who I was, she introduced herself as Joan, and said she was the original buyer and had been living there for seventeen years. She invited me in.

I was floored by what I discovered. She'd preserved the house almost like a museum. When it was time to repaint the downstairs, she'd brought chips to the paint store so she could replicate the color exactly. My bedroom had not been repainted, because she felt the angsty song lyrics I'd written on the wall at age fourteen could not be effaced. My brother's room hadn't been repainted either, because he'd created an elaborate collage mural by cutting out characters from comic books and gluing them to the wall. The mural was at least six-feet square, and it was still there.

I was able to satisfy Joan's curiosity about the construction. There had been no indoor plumbing when my father purchased the place, and the kitchen was collapsing. Once he bought the house, the kitchen was gutted and rebuilt, and the kitchen floor was shored up with construction in the basement. My dad and a friend had torn down a barn so the weathered barn boards could be used for all the cabinet faces. We'd added a den by dividing the cold pantry in half, and had rebuilt inside the remaining cold pantry as well. I showed her which bedroom had belonged to whom, and she was delighted to learn that the small front bedroom had been my father's office—she never could figure out why such a little room had needed so much wiring. (Home computing in 1977 was pretty unusual.)

We talked and talked. Isaac stayed in the car with Arthur, who had a bad cold and was sleeping; we didn't want to wake him. Joan had lots of questions about the house, and I wanted to know which fruit trees ended up producing. She told me that the land was sacred to her, that this land, in this spot, had a special presence. We understood each other perfectly. Standing in the yard, almost exactly where I'd once worshiped with a hand-dipped candle, I said, "The Moon rises right …" We both said "there" together and pointed at the exact same spot. The moonrise, right there, meant a lot to us. I told her, "This wasn't a happy family. There was a lot of pain here. But this house, and this land, was always a source of happiness to me." She told me that her daughter had died, and the house and land were what comforted and healed her and her husband. Later, when her husband died, she felt the same. She hoped to die there.

I'm sure she wasn't a Pagan; nonetheless, she and I shared a religion, an altar. We'd heard the same holy voice and worshiped it in the same place.

Finally, Isaac came in with the baby, who was fussy and congested. Joan greeted them warmly, and before we left, she gave us jars of jelly from fruit grown in Ashfield. We hugged like old friends.

I wanted Isaac to make a U-turn and head back to Bear Swamp Road when we left, but he pointed out that we'd passed the other end of Bug Hill Road on the highway—we could just go straight. "No way," I said, "that road isn't passable; we'll only get a few hundred feet."

"Deb, it's been seventeen years! They've fixed it by now."

"Isaac, you don't know this part of the country. I guarantee you, they haven't fixed it."

"You're being nostalgic," he said. "Of course they've fixed it." He drove straight ahead.

After a few hundred feet he had to make a U-turn, because the road wasn't passable.

Isaac and I spent our entire relationship traveling. We met at a festival and went to many, many festivals together. We loved road trips and never had a road-trip fight. We enjoyed the same stupid tourist traps and odd roadside sights. Within a month of moving in together, we began a three-week excursion, and within six weeks of deciding to separate, we chose to take another three-week trip together, despite the state of our marriage.

Our host, Doc, brought me and Isaac, as well as Oberon and Morning Glory Zell-Ravenheart, to the first-ever Pagan festival held in the

Australian state of Queensland, in August of 1998. Of course, such an event is planned many months in advance. We'd asked Doc to buy a third ticket—for Arthur—in lieu of an honorarium. It was a thrilling opportunity!

When we decided it was time to end our marriage, the trip was just around the corner. Realistically, I knew I didn't have the fame or renown that Isaac or Oberon or Morning Glory did. I was confident in my abilities as a speaker and teacher, yet I wasn't someone that an organizer was eager to fly in from a faraway place. I was invited as Isaac's wife, so I asked Isaac if I could still go with him.

He said of course. He recalled that we'd always had fun traveling together, and that was true. It turned out to be prophetic as well; our time during this trip was easy and even joyful. We got along so well that no one could have guessed we were divorcing.

The flight from New York to Tokyo is about fourteen hours, and then it's about nine hours to Brisbane. On the trip out, we had a five-hour layover—too short to visit Tokyo, too long for comfort. When we arrived in Australia, there was no one waiting to pick us up. We paged Doc and wandered about, dazed from the long trip. Immediately I began to get a taste of Australia. I asked directions from a man who looked for all the world like Crocodile Dundee. He exclaimed, "You're from New York, aren't you?!" When I said yes, he said he'd been to New York and loved it, and then asked, "You're *Jewish*, aren't you?" He was so excited, and so unaffected, that I hadn't the least thought of being offended. He was ridiculous yet charming.

Every culture has its character. Within the United States, New Yorkers are known for being in-your-face, fast-talking, and aggressive; Midwesterners for a pleasant and trusting demeanor; and Californians for being mellow and trendy. Obviously there are many exceptions, yet these stereotypes exist for a reason. Just as we enjoyed discovering the Canadian character, Australia held interpersonal delights for us as well. My airport acquaintance was in many ways a typical Aussie: surprisingly blunt yet friendly. I found Australians to generally have the outspokenness of New Yorkers with the open warmth of Midwesterners. I loved them and would gladly have stayed longer.

Isaac finally phoned Doc, who had completely forgotten us. He was in a tizzy about picking up the Zells on Thursday, and here we were on Wednesday. It all got straightened out, and we met our host and drove to his home outside of Brisbane, on a rough piece of land. He had an unheated guest house. At first he insisted that, since we were a married couple, we had to have a bed together and he'd give us his own bedroom, but we took him aside and explained the situation. The guest house was a better fit for us. August is winter in Australia, but Brisbane is subtropical and the weather was pleasant. We were a little underdressed, and I'm one of those people who's always cold, so Isaac and Doc went out and bought us all sweaters.

The first couple of days were quiet; we socialized and had fun with our language differences. When Oberon and Morning Glory arrived, they were exhausted (naturally), so Thursday night we went to the movies. *Dark City* remains a favorite film of mine.

Practically from the moment we arrived, Doc began teasing me about being a traditionalist. His teasing was in part playful and in part born of a genuine desire to have the argument, to debate the theology, because he just didn't understand why a traditional Wiccan does certain things.

In particular, Doc had a bee in his bonnet about assigning the elements to the directions. Didn't it make more sense to place the elements *where they occurred naturally*? Wasn't it weird, and annoying, and not at all magical, to invoke Water in the west, when a body of water was visible out an east-facing window? Wasn't Paganism nature-based, and therefore, shouldn't we take our ritual cues from nature?

I talked about how the elements are more than just their natural manifestations. Elements are primal forces of the universe. The water of the ocean or of a river is just one piece of all that is Water. I might have added that the water of the ocean, like anything in manifest reality, also has components of Air, Fire, and Earth. Our plane of existence has no truly pure elements. The ocean has salt and other minerals (Earth), oxygen (Air), and heat (Fire).

Another point is that, in Wicca, we are not creating ritual space in the world. We are "between the Worlds of men and the realms of the

Mighty Ones." We erect sacred space outside the bounds of the Earth, and bring it into being. Occultists have long spoken of "building the astral temple"; that temple needs to be the same for everyone building it. Our ability to share this sacred space is a great source of power. It can be anywhere because it isn't in a "where." Sacred space can be in the hospital room of a person being healed, or it can be on a trance journey, wherever that leads, or it can be among the Gods.

I also talked about ritual mind: We gain power in our rituals through repetition. It's a tricky thing. We don't want to get bored, but when we do the same thing at the same time, we cue our consciousness as to what is going on. Just as ringing a bell made Pavlov's dogs salivate, repeating certain behaviors in ritual makes our minds ready for magic.

There's also the power of cumulative magic. Repeated activities don't just trigger the mind; we're more than laboratory dogs. We imbue things with power by repeatedly giving them energy. When you use the same athame over and over, it acquires energy and is a truer manifestation of your will as a result. When you use the same Tarot deck over and over, it acquires energy and allows you to be more psychic.

We tend to visualize energy as physical. There's some*thing* we're putting into the athame or the Tarot deck, as if our hands were wet and therefore the thing we touch gets wet. In part, that's true; our aura acquires energies that can be conveyed through touch, and some objects store that charge quite well.

But there's more to it. We're not the only ones using athames and Tarot cards. The Tarot has been used for divination for over two hundred years, and the symbols it uses are older still. Many thousands of people have put their thoughts and belief into those cards, for all those years. Even though we can't see a clear physical connection, the energy of the collective unconscious makes a powerful difference as well.

The fact that thousands of other magicians are using a system *right now* in which east, south, west, and north correspond, respectively, to Air, Fire, Water, and Earth makes that system a powerful one to use. And that system has been in use for hundreds of years.

I emphasized this last point a lot: the power of repetition, the way an idea creates an energetic reality that resonates with multiple people through time. That power can then be condensed in ritual.

Doc delighted in showing us the sights and was passionate about taking us to a particular beach. His group used to do ritual on that beach, and he loved its sacred energy. It was in an inlet, and the water was to the south.

"Isn't this place fantastic?" he enthused. "We had such amazing rituals here. It was so powerful, and stayed with us so deeply, that even today, we all still place Water in the south no matter where we are."

"You've just proved my point," I said, and Doc laughed. The group mind, the power of repetition, the magical experience of Water that transcended any specific body of water, had led him to create his *own* tradition. Although he had no intention of changing his practice, he fully understood my point of view during that conversation.

The festival itself felt like any Pagan festival anywhere. Despite cultural differences and some language confusion (Australian slang tripped us up a few times), it was easy to recognize my tribe among the Pagans of Oz. When a conflict arose about whether children would be allowed in the main ritual, the Australian personality really came out. The people on both sides of the argument were in-your-face angry, and the arguments were intense—no beating around the bush! For a Pagan festival, it was a relatively small crowd, with an "everyone knows everyone else" kind of feeling.

When the pre-ritual announcements were made, attendees found out that children would not be permitted in the ritual. There was also no childcare available at this festival, and a whole bunch of parents got really angry; not only were the kids being excluded from the experience, but so were they. Oberon and Morning Glory stepped up, creating a marvelous ritual for the kids that was in many ways more fun than the "official" ritual. But what I remember best was the shouting match that functioned as community in action. Instead of muttering, gossiping, or complaining, they got up and objected with full force, and as a result, something new—the children's ritual—emerged. Perhaps it was ironic that the solution was provided by visiting Americans, but the

Pagan community in Australia, especially in Queensland, was relatively new. We Americans were there, after all, to share some of our longer experience.

A number of people asked me my opinion about when Australians should do their holidays. Wicca, which originated in England, has a Northern Hemisphere calendar, placing Winter Solstice (for example) in December. But the actual Winter Solstice in Australia occurs in June. Speaking with a wide variety of Pagans at this festival, it seemed that group practices were divided about fifty-fifty: half of these Aussie Wiccans celebrated festivals when they occur astronomically, thereby connecting to the land and sky surrounding them, and half celebrated according to a British Wiccan calendar, thereby connecting with the group mind of Wiccan tradition.

I refused to give an answer. I'm not Australian, and I'm not connected to that land and that sky, so any opinion I had would just be so much noise. However, I spoke to one couple who had emigrated from Europe. They felt deeply that Winter Solstice was connected with the Christmas season. They wanted to celebrate when they always had, and they felt they were being mocked for doing so. It seemed to me that, more than anything else, they were looking for reassurance that their practice of using the Northern Hemisphere calendar was valid. For them, celebrating the native Australian way just didn't feel right. In that case, I assured them that they could practice as they always had. I live in a part of the world where I meet and spend time with immigrants every day; they all seem to retain a deep connection to their native land. I suspect that if I lived in Australia today, I'd follow a Northern Hemisphere practice, because my deep inner connections would still be to the United States.

When the festival was over, we had a little over two weeks to tour the country. Isaac and I had a rough route mapped out, with some tourist sites and a lot of room to explore. Arthur's goal as an eight-year-old was to hold a koala. Doc took the five of us (Oberon, Morning Glory, Isaac, Arthur, and me) to the Alma Park Zoo. There, the park ranger held the koala and allowed visitors to touch it. This wasn't at all what Arthur wanted, and he was adamant on the subject. We looked at our plan and saw that the Lone Pine Sanctuary—the only place in the world where one can hold a koala—was right by the airport, so we scheduled a visit for our last day. This meant we had to endure two weeks of Arthur asking when he could hold a koala. At Alma Park, there's a kangaroo petting zoo, and a kangaroo actually allowed me to pet her joey while it was in the pouch. That was a stunning moment!

It was also at Alma Park Zoo that I encountered the lesbian peahen.

Peacocks and peahens wandered freely about the zoo. As they did so, they engaged in sexual-display behavior. The male would open his big fancy tail and thrust his butt upward to make it look very fine indeed (peacocks would wear high heels if they could), while the female feigned disinterest. Parade, thrust, parade. Snore, yawn, snore.

Sometimes two or more males would be parading and butt-thrusting in front of a group of yawning females. Peahens would scratch their armpits if they could, just to complete the picture.

Now, I'd noticed this one peahen earlier. Let's see…what's a good name for a lesbian peahen? I'm thinking Darla. So Darla was wandering around in a very aggressive manner, and chasing other peahens, and generally behaving rather peacockish. I was watching two peacocks parading and preening in front of a group of peahens, when up came Darla. She went over to the peacocks, turned to face the peahens in parade position, and started thrusting her butt. This was somewhat amusing, because peahens have stumpy butts. But clearly she was moving exactly the same way as the males, and she was spreading what few tail feathers she had.

I ran and got Isaac and the Zell-Ravenhearts so they could see it for themselves, because I knew no one would believe me unless I had witnesses.

So here's to you, Darla, wherever you are. You're a testament to the diversity of nature.

I was awed by Australian wildlife. Waking up at Doc's, we heard the "laughter" of the kookaburra. At the festival in Joyner, we saw a dozen or more koalas in trees. This thrilled the natives just as much as it did us, since koalas were endangered and they'd only recently reemerged in such a visible way. The sounds and smells of nature in a foreign land awakened us to how far from home we truly were.

Our plan was to head as far north as Lady Musgrove Island—the southernmost point of the Great Barrier Reef—and as far from Brisbane as we could get and still have time to turn around and get back in time.

We visited an expo in Brisbane and toured everglades in Noosaville. In order to visit Rainbow Beach, you needed an off-road vehicle, so we signed up for a tour that would take us there. The tour brochure said to "bring togs." We had to look in the glossary of our Fodor's guide to figure out that meant bathing suits.

Rainbow Beach was characterized by colorful stripes in the dunes. The Aboriginal Kabi say that Yiningie, "the spirit of the Gods representing Rainbow," was killed fighting an evil enemy, and as he fell he colored the cliffs. From the beach we spotted whales just offshore. We also walked around inside a shipwreck that had been there since 1959.

We made it to Lady Musgrove Island, which was breathtaking. The reef was pristine, and the water was astonishingly clear.

The highlight of our tourist activity, though, was whale-watching in Hervey Bay. Arthur, who had endured quite a few excursions by then that decidedly had *not* involved holding a koala, would only deign to participate in this trip if he could bring a book along, in case he got bored.

I'd imagined that whale-watching would be like what we experienced at Rainbow Beach. Someone would say, "There she blows!" and we'd see a whale just at the extreme range of our vision, and then we'd all pat one another on the back that we'd seen that amazing thing. Boy, was I wrong.

At first there was, indeed, a "there she blows!" moment, and then the whale came closer. And closer. And then another came. And another. Soon we had four humpback whales surrounding our boat (the "Spirit of Hervey Bay"). If someone had fallen overboard, they'd have landed right on top of one. The whales started playing with us, diving under and coming out the other side, seemingly quite aware that they were rocking and splashing us. Our captain radioed another tour company's boat to come to our location, and then the whales had two boats to play with, chasing back and forth between us like we were pets. It had been more than ten years since we'd met a pilot whale in San Diego; we had the same palpable sense of being with spiritual "people," but this time they weren't babies—they were massive. It was in every way extraordinary. I still wear the little humpback-whale charm I purchased as a reminder of a peak experience I'll always treasure.

By now we were on our way back to Brisbane, but our itinerary was roomy. An hour or so outside of Hervey Bay, we saw a big, funky-looking billboard for the "Bauple Mountain Fairies."

I *love* fairies.

A second sign directed us to turn onto a narrow road. We drove about a mile, but it seemed much longer. It was windy and unmarked, and there was no sign of any kind of a fairy village or retail store ... or anything at all. We pulled over to turn around, and as we did so, we found ourselves next to a tiny sign that said the Bauple Mountain Fairies were just ahead. So we got back in the car and continued on our way.

After another half-mile or less, we were at a charming store that was worth all the trouble. It was three big rooms of fairies, fairies, fairies, with everything from life-size dolls, to tiny toys, to silver jewelry. There were fountains and flowers and a beautiful atmosphere. The owner was a charming woman who'd been fighting with the town to get better signage. We told her that the magic words were "American tourists." Tell the town, we said, that *American tourists* were trying to find the place. We all laughed. We shopped for quite a while, soaking in the beauty of the place and purchasing a few items. It was magical to find such an unexpected place off the beaten path, and it was everything I love about travel: the unplanned encounter, the instant warmth, and the hidden treasure of finding something and someone new.

Finally, on the day of our departure, we visited the Lone Pine Koala Sanctuary. It was an amazing zoo, but of course the highlight was holding a koala. The zoo made money for protecting koalas by selling photos of visitors holding them (and not allowing you to take your own personal photos), and we were happy to buy one of each of us. Koalas are amazing animals. They clung to us fiercely, as soft and sweet as teddy bears.

The trip home wasn't quite as bad as the trip out. We begged them, at the airport, to upgrade our tickets. We were willing to pay quite a bit for comfort, having experienced the trip once already, but our tickets were not upgradable, and we would have had to buy three new tickets at approximately the cost of a new car. On the other hand, the layover in Japan was overnight, and the airline provided a hotel room and a buffet breakfast. We ate a lovely dinner in the hotel but were too spent to venture out into another country, so we never did see Japan.

Arriving home was wonderful. International flights arrived on the third floor at Kennedy Airport, so we came down a long escalator into the main concourse, and it seemed that all of New York was laid out before us. Australia is a relatively homogeneous country—at least the parts we were in—and the diversity of faces we saw and the languages and accents we heard in New York made us happy. "Goddess bless America," we said to each other.

Chapter 15

LIFE CHANGES

Around 1996: Isaac and I posing with a snake
at a birthday party featuring exotic animals

> But when one partner has adult attention deficit disorder
> (ADD ADHD), time management can be as big a thorn in the side
> of your ADHD marriage as those classic marriage problems:
> money, sex, and communication.
>
> —*Help Your Spouse Keep Dates: ADHD Time Management*[13]

The year 1995 was eventful.

There was a ten-day period that spring during which we performed four major rituals. First, I elevated a couple to second degree. Let me pause here to note that this sounds like one ritual, but it's two in one: two full second-degree rituals packed into one busy night. It took *hours*. And without giving away any secrets, I can freely say that second degree is the most complicated of the degrees to perform.

Two days later, I initiated a new member of my coven.

The following weekend, Candace founded her own coven and initiated its first member. This was done as a joint rite with Stormcircle, since Isaac was functioning as her "bootstrap" High Priest, just as I'd founded my own coven with my initiating High Priest. It was another huge, lengthy ritual. The following night, we initiated the second member of Candace's new coven.

I have a running joke that when you do good deeds in life, when you "accrue good karma," you're rewarded with beachfront property in the Summerland. After all, what's the fun of being dead if you have to walk to the beach?

---

13. Rick Hodges, "Yours, Mine, and Hours: Understanding Your Partner's Time Style," *ADDitude*, www.additudemag.com/adhd/article/755.html, accessed November 8, 2012.

During that last initiation, I caught Candace's eye and whispered, "Beachfront."

Also in 1995, Isaac and I settled our lawsuit with Showa Denko K.K., and things changed for us pretty rapidly.

Just a few years earlier, we'd been dirt poor, as in rolling pennies to buy milk poor, or sneaking in when the landlord wasn't around to avoid a confrontation poor. At first, it was hard even for Isaac to qualify for SSI disability; EMS was such a new disease that it wasn't in the SSI databases. With the help of a lawyer who specialized in disability qualification, and by networking within the community of EMS sufferers, he was able to make that happen. Meanwhile, I went from being a stay-at-home mom with a few freelance jobs to working full-time. We were still struggling financially, but by 1993 we at least owned a car capable of passing inspection, we were current on the rent, and things weren't so scary. Nonetheless, we lived paycheck to paycheck and had few luxuries.

When the settlement money arrived, the first thing I did was buy a new mattress. We were sleeping on the mattress I'd given birth on; it had caved in on one side, so I was essentially sleeping in a sink hole.

Next we started house hunting.

Isaac wanted a big yard. I wanted a great school system with a good program for gifted children. Arthur wasn't yet diagnosed with anything, but he had shown enough unusual abilities that it seemed a given we'd need those programs. We also needed a ranch house. Isaac used two canes to walk, and there was no telling how much worse he might get. With EMS we were in uncharted waters. Some of the ranch homes we were shown were "split ranch" and had stairs, and one had a steep hill up to the front door, but we needed a level house that could be adapted to a wheelchair.

The place we found in Congers was beautiful. The front of the property was level, there was only one stair to the front door, and the doorways were wide. There was a wide staircase to the finished basement—the width meant we could easily install a lift if needed.

It was a luxurious property and an enormous change. In Dumont, we had only six rooms, some of which were tiny. The "dining room" seated three, and the kitchenette zero. Arthur's bedroom and Isaac's office sacrificed much of their space to sloping attic ceilings. It was a nice apartment and I liked it a lot, but we were ready to spread our wings.

In Congers we had nine rooms, with hardwood floors throughout. Everything was huge. The house had been built by a custom home builder as a gift to his wife, and it reflected his attention to detail.

The best part was the temple. The finished basement had a twenty-four-foot room with a fireplace (in the north—Doc would have laughed) and a huge closet. We made the room a dedicated temple—no more tearing apart the living room and standing the couch on end to cast a circle! Isaac labeled all the shelves in the closet, so everything we used in ritual was organized. Goblets, candles, incense … all had their place. We would host major rituals there—even a handfasting—with up to thirty-five people. Between that and the huge kitchen, the library, and the comfy space to socialize, well, there were people in the house constantly, and we loved it.

Organizing Ritual Storage

Suppose you're lucky enough, as we were, to have a closet in which to keep your Pagan supplies organized and stored. How would you go about it? Here are some useful categories to help make your ritual life easier. Currently, I don't have such a closet; I use an old bureau I moved into the basement when I bought new bedroom furniture. But the same principles apply.

- **Basic altar setup:** It makes no sense, and isn't handy, to separate the things that go onto the altar every time into meaningful categories. Just have one space where "the altar stuff" goes. The organizing is for "extras."

- **Special occasions:** Here's where you put your holly crown for Yule, your painted eggs for Ostara, and your Loving Cup for handfastings.

- **Private:** Clearly mark as private anything that other Pagans in your house shouldn't touch, and set these items aside.

- **Cups:** Since I allow people to have their own cup for cakes and wine, I keep a bunch of spares.

- **Candles:** Have a space for candles that is away from any heat source. Keep dark-colored candles away from white ones, or wrap each color group in paper towels. (Yes, I have white candles with red blotches. That's how I learned this.) It's really handy to have an assortment of colors, especially astrological colors, for spellwork.

- **Incense, charcoals, and herbs:** Clearly label incense so you know what it is. Herbs and incense should be dated for freshness. Charcoals should be kept in an airtight container.

- **Spell leftovers:** Spells that are in progress often leave leftovers. For example, my coven has done protection spells for a number of soldiers in Afghanistan and Iraq. We keep each soldier's picture in the "spells" box until he or she comes home.

~

It was the fact that we moved that led to Arthur being diagnosed. In Dumont they'd denied there was a problem, despite plenty of evidence. As we were visiting the school in our new town, we met the school district's psychiatrist, and he gave us excellent advice. Soon we had a neurologist and a diagnosis that allowed Arthur to qualify for special education services. It made a huge difference.

In less than a year, we went from being low income in a rundown apartment with a stack of bills and an out-of-control child, to being homeowners with sufficiency, a new car, and a kid who was miraculously changed by medication. On the one hand, Isaac's illness loomed over us with as great a terror as ever, but on the other hand, life was pretty damn good.

Then Isaac started to get better.

He never got *well*, but he improved dramatically. Within a year, he was using only one cane, and only occasionally. He still slept a lot, but less, and he was less fatigued during his waking hours.

It was always a possibility that Isaac's health would improve, just as it was always a possibility that it would decline. The gradual increase in the scope of his disabilities over the previous five years had left us with little hope. During that time, we'd seen many doctors, tried many alternative therapies, and done a great deal of magic. EMS stubbornly held on, taking more and more of his mobility, memory, and energy.

Maybe settling the lawsuit released psychic energy around the notion of sickness. Maybe the freedom from constant financial worries made a difference. Maybe the magic worked in a limited way. We could never know. About 80 percent of EMS sufferers were female, so what little statistical and demographic information existed didn't necessarily apply to a male patient.

My marriage to Isaac Bonewits, until the last year, was a happy one. We loved each other, we connected to each other, we shared most of the same values, and we functioned as a partnership in the world. Most importantly, we had a child, created a family, and built a life. Certainly we had problems. Every married couple does. There were things about Isaac that drove me crazy, big things that enraged me, and little things that frustrated me. Yet when I look at my friends and family who have been married for thirty years or more, I see many of the same kinds of things, and I know that none of them would have driven us apart. Once you're divorced, it's easy to look back and say, well *this* and also *that* and, my goodness, *that*! Of course, there *were* specific factors that caused us to divorce, and paradoxically, one of those was that Isaac started to get better.

For five years, I had held my breath. For five years, I had known he could die. For five years, I learned to live with a husband who was almost never really *there*. Isaac continued to travel and work as a Pagan priest, and he slept a minimum of twelve hours a day, so the hours available to interact as a couple were very few. During many of those hours, he was in pain. Early in his illness, I learned to shield myself from him; his intense pain was easy to absorb empathically in the simple act of loving him and trying to help. I had to shield myself further in order to accept the vast distance between us that his illness caused, an illness that sometimes made it unbearable for him to be touched, and that nearly destroyed his libido even when he did enjoy being touched. We loved each other, we cuddled, and we talked, but I was psychically shielded from his pain and emotionally shielded from the absence his illness necessitated and from the fear of what might happen to him.

As Isaac improved, a lot of things changed at once. First, when he was able to reenter our marriage more fully, there were connections between us that had atrophied from disuse. In some ways, he was like a stranger to me. In other ways, he *was* a stranger to me—the disease had caused some personality changes. The release of pent-up emotional shielding was also draining and confusing for me. I wasn't conscious of any of this. I didn't know why I felt as I did, but in retrospect, it's clear that I had made a long series of unconscious choices about how to manage Isaac's illness, and some of those choices damaged me, and damaged us. Some of those choices were impossible to reverse. Some of those shields refused to come down no matter how hard I worked on them.

It's also true that we had set aside many of the small issues that commonly arise between couples, because our life was in a constant state of crisis. We had struggled, and struggled, and struggled. You ignore small problems when the big ones demand all your attention. But everyone knows that small problems, when they pile up, *become* big, and there was a huge pile of them now that we had a chance to notice.

There was one failing of Isaac's that had always been a major issue for me: his "disappearing act." He was absolutely incapable of being on time or of communicating his whereabouts. If he was expected home from work at 7:00 PM, he might call at 10:00 to tell me he was working late, or he might not call at all. He often pulled all-nighters at work without letting me know. It wasn't that I didn't trust him—he was absolutely and without a doubt at work when he said he was at work—but not hearing from him was agony for me. In the early days of our relationship, still fresh from John's death, his absences terrified me. I saw death around every corner.

Isaac said he felt my fears were irrational, and didn't want to accommodate them. I countered that, rational or irrational, wouldn't a loving partner want to alleviate them?

In time, the fear—that his absence meant he'd died—left me, but his disappearances never stopped driving me crazy. People with AD/HD, like Isaac, have no sense of time. Isaac would become caught up in whatever he was doing to the exclusion of any awareness of anything else—how long he'd been doing it, who might be waiting for him, or where else he might need to be. Not only was he extravagantly late, but he also didn't stay in touch on his frequent trips out of town. This was in the days before everyone had a cell phone, and even when he finally got one, he'd forget to charge it or to have it on him.

Isaac would be hours or days late, he would routinely miss planes, and he would pay financial penalties for missing deadlines. It was maddening.

Other people can and do handle this sort of thing with equanimity, and the Gods know I tried to be at peace with it, but it infuriated me, hurt me, and frustrated me throughout our years together. It was my one and only irreparable issue. There are people who are punctual, and there are people who don't mind lateness. But Isaac and I just weren't compatible about this, and it never stopped being a problem.

There was one time, in 1993, when he flew out of state on a Thursday and I didn't hear from him until Saturday. He'd left home without giving me the name of the place where he was lecturing or the name or number of his hotel. When we finally spoke, I was at wit's end. I said: "There will be a last time. I know I married you for 'as long as we both shall live,' but I am telling you now that if this doesn't stop, there will be a last straw. There will be a day when I can't handle it anymore. And I beg you to change it, because I don't want that to happen."

When I brought this up as our marriage was ending, he was angry that I still held a grudge about an event five years earlier. But that wasn't why I brought it up. I just wanted him to remember what I'd said—that there would be a last time. Finally, that last time came.

Isaac and I went to the Starwood Festival every year. In fact, I'd only missed one since 1982. It's easy, when playing and wandering at a festival, to spend no time at all with your spouse, so, on my suggestion,

Isaac and I planned a "date night" for Friday at Starwood 1997. We were to meet at 6:00 PM in the food court.

At 6:00, I was there, waiting with Arthur. In those days, Arthur took Ritalin. As soon as his medication began to wear off, he would become intensely hyperactive. He would spin, run, jump, shriek, and generally behave like the Tasmanian Devil. Isaac had Arthur's meds on his person, and 6:00 was medication time.

Isaac showed up at 8:00.

I completely flipped out and just could not control my anger. Isaac said, "Why didn't you just go back to the cabin and get the other bottle of meds?" In truth, that hadn't occurred to me. It was maybe a ten-minute walk, and, to my mind, Isaac was *on his way*. Now I felt abandoned, I felt like our special "date" meant nothing, and I was burnt out from caring for a kid in a hyperactive state. Isaac didn't see the big deal; the divide that had always been between us on this issue couldn't have been clearer. He saw someone who flipped out (which was true), and I saw someone who was unreliable (which was true). He didn't think being unreliable in this way mattered at all, while I thought flipping out was normal and justified. This wasn't an unusual case—far from it. I was always irrational, as far as Isaac was concerned, and he was always disappearing, as far as I was concerned. This was just one more incidence.

I felt a switch being flipped. I'd reached my last time. The moment that I'd feared had arrived. I asked Isaac for a divorce.

We talked and talked, and finally I agreed that we would go to marriage counseling.

Being at Starwood, there were plenty of people to get advice and input from, and plenty of friendly shoulders to cry on. One thing this festival is famous for is its enormous, house-size bonfire. I danced around it every year. It was sacred to me. On Saturday afternoon, when a friend asked how I was doing, I said I'd be okay; I would throw all my anger onto the fire. That may have been the wrong thing to say, because I was taken from the bonfire in an ambulance.

One minute I was dancing around the fire, and the next I was on the ground. Quickly, strong hands lifted me and moved me away from the danger of being trampled, but I couldn't stand up. Oberon Zell, Frank

Dalton, and a man I know only as Mouse were my rescuers. My knee must have looked horrible, because they wouldn't let me even try to stand on it. They got a station wagon down to the fire, put me in the back, and drove me up the hill to the first aid station. The station wagon drove at walking speed, with the back open and Frank walking beside me. It was terrifying. If Frank hadn't been there, I can't imagine how much worse it would have been, but he never left my side.

I was in pain and in shock, and I don't know how the decision was made, but an ambulance was called. Someone brought Isaac to me, and our friend O got pulled out of his fire trance to babysit Arthur while we were gone. Isaac and I may have hit rock bottom, but he was my husband, and he stayed with me and held my hand until the ambulance came, and then followed us in the car to the hospital.

It was a hellish night. The hospital was awful. There was no physician on duty, and I was there for hours. I spent the first forty-five minutes *begging* for a bedpan, which they wouldn't give me until all the paperwork was done. Finally, I left with a knee immobilizer and instructions to see a doctor. Imagine that—I was in the hospital all night, and they thought I should see a doctor! What was I *there* for?

Everything takes time. First, see a physician to get a referral to a specialist. Then get an MRI. Then see the specialist. None of that happens right away, because everything requires an appointment. Then schedule surgery. I didn't have the arthroscopic surgery until September—seven weeks later. I had a torn ACL and medial meniscus. My left knee has plagued me with one problem or another ever since.

Meanwhile, Isaac and I started seeing a marriage counselor. I was in physical therapy three times a week and marriage counseling once a week. Eventually, the counselor suggested twice a week, and I cut back on the PT. It was a grueling year.

Marriage counseling is the most emotionally intimate and difficult work I've ever done. Almost any other form of therapy is about what happens outside of the therapy office—you're addressing what happened last week, or twenty years ago, or earlier that day. But in marriage counseling, you're right there, with your marriage, in the room.

You're addressing what's happening as you're being counseled. It's immediate and therefore intense.

We would go on dinner dates after counseling. We were drained and needed the down time, and we *wanted* to be married to each other. I was pessimistic about our chances, but I'd agreed to this process and I was fully committed to it. Our dinners were always fun. The counselor felt we had a great connection and a really good chance of making it work.

In January, Isaac announced he was taking a leave of absence from the coven. (In reality he was resigning, but as usual, big decisions in a coven are for a year and a day before being made final.) Many people close to us thought he did so because of our marital problems, but that wasn't true. He'd simply come to see that being a Gardnerian was not his path.

While Isaac didn't leave because of our problems, his leaving definitely had an impact on them. Our work together in the coven was one of the few remaining areas where we were actively and successfully functioning as partners. His departure from it kind of drove a nail into the coffin of our marriage.

Even though we were still having good times together, still connecting, and still sharing a lot of warmth, Isaac was also still disappearing— sometimes for days—and I was still flipping out. Except now, we never had little fights. Every fight, no matter how small the issue, was suddenly massive, the kind we'd had maybe five or six times during our entire marriage. And for the first time, we were starting to fight in front of Arthur. I imagine this was due to the pressure cooker and laser focus of marriage counseling, but it was exhausting and it felt destructive.

At last, I felt we should end it while we could still remain friends, while we still had love and regard for each other, and while we still were able to *stop* fighting. I was full of doubt; indeed, that doubt never fully left me. Ending my marriage was the last thing I wanted. But Isaac responded to the fighting by withdrawing from me. He'd always had that tendency to withdraw, which was part of his "disappearing," but now he managed to completely reverse his clock, working on the computer throughout the night and going to bed around the time I left for work. We weren't "not speaking," yet we barely spoke. I was lonely, yet I lived with my husband. I felt like, maybe loneliness was more honest when you didn't have a partner there "with" you. Part of me felt weak, a failure; I wanted to make it work. Part of me was relieved to have it end.

I said, "Let's not break our vows; let's reframe them," and that's what we did. We took our "as long as we both shall live" vows seriously, and framed them as a vow of friendship and co-parenting, and that never changed.

Isaac moved out at the end of September 1998, just five weeks shy of our tenth anniversary. The first month or two were hard; we were angry and nasty to each other. But as we calmed down, we quickly went back to being friends. We had an eight-year-old when we separated, so we saw each other often, and soon it wasn't just a "drop off Arthur" visit, but also a beer and a long chat. When a new kid-friendly movie came out (*Harry Potter* or a Pixar film or whatever), we'd often take Arthur together, and go for a meal afterwards. We were still a family.

In Stormcircle, we were sad to have Isaac leave the coven. At the same time, there was a flurry of excitement. There were some aspects of Gardnerian ceremony that the rest of us were eager to experiment with but that Isaac had vetoed. A coven is ruled by the High Priestess, in partnership with the High Priest. Although she has the final say, a true partnership is best, and in fact, the coven as a whole functions best with consensus. I rule because everyone agrees: consensus dictatorship.

The experimentation was fantastic, but I quickly learned how much I had depended on Isaac's power as a magician. Just as I don't see auras, I also don't see most magical energies that other people describe; they're invisible to me. I feel them, but in a coven situation, when we're all creating magic together, you don't necessarily know what's coming from whom—in fact, as we form a group mind that is greater than the sum of its parts, it's beside the point! It surprised me, then, how much his departure weakened us. We worked hard to bring ourselves up to where we'd been before, but, just as I learned to sense the energy of circles by being in a low-energy one, I was now learning about Isaac's power by experiencing its absence.

Chapter 16

NEW BEGINNINGS

Three of my books: *The Elements of Ritual,*
The Way of Four, and *The Way of Four Spellbook*

Triple portions of thanks to Isaac Bonewits, who has taught me
so much, and who has been as understanding and helpful as it is
possible for an ex-husband to be.

—*From the acknowledgments page of my book* The Elements of Ritual

When Isaac moved out, I took a hard look at the traveling I'd done for
the years we were together, and realized it was probably coming to an
end. I had been invited to speak at events primarily as the wife of a
famous author, and been given opportunities that would otherwise go
only to published authors. One event organizer basically said to me,
"We'll talk if you write a book." Without feeling sorry for myself, I saw
that the facts didn't add up to me getting many more opportunities of
that kind.

But in the spring of 1999, I was invited as a featured speaker to
Craftwise in Connecticut. This was an event run by Cate and Frank
Dalton, making it twice that Frank had rescued me. It made me feel
valued, and like the work I had been doing really meant something.

When I got home, though, I asked myself if I wanted to spend
my time promoting a career as a "famous Pagan." I really didn't. The
lessons I'd learned as an ADF organizer were still true: Public work
was important work, but what I valued most dearly was at home. If
I worked too hard publicizing myself, I risked losing touch with what
was truly right for me.

I decided to sell the house. It was beautiful—I loved it—but the cost of buying Isaac's half would have left me with an impossibly tight budget. Once the decision was made, I suddenly *hated* the house. It was huge and empty and echoed with the marriage that used to be there. I was struggling to relearn how to manage my life without a house-husband, and smaller seemed better. I bought a condo, because having a management company that provided maintenance felt like an excellent stepping stone into independence.

FINDING THE CONDO:
A LESSON IN MAGICAL LANGUAGE

In chapter 2 of *The Way of Four Spellbook*, I told the story of how I found my condo:

In 1999 I was looking to buy a condo. Because my requirements were quite specific, there were only two condo complexes in the area in which I was interested, and neither had any available units. The realtor had been unable to show me anything for days and days.

I drove to each complex and picked up a stone from within its residential area. I used the two stones as focal points for a spell, and the words of the spell were something like, "A home for me! So mote it be!/A home for me! So mote it be!"

The next day the realtor called. A one-bedroom unit had just opened up in one of the complexes. Unfortunately, I was looking for a two-bedroom. Since it was an opportunity to see the complex from the inside (and since it was clearly a manifestation of my spell), I looked at the unit, which was lovely but far too small. I spoke with a friend later that day and explained what I had done and the results, and she said, "You left out Arthur!" To which I could only reply, "d'OH!"

So that night I started over. This time the words of the spell were, "A home for my son and me! So mote it be!/A home for my son and me! So mote it be!"

The next morning the realtor called. This time a *two*-bedroom had just opened up, and it is in that two-bedroom that I am living and writing right now.

The lesson I was illustrating in the book was about magical language, and speaking exactly what you mean when you do a spell. The experience also illustrates other good magical practices. First, use focal objects that have a direct connection to the work. Second, use rhythmic repetition to raise energy. I repeated my spell over and over, inducing a light trance while staring at a lit candle that was placed between the stones. (I still have those stones, melted wax and all.) Finally, my friend and initiate gave me great insight, and her presence in this story is an example of the value of a group of practitioners working together. Our friends and circle mates often see things we miss.

I hoped that having a new home that I hadn't shared with Isaac would help establish some boundaries with him. He was letting himself in. I'd come home from work, and he'd be inside with Arthur. There was always a half-second of seeing his car in the driveway before I recognized it, or of finding the front door unlocked before I realized I'd seen the car, and that half-second always stopped my heart with fear. "Who's here?" I'd wonder, and then I'd realize it was Isaac. I kept asking him to call to say he was there before I arrived. At first he didn't understand. Then he did, but he'd forget. It was the flip side of forgetting to call when he was away. I hoped he'd feel less "at home" in a house he hadn't lived in.

In fact, that did help. He had a key to the condo and would let himself in, but he was more careful not to frighten me.

Isaac was also incredibly helpful. Splitting up our stuff had been a major process. Over two-thirds of the books were his, and I still miss that magnificent library. We'd spent weeks with piles of books on the floor, determining whose was whose. When we were finished, he said, "Okay, honey, now we have to do with the music what we did with the books." I laughed and laughed. There were maybe three CDs or cassettes in our entire collection that we both even *liked*.

Then I realized the tools were all his. With Isaac moving out, I'd have to do all the household repairs myself. I was losing my handyman *and* my toolkit. So, as a "divorce present," he bought me my own toolkit and power drill. (The power drill was a hand-me-down. He upgraded his own.)

I loved doing little fix-it things around the house, and when Isaac came over, I'd show off the latest picture or shelf I'd hung. Invariably, he'd roll his eyes and rehang it "right." After a few weeks of this, he came over one evening and I handed him a new wall-mounted coat rack. "Let's save a step," I said. He did a nice job, too.

I could start a thousand stories with "Isaac always said…" He had a lot of ideas that he often mentioned. He had funny shticks he liked to repeat, and catch phrases he enjoyed, but he also repeated Big Ideas: things about Paganism, or how community works, or politics, or love. His theories were wide-ranging and sometimes dazzling (and sometimes a little crackpot).

One that has always stayed with me is his understanding of Pagan groups. Isaac would say that a Pagan group—whether a small coven or a nationwide organization—reproduces by fission. At a certain size, it is the nature of an organic group to split into smaller groups, and those groups, if they survive, will themselves grow until they split. When you're in the middle of such a split, the reasons are very important, and the stresses are very real. But the longer view is that these conflicts blow up in part because it's simply the natural life cycle of a Pagan group—and I doubt it's unique to Paganism.

The reasons that Stormcircle broke up were painful, and personal, and complex. The were anything but petty; they were about huge life changes among individuals, and deep, long-lasting breaches of trust. Yet, Stormcircle was also at the end of its natural life cycle. Stormcircle Pagan Way started in 1986, the coven started in 1990, and the whole thing broke up just before New Year's 2000. That's a long life for a Pagan group.

The break came in two steps. First, one member of the coven left, and made kind of a stink about it. We've made peace and are good friends today, but at the time, it was one of those things where everyone was gossiping, everyone had an opinion, and everyone took sides. He ended up joining a downline group of mine.

In Gardnerian Wicca, you trace lineage back to a High Priestess who worked with Gerald Gardner. Other lineaged traditions similarly trace back to a founder. I was initiated in Susan's circle, and she was initiated by someone, who was initiated by someone, who was initiated by Gerald. Susan and those someones constitute my "upline." I also have a "downline," people who trace their lineage through me—my initiates, those initiated by my initiates, and so on down the line.

By 1999, I had two local downline groups and some starting murmurs of additional groups. We were accustomed to gathering together for big celebrations like Beltane and Lammas, but now things were sticky. Not everyone was comfortable with everyone else, including me. Our gatherings had always come together under the name of "Deborah's group" or "Deborah's clan," but now that didn't suit everyone. Certainly one of my former people being in a different group was all kinds of awkward.

The next gathering that was held was announced as being "the Clan." Not "Deborah's" anything, just "the Clan." At first, cutting my name out rubbed me the wrong way. It was a blow to my ego and felt rude. However, I kept those feelings to myself. The new name created a way for people to gather together without taking sides.

Over the years, the Clan has thrived. There have been nine, maybe more, groups (mine and downline) affiliated with the Clan, some now defunct, as well as unaffiliated individuals—former group members, for the most part. It turns out that those early ego wounds were worth it. The Clan is open and pod-like, without any top-down structure. Even if I'd never asserted any authority of any kind, the simple act of calling it "Deborah's" would have created a hierarchy. A "clan," though, allows each group to be autonomous, which is as it should be in the

Gardnerian tradition, and keeps us all healthy and sane. Each person's home base is always her own coven or Pagan Way or (for a solitary) the shrine on her bureau; we can come together in fellowship. People can leave one group for another and still be Clan, and if there are a couple of people who aren't quite on speaking terms from time to time, we're big enough to be together and yet still avoid problems while they are in the process of being resolved.

The Clan has given me, and all of us, a model for knowing that these things *will* be resolved. There was a huge tumult when that first person left my group, and everyone knew it. Yet now, everyone can see the two of us hanging out, hugging, and circling together. It's the standard I hold people to: "*We* made peace, so I know *you* can." It gives me patience as well, because it took us years to make peace and rediscover our relationship. Meanwhile, throughout that long time, the Clan continued to grow and nurture the people who entered it.

In my life, I've seen people be at war with each other or refuse to speak, and five years pass, or ten, and then somehow, peace comes. Now, I look at the things that tear people apart, and I think, "Peace will come." This is especially true when bonds of the Craft exist: The pain is greater, because mystical intimacy is deeper, in its way, than even sexual intimacy, but the bonds are there. I believe they are past/future life bonds, and we are drawn together. The Clan, in its loose, informal, funky way, facilitates a process of reunion and love.

Back to 1999. One person had left, and the rest of Stormcircle banded tightly together. Then suddenly, and from another direction entirely, the shit hit the fan. A personal and painful (and truly not petty) dispute between two members broke everything apart. The final flurry of accusations and resignations took less than two weeks.

I moved to my current home in September of 1999. We had two rituals here, then Stormcircle was over. I was bereft. The relationship I was in ended at about the same time, and my heart was broken. I wasn't friendless, but I felt like I was. Most of my social circle had been in my coven or downline. My downline was in the process of shifting into becoming the Clan, and things there were still awkward. Barbara was and still is my best friend but had moved to Florida years earlier.

Other than Isaac, Arthur, and my blood family, the people I saw and spoke to on a day-to-day basis were all gone. It was a dark time, and I shed many tears.

It was clear to me that I'd missed some essential trick about not making the whole High Priestess thing personal. The wounds felt *very* personal to me, and I didn't know how to feel less involved. I announced to my downline that I was taking a year-and-a-day sabbatical from teaching the Craft.

I went to Starwood while still on my sabbatical, still feeling wounded, and still longing for the lover I'd broken up with that previous December. At Starwood, I got a card reading from Skip Ellison, someone I knew through ADF who would, in a couple years, become its Archdruid. I wanted a reading about my love life. What Skip said, though, made no sense to me. It had no connection to what was actually going on.

Then I said, "Wait a minute. This isn't about my love life. It's about my writing."

It was all there: A creative start that had stalled. A long-abandoned project that could somehow not be revived. It was a reading about the book I'd started in 1987 and had given up because I'd managed to disprove my own theories. There was also very clear advice: Throw everything away and start over.

I was excited! This was the first time I'd felt hopeful about writing a book in years. I'd always felt a bit ashamed that I'd never finished. Many people, including well-known writers, had asked me when I was going to write a book, and all I could say was that I'd written myself into a hole I couldn't get out of.

When I got home, I began right away.

I looked at the old manuscript to remind myself of its scope and intentions, then put it aside. Skip's reading had clearly said to forget about the old and start fresh. I got about fifty pages in with completely fresh material, but my resolve weakened. I started looking at old pages, seeing if I could salvage some of it, and became bogged down.

While I was writing this book, the idea for another book came to me. It came full blown: I knew the concept, the structure, and the individual chapters. It was all a piece in my head. Quickly I opened another document, jotted down the outline of it, and went back to the book at hand.

However, the new book kept calling to me, and now the original book was back in the swamp, entangled by old writing that I couldn't seem to get past.

By September, I had given up on my myth book and was working full-time on my new book. I even had a title: *The Elements of Ritual*.

Writing *The Elements of Ritual* was a lot like teaching a class. I visualized my readership clearly; they were my students, and I was always speaking to them. The book itself is almost entirely stuff I'd taught in Stormcircle. The outline of ritual steps was a class (often a two- or three-part class), the four elements introduction was a class (or two), learning different ways of calling the quarters was a class and a homework assignment, and so on. The need to teach was expressing itself in a way that protected me from being personally wounded by students. Writing it allowed me to continue to teach while I was healing. I owe the book very much to Skip's reading, but equally to the breakup of Stormcircle, which left my need to teach unfulfilled and seeking a new outlet.

I started writing *The Way of Four* almost immediately upon finishing *The Elements of Ritual*. I started *The Way of Four Spellbook* right away too, then stopped, wrote my book about James Bond movies, and went back to it.

It's daunting to write a book. Most people who can write something short feel like a writing a book is a whole different animal; it's mountain climbing as compared to hiking in the woods. For me, I break down every book into an outline detailed enough so that I'm always working on something short—on a section of the outline rather than an intimidating whole. Finishing *Elements* let me know that I was capable of writing an entire book, and that opened a door for me. It wasn't scary to start *The Way of Four* because I trusted my ability to finish it. After all, I'd already finished one.

Writing books was, frankly, great for my self-esteem. I love being a writer. I love going into Barnes & Noble and seeing my books on the shelf. Being a published author put to rest, at last, my secret fear that I was riding Isaac's coattails and perhaps I really wasn't all that.

One thing that Isaac and I learned was that the concept of "divorced couple remain friends" violated a cultural narrative in a big way. I can understand people being surprised at our continued friendship—most divorces *aren't* friendly—but it seemed to run deeper than that. I saw this in many places, including a number of people who wanted to know which of us would be avoiding Starwood that first year. Of course, the answer was "neither."

When I finished writing my first book, no one cheered louder than Isaac. (I mean that literally; he had quite a piercing cheer.) When I was looking for a publisher, he helped. When I opened my first royalty check, he whooped and hollered at my success.

I may even have inspired him or awakened some competitiveness within him, because, after years and years of enduring a crippling writer's block, he finished *Rites of Worship* shortly after *Elements* was accepted for publication. *Rites* was the book he had been "finishing" when we'd first started dating more than a decade earlier. He wrote it and wrote it, added to it and perfected it, and couldn't let it go. *Rites of Worship* (now in print as *Neopagan Rites*) is actually just a small piece of that original, gigantic manuscript. If it *was* competitiveness, I am pleased to have sparked something that got such a marvelous book into print. In fact, Isaac wrote four more books after that (one co-authored by his fifth wife, Phaedra), which was wonderful to see after such a long and frustrating dry spell.

Now that I was published, I began to travel on my own. Having traveled all those years with Isaac, I was well educated in the things that could go wrong, and that helped me a lot. I'd already been through showing up to speak at an event that the organizer didn't advertise (so it had no attendees at all), and being given incomprehensible directions, and having nothing to eat or drink when I arrived. I have still, over the years, been forgotten at an airport, and been scheduled to speak at an event an hour earlier than I told them I would arrive. Nonetheless, experience helped me avoid many difficult situations, and I was again on the road, meeting new people, having adventures, and teaching ritual, spellcasting, and mythology.

Chapter 17

ANAHATA

2006: With Claudiney Prieto in Brazil

Anahata is the heart chakra. May our hearts be open.

—*From the Anahata Pagan Way letterhead*

Life had its ups and downs. I lost my job, had two more knee surgeries, and found another job. I wrote, received excellent reviews, traveled, and taught at festivals and events. My love life was bumpy, as was parenting. In other words, there was the usual assortment of pluses and minuses in a basically happy life.

We have a local men's group called the Hermes Council, consisting mostly but not entirely of Clan men, that has been running for many years. When it was time for Arthur to have a coming of age ceremony at age thirteen, Isaac asked them if they would do it, and they agreed, provided that Isaac and Arthur joined Hermes, and didn't just use them for the ceremony and then depart. Honoring the secrecy of that rite, Arthur has never revealed its particulars to me—I'm not a man, and therefore not part of Hermes Council. Nonetheless, the ceremony clearly had a powerful impact on him. He treasures the gifts he was given during the rite, and he is still a Hermes member, as was Isaac, even on his deathbed.

It was as a result of this rite that I was able to finally have real healing with the person who'd departed my coven years earlier. He'd been an important part of Arthur's ceremony, and that opened a door. We walked through that metaphorical door, sat down, and really talked.

Sometimes people apologize, and it's between clenched teeth, or it's given merely because it's the right thing to do. Other times, apologies are heartfelt, and all the energetic bonds holding the hurt and anger in place just fall away. It's not that love is *restored*—love was always there, just hiding underneath all that pain.

So, I was at peace with my Clan and in loving relationship with many wonderful friends. I was parenting, working, creating, playing, and living. But there was a missing piece.

It was time to start another Pagan Way.

Arthur inspired me by asking if I would train him formally. He'd picked up a lot of Pagan knowledge, just living with Isaac and me, but he'd also ignored Pagan studies, basically assuming that, being raised as a Pagan kid, it would come naturally to him. He realized he was wrong, though, and was ready to make up for lost time.

When I first started thinking about starting a new Pagan group, I was skittish, but gradually I began to feel that the way to approach this was not with a plan on how to avoid getting hurt, but with an open heart. It's great to learn not to take things personally, but it's also important to me not to be too guarded. I approached a member of the Clan about being my High Priest, and we named the new group Anahata, which is the heart chakra, symbolizing our open hearts and the loving environment we hoped to create. We started the group in September of 2004.

My partner, Dave, is the father of the boy (now a man) who was hit by a car all those years ago. When we began working together, we didn't know each other well. To me he was mostly the husband of a good friend; we built a friendship and a partnership simultaneously.

People in the Craft community tend to idealize the "couple partnership"—a romantically involved couple who also work together as magical partners and are sometimes known as a "perfect couple." I had that partnership with Isaac, although I'd hesitate to call us "perfect." I have also worked with a broad range of partners in a wide capacity of situations. I've had gay male partners, ex-boyfriends, male and female lovers, and in one case a (heterosexually) married woman. Each partnership has had a different flavor and brought different gifts to the ritual. Many times, I've envied couples who create long-term magical partnerships, but I also know that the ability to discover, often on the fly, how two energies can interlock is a powerful skill. I have, from time to time, suggested that longtime couples mix things up, working with other people in their groups, so they can experience the ways that energy shifts in different combinations.

With Isaac, I was a willful, verbal, outspoken High Priestess, and Isaac was a willful, verbal, outspoken High Priest. We worked well in concert with one another, and we played off each other.

With Dave, I'm willful, verbal, and outspoken, and Dave is musical, quiet, and gentle. He creates a space in our rituals that I'm incapable of creating or sometimes even of understanding, but I recognize the power of his energy and the way it makes our rituals different.

As these relationships change—indeed, as the makeup of a coven changes—the rituals have to change as well. You can't just plug in the old rites you used to do with the new group of people. Yes, there's a Book of Shadows, and yes, I use it, but the stylistic and magical choices we make must be influenced by the energies gathered, and it is the individuals who bring those energies. Where Isaac would recite an invocation and create great power, Dave will set the words aside and drum the invocation. Naturally, that changes the energy for both the people and the non-corporeal entities called.

When we first started working together, I couldn't understand why Dave whispered so much. He would speak parts of the ritual so softly that you'd have to lean in to know what he was saying. He's not shy, just soft-spoken, yet for a long time I assumed he either didn't understand how to use his voice powerfully or was in some way self-conscious. In fact, though, when we led a large public Samhain together at a bar/restaurant, he used a big, booming, theatrical voice that everyone heard.

As I came to understand my partner, I came to see that he doesn't experience *power* in words. He enjoys wordplay, puns, and jokes, and can tell a good story, but his true inner power is nonverbal. He says just enough to make sure words that should be said are said—or whispered, if he can get away with it—so that he can focus his energy elsewhere. In public, words are more important, but in a small group where he can trust people to pick up on the energy, he whispers. It's utterly different from the way I work, or the way that any other partner I've had has worked, but for Dave, it's effective.

I am the opposite in that most of my power comes from words.

Perhaps the most crucial lesson for people to learn in their development as Witches and as individuals is that their source of power and their failing are generally the same thing. For me, it's all about talking. As a child, I was constantly in agony, knowing that I talked too much, knowing that I stuck my foot in my mouth, that I embarrassed myself. I would always promise myself to talk less, and I would always fail.

Learning to be silent when it's appropriate, learning what not to say and when not to say it, are social necessities. At the same time, my "talking too much" has become my magic. Not only do I write and speak for a living, but my spells are empowered by spontaneous bursts of words.

While Dave drums, moving power into our work through music, I often speak directly into the spell, spinning a web of words. I use declaration and description to build power around a goal, usually speaking off the cuff. Sometimes the group will use a single chant or couplet, and I will build around it.

Without self-acceptance, I could never have truly found the power of words, because I'd be too busy fighting them.

HEALING THE SICK: A SPELL OF WOVEN WORDS

In this made-up example, the patient is named Joseph Jones and we have already invoked Brigid, both because she is a goddess of healing, and because Joseph is a musician and she is a goddess of bards.

Coven recites:

Joseph is healed, Joseph is well.
Brigid, bless this healing spell.[14]

Woven words: (These are recited by one person, or more than one, as the coven recites, drums, and chants.)

Brigid, look upon this healing spell.
Look and find it worthy.
Look and find Joseph.

---

14. Okay, it's not brilliant poetry, but it doesn't have to be. The key is for the words to be simple and easy to remember.

Find Joseph and heal him.
Aid us as we heal him.
Joseph is healed and we heal him.
We invoke you, Brigid, to heal.
We invoke our own power to heal.
We heal.
We heal Joseph.
Joseph, Joey, Joe,
We heal you.
Joseph, we heal you.
Joseph Jones, we heal you.
Lady of bards, we invoke you.
Heal this bard.
Joseph, we heal you.
Lady of healing, we invoke you.
Heal this bard.
Joseph, we heal you.
Joseph, Joey, Joe.
Joseph Jones, we heal you.
(Continue like this as long as feels right.)
So mote it be!

Coven responds:
So mote it be!

~

I was trained to be very sensitive to the whole notion of "coven raid-ing." Inviting someone to join your group if he or she is a member of someone else's group is a serious breach of Wiccan etiquette. Many groups do not allow people to be a member of more than one group at the same time, while others allow you to attend other groups' rituals only with the express permission of your group's leaders. In the 1960s and '70s, with no access to groups via the Internet, it was all word of mouth. Reputation mattered a great deal. Rumors flew fast and furious.

If newer members of my group received an invitation from another group, they couldn't know if they were going to be attending a nice circle or walking into a hornet's nest. Carefully vetted permission from leaders who knew the community helped prevent awkward situations from arising. Even today, a lot of this still applies.

If I take a student into my Pagan Way who has been a member of another local group, I call or write the leader of that group. Mostly I'm checking references, but I'm also preemptively ensuring that the other group won't feel slighted. I've written about the several people who've left my group over the years without formally resigning. I wouldn't want another High Priestess to believe someone was still a member of *her* group when that person had joined mine.

Gossip isn't always a bad thing! Our ability to communicate through the grapevine keeps us connected and keeps us honest with one another.

Sometimes, though, it's awkward, perhaps never more so than the time I took a student who had been a member of a group run by one of Isaac's former paramours. Their relationship had ended badly, and on the few occasions that we'd met after Isaac and I were married, she had been frosty. I certainly sympathized with being stiff around an ex, and I didn't blame her for it, but it made it uncomfortable when I realized that screening a particular student meant I needed to talk with someone who had previously been so cool toward me.

She was perfectly friendly and very informative. She suggested I talk with her husband, who had done most of this person's training. We met at the local Renaissance Faire, where the woman worked. I'd never met her husband, but he picked me out of a huge crowd because he'd seen me with Arthur, and the resemblance was so strong between father and son that it was enough! We had a good, long conversation. The whole thing validated my appreciation for the value of this kind of communication. This couple, despite our odd personal connection, had been professional. They'd taken Wicca seriously enough to realize that our duties as priests and priestesses were more important than the human drama of past romance. In that sense, we were very much on the same wavelength.

For all the effort I went to, that student washed out pretty quickly. She RSVP'd for Yule, and I bought her a present, which she never got, because she didn't show up for the holiday or ever again. I never heard from her. Later, I ran into a friend of hers at an event, and he asked me about her. She'd disappeared from his life at about the same time. Twenty years ago, I'd have found it all very odd, but I've gotten used to strange disappearances.

At her second ritual, the former student of Isaac's ex got permission to bring a guest. Tracy was funny and earthy and we all really liked her. She expressed her intention of joining the group, which was good news as far as we were concerned. I got a few e-mails from her after that— Tracy had a bad habit of forwarding cute sayings—but then she, too, disappeared.

Dave and I started with Arthur and three other students. Three years later, quite a few people had come and gone. We still had Arthur and one of the original three, as well as several other good people.

One of those good people had a friend he'd met through a local Pagan group. He thought she'd be a good addition to Anahata, so with permission, he brought her to a ritual. Naturally, it was Tracy. Once again, my life moved in circles, with a connection, and then, years later, a reconnection.

Tracy had been through enormous upheaval. She'd lost both parents and her sister within just a few months, and she'd adopted her nephew when her sister died. With all that grief and chaos, it was no wonder she wasn't able to keep in touch with Anahata for a few years.

I always watch for synchronicity: meaningful coincidence. You can't prove anything by it, but a cluster of odd and seemingly random connections can be a resonance of karmic energy. In other words, footprints—you've been this way before. When I find a lot of synchronicity floating around my relationship with another person, I suspect that we may have a past-life connection, and I pay close attention to the person. By itself, it wouldn't compel me to make any decisions, but it's interesting to make note of.

Tracy's a great example of this. Not only did she circle into, out of, and back into my life, but I was in for a big surprise the first time I visited her home. Her backyard faces the house where my mom used to live—where I lived with her in the early 1980s. If you walk across Tracy's backyard, through the house she's back to back with, out that house's front yard and across the street, you'll walk straight up to Mom's old front door. That was eerie enough, and then I realized that Tracy had a phone number that was almost identical to the one Mom had in that house.

Echoes. Tracy is still a beloved and powerful part of my group. I could tell similar stories about many of my current and former coven members.

In 2006 I was invited to speak at a Wiccan conference in São Paulo, Brazil. It was a thrilling opportunity for me, although at first I was nervous about it. The trip was a bit of a whirlwind. I didn't schedule it properly or set aside enough other things, so I was there for only five days, half of which were spent at the Conferência de Wicca & Espiritualidade da Deusa no Brasil (the Conference of Wicca & Goddess Spirituality in Brazil).

Travel itself always excites me. Little things awaken me to being in a foreign country, like arriving at my hotel and seeing *Q* and *F* in the shower, and not knowing which is hot and which cold. For me it's pure joy. I feel as if I'm part of the whole world when I notice the small differences from place to place.

On my first morning in São Paulo, I used my minimal Portuguese and the hotel clerk's minimal English to purchase a card to use the hotel's Internet café. I was so proud of my ability to conquer the language barrier. Indeed, I expected that not speaking the language would be a downside of the trip, but instead it was half the fun. My hosts had told me that every educated Paulisto spoke English. In practice, this meant there was a class divide. Waitstaff, clerks, and maids spoke no English, and these were the people with whom I needed to speak. I found the small successes in making connections glorious. I signed for my lunch bill. Hurray! I got the maid to clean my room. Hurray! Brazil was my first time in a non-English-speaking country, so it was all new to me.

I fell in love with the *sound* of Brazilian Portuguese. Being from New York, I am used to hearing Spanish spoken at a breakneck pace—too fast to make out individual words. In Brazil, I understood the words that most people were saying, and could repeat them back, even if I didn't know their meaning.

The event opened Friday night with a belly dance in honor of Lilith, then all the presenters introduced themselves. Next the lovely dancer gave a second performance, this one in honor of Aphrodite.

On Saturday, one of the festival's core organizers suggested I read Tarot at the conference (which I did with the help of Lulu, my translator). I had somehow neglected to bring a deck, so we went shopping in Liberdade, a Japanese neighborhood as dense and interesting as New York's Chinatown. There were thousands of tiny stalls and booth-size shops. On Saturday and Sunday I taught, read Tarot, taught, and read Tarot.

I did five readings in a row that were dead-on: "You're in a legal conflict with a man who has disappointed you, and you're involved in athletics" were my first words to a woman who then revealed she was a gym teacher in the midst of a divorce.

Then P. came in. I read the first cards.

"No," she said.

I read the next cards.

"Not at all. I just don't relate to that."

Next cards.

"In fact," she said, "it's the opposite."

You get that fear in the pit of your stomach. Every reader knows that fear. I never doubt I'm good, but sometimes everything just stops working, and it's pit-of-the-stomach time.

I took a deep breath, let go of the fear, and breathed in the knowledge that I was in the right place, at the right time, saying the right thing.

"This isn't working," I said, washing the layout and pulling in all the cards.

"It never works for me," she said (through Lulu, who was translating). "I've had readings before, and this is what happens."

Ah! This told me something. This was about *connection*.

"Listen. We're going to do this. Look in my eyes and stay with me. Don't look at Lulu; she can translate without seeing your face. Stay with me."

I shuffled the cards without breaking eye contact, and fanned them out on the table.

"Now let's stay in contact here." I placed my hands gently over hers, and asked her to pick a card from the fan. I read the card.

"Yes."

We did it again. Eye contact. Hand contact. Slowly pick a card. Read it.

"Yes, that's true."

Six cards that way. Six isn't a lot for a reading, but the process was slow. And powerful.

"That's all we're reading," I said. "You've broken through. There was a wall, but we broke it down together. You never again have to say that readings don't work for you. You can always break this wall."

We hugged. *Obrigada*, P., for one of the highlights of my trip.

My most popular lecture was on Gardnerian Wicca. Because there had been some controversy in Brazil's Wiccan community on that very subject, people were eager to hear what I had to say. I was in the big main room for that one, and I'm sure I had over a hundred attendees.

In that big room, we used a microphone. Since we had only one, we handed it back and forth, which was a pain in the neck.

Not surprisingly, we spent some time discussing the issue of fraudulent claims. It's quite common for people to claim they are Gardnerian, and most Pagans wouldn't begin to know how to verify such a claim. I talked about how we network and know one another, and how rare it is for someone whom no one knows to be a true Gardnerian. Nonetheless, people try to establish claims based on unknown or unavailable connections. "For example," I said, "within a month of Doreen Valiente's death, there were at least four or five people who emerged from nowhere to claim initiation by her."

I handed the mike to Lulu, who translated and handed it back.

At this point, I was about to say, "What a surprise," when I realized I knew that phrase in Portuguese.

"*Que surpresa,*" I said, dryly.

I got the biggest laugh of the day and a huge round of applause.

The main ritual was Sunday night. I think the spiral dance in that ritual was the best I've ever seen, bar none. It was tight, it didn't devolve into chaos, and the song carried the movement. It was beautiful.

After the conference, I had a few days to tour Brazil. I was quickly becoming friends with my hosts and their friends: Claudiney, Lulu, L., C., and R. are all still dear to me.

One night we had dinner at C.'s home, and Lulu arrived about an hour late. Fond as I am of her, I was a little disappointed when she arrived, because half the fun that evening was wriggling around the language barrier without my translator. Indeed, every time a Brazilian and I really understood each other, I wanted to do a happy dance.

At one point, R. said he liked '80s music, which I happen to collect. We nearly got kicked out of a restaurant when a bunch of us burst into "Mickey" by Toni Basil! Loudly.

Often, Brazilians don't hear the American name for pop songs on the radio, or the names of the original performers, so we sang a lot to each other, figuring out names from melodies. I sang "I Ran" by Flock of Seagulls. They got very excited, and L. told me her brother had been trying to find the name of the group for some time. They had me repeat it, but none of them knew what a seagull was, so they couldn't translate it.

"It's a white bird that lives near the sea and eats garbage."

"Like this?" R. made a motion in the shape of a beak.

"No, that's a pelican."

"The one that brings babies?"

"No, that's a stork."

I was wracking my brain. How could I communicate this? Where had they seen a seagull … Aha!

"Have you seen *Finding Nemo*?"

"Of course!"

"Mine! Mine! Mine!"

"Ooooh!" they said, and all burst into a chorus of "Meu! Meu! Meu!" (thus preventing me from ever forgetting the Portuguese word for *mine*).

⌒

On May 27, 2007, I got a terrible phone call. Orien Rose Laplante, the eight-year-old daughter of two Clan members, had fallen out of the family boat. Her head had been sliced through twice by the propeller; she was having emergency surgery.

We gathered immediately that night, as we had before. The Clan was much bigger now than the two covens that had gathered for Joey. More than two dozen people came together on the Sunday night of Memorial Day weekend, many traveling distances and changing plans. As we prepared the ritual, we were in touch by phone with the Laplantes, who gave us detailed information on our magical goals. We learned about tissues, swelling, infection, and so on. Our visualizations were up-to-the-minute with the surgeon's specific description. Our work was long and intense.

Riding home, I asked, "Is it wrong to feel so good?" A child's life was in terrible danger, yet the way we drew together, the way we poured power and love into our work, felt ecstatic. I was *flying*.

Orien Rose's recovery was in every way miraculous. She easily could have died—from one of the slices, from septic river water infecting her brain tissue, or from the surgery. She was released from intensive care, then from general hospital care, and then from the rehabilitation hospital, weeks earlier than expected in each case. All of it should have taken many months, but she was home by mid-July.

There were many rituals, and many prayers, from all over the world. I led rituals and participated in those led by others. I organized large groups of people, and lit candles home alone. Sometimes I took the lead, but often I did not, because this was much bigger than me, and the Clan was now much bigger than me. Indeed, many, many rituals, prayers, and other spiritual work on Orien's behalf had nothing to do with the Clan.

Orien Rose's recovery is a testament to many things: to the power of magic (especially magic done well—we were always specific, focused, and clear), to the power of love and community, and to the flow of the miraculous that runs through our universe even when we don't see it. Her parents and her community were amazing, and I was blessed to be a part of it. Healing felt real to all of us, and even Orien Rose's surgeons were transformed through witnessing her amazing recovery and the amazing power of her network of support.[15]

Joey is a young man now, and Orien Rose is becoming a young woman, and I am able to watch my Clan grow through the miracle of healing. It's a great gift.

---

15. Christine Laplante has written a book about her daughter's accident and miraculous recovery called *Sirens from across the River*, which I hope will be published soon.

Chapter 18

DAGDA'S CAULDRON

2008: Arthur with his proud parents
at his high school graduation

Isaac sits with the Shining Ones and eats from Dagda's Cauldron.
The mortal world is a poorer place without him.

—*From "Philip Emmons Isaac Bonewits, October 1, 1949–August 12, 2010"*[16]

When Isaac first told me he had cancer, he treated it like it was no big deal. He didn't even ask for magic. This was October of 2009, and he explained to me that he had a choice between surgery and chemotherapy. He'd elected the chemo. We both knew his immune system was compromised from the EMS; he healed slowly and often had bizarre reactions to the simplest treatments. Surgery seemed like a very bad idea, and he was confident—apparently the oncologist was confident—the chemo would be effective and finished in six months.

That's not what happened.

The facts about Isaac's illness kept changing, and hearing them was hard. Sometimes Isaac filtered what he said to me through his own wishful thinking, and sometimes I listened through *my* wishful thinking. Speaking and listening, accurately and forthrightly, was strangely elusive for two people who'd always been as blunt as we had.

When Phaedra moved to New York to live with Isaac, my relationship with my ex-husband changed. That was to be expected; I missed our hanging-out time, which was dramatically curtailed, but I accepted it because that's what always happens when someone who was single now has a partner, and it's even *more* what always happens when that someone is your ex. In the back of my mind, though, there was always

---

16. Deborah Lipp, "Philip Emmons Isaac Bonewits, October 1, 1949–August 12, 2010," *Property of a Lady,* August 13, 2010, http://www.deborahlipp.com/wordpress/2010/08/philip-emmons-isaac-bonewits, accessed November 8, 2012.

time, so I put the desire to spend time together off into an indefinite future.

Now, though, time was diminishing. As soon as I understood that Isaac was really sick, I understood also how very deeply I still loved him.

In February we learned that the first round of chemo hadn't worked. The possibility of a second round working was shrinking. At some point it seemed like he was going to get better, then like he probably would, then like he might. At some point it seemed the doctor was saying he had five to ten years left before the cancer would inevitably win, then she was saying it was one to five. In May it was six months to a year. He died in August.

I did what I could to help. If Isaac needed a ride to or from the hospital, I could do that. The chemo caused cold sores, and chewing was painful, so I brought avocados, which I knew he loved. His apartment was in chaos, since his wife had her hands full dealing with Isaac's illness, so I did dishes and wiped down counters whenever I was over.

I did a lot of magic. I listened closely to Isaac, to the specifics of what he needed. We devised Water spells that would flow healing gently over him, because his pain levels were intense and he couldn't tolerate much. When that didn't work, I got his permission to try a very aggressive spell. Using myself as the subject, I did magic of pain, trying to burn off the cancer with the intensity of it. (You can raise power with pain just as you can with pleasure, but it's difficult to control, and few people try it.) Then we tried gentle Fire energy, which fell in between the two.

I did magic on my own, at my private altar, using my wedding ring as a connecting totem. I did magic with my coven, and with my Elders group. (By now the Clan had a large number of third-degree priestesses and priests, and we had begun having thirds-only circles.) We drew down Isaac's patron goddess and asked her guidance. She gave specific instructions, which Isaac followed.

In May, he knew he would die. He asked me to bring Arthur to him in the hospital and leave them alone for a while. Arthur was, by now, home from college. His AD/HD had gotten the better of him, and he had not thrived there. After father and son spoke privately, Isaac and I spoke at length. He was very concerned that I inherit his Gardnerian things, and we discussed his athame (more about that later).

Isaac had learned that he had a rare cancer, usually seen only in people with AIDS, that targeted immune system disorders. After all those years, the EMS had finally beaten Isaac; it was the EMS—an immune system disorder—that had made him susceptible to this.

I was scheduled to be the featured speaker at Free Spirit Gathering, and Arthur was invited to present two Young Adult–track classes there—his very first gig as a speaker. It was something we were excited about, and I'd been helping Arthur prepare for months.

We were to leave on a Tuesday morning. On Monday, Phaedra called Arthur and told him that Isaac was going into hospice care (at home) and that he was needed to care for his father. By the time I got home from work, Arthur had moved out of our house and into Isaac and Phae's apartment.

I was blindsided, shell-shocked, stunned, confused, speechless. I couldn't get clear information—Phae didn't want to talk to me, and I wasn't sure Arthur was conveying things accurately. I had *just spoken* to Isaac, and he was hopeful about future chemotherapy. I was suddenly living alone, and I was supposed to leave town in the morning.

Arthur insisted I go on the trip as planned, although I wanted to stay with him. Since I was apart from Arthur and Isaac anyway, it made sense, and I was a quick three hours from home if I was needed. It was horrible, but it was also right for me. A good festival (and Free Spirit is definitely a good one!) creates a bubble of sacred space. A lot of Clan members were going to be there, and I needed the support. I called Arthur twice a day, and spent almost the entire festival crying. That sounds terrible—it *was* terrible—but it was also good. In sacred space I was open and vulnerable, and the tears flowed with ease.

Over a meal with Orien Rose's mother, Christine, I said, "I'm so happy that Orien Rose is well, but I'm so *angry* that our magic for her worked, and the same magic for Isaac didn't work." It's the mystery of life. We shout our magic into the wind, and sometimes it's heard. Sometimes fate is too great and too implacable. And all of our lives must end. Magic gives us great power over many things: We can find jobs, homes, and lovers, improve fertility, heal illness, and create miracles. But we don't have power over death. No one does.

Isaac faded rapidly. I visited often. Sometimes I sat with him; I brought over photo albums to reminisce with, and we talked about many things. Sometimes, when Phae was there, I took Arthur out. Isaac could not be left alone, even for a few minutes, and Arthur didn't have a driver's license, so, other than walks he took when Phae was home or the hospice nurse was there, he never left the apartment. It was an enormous relief for him to see new scenery and eat different food.

My son grew up overnight. When I left for Free Spirit, he was a kid barely out of his teens, and when I returned a week later, he was a man.

There was a day when my mother came to sit with Isaac so I could take Arthur out for a special event in New York City. When I arrived to pick up Arthur, Isaac was having an attack of unbearable pain. Arthur gave him medication, but in his disorientation, he refused another dose. He called for Phae, and she left work to go to him at once. All my mother and I could do was sit with him and try to calm him while he waited.

There was a moment when Mom and I looked at each other with the same vision: Twenty years before, she and Isaac had sat by my bed while I moaned with the labor of life, giving birth to Arthur. Now she and I sat by Isaac's bed, with Arthur nearby, while Isaac moaned with the labor of death. It was a perfect parallel.

Throughout his life, Isaac had been in the thick of the best and worst of the Pagan community. For that matter, so had I—some before I met him, some experiences we'd shared, and some after we separated. We'd seen the gossip, backstabbing, and pettiness that any small and highly involved community will naturally have, as well as the goodness, kindness, and deep love of humanity and of the Gods that most Pagans share.

Isaac told me he'd made a conscious choice to allow the news of his illness to be spread publicly, in order to allow as much magic to be worked from as many quarters as possible. The loss of privacy was a trade-off he was willing to make.

I was fearful of how the Pagan community would respond. I thought they would ignore him, or minimize his importance to Paganism, or insult him, or I don't know what. While those thoughts were rooted in experience, they were mostly an irrational way of quantifying my grief. Grief becomes so huge that the mind seeks to place it in a box, assign an explanation to it, or have a target at which to aim the negative emotion. My target was a straw man Pagan who would behave badly.

In fact, 98 percent of people were extraordinary—compassionate, respectful, and kind. The support of the Pagan community was one of the things that kept me going. From all corners of the world, kindness and love poured in.

But it wasn't all sweetness. There were a few vultures, hovering about and looking for scraps to scoop up. Somehow, in the last few days of Isaac's life, rumors started to go around the Internet that he had already died, and I began to receive condolence messages, some from strangers, and even demands that I explain whether these rumors were true. Someone put a date of death on Isaac's Wikipedia page four days before he died. I urgently needed these rumors to stop, even while knowing that they were off by only days or hours. Friends were incredibly helpful in sending out messages that Isaac was still with us during a time when I felt unable to communicate with anyone except those closest to me.

Isaac's two brothers and two sisters came to say goodbye. For a while after our separation, one of Isaac's brothers had moved in with Isaac, but I'd never met the other siblings. His younger sister flew in on a Tuesday night, and I picked her up at the airport. In the morning I drove her to the apartment and then went to work, and then went back to the apartment that night. The rest of the siblings drove out together and arrived Wednesday evening.

It was remarkable seeing all the Bonewits siblings together. They looked alike and sounded alike. Isaac had a distinct nasal twang that I knew, having met my father-in-law in California, was his father's voice. It turned out they all had that voice to some degree. Everyone had always remarked on how much Arthur resembled his father, but he was the spitting image of one of his aunts.

We all sat with Isaac that night, speaking with him and expressing our love. I took the sisters back to my place for the night, and in the morning we got the call. He was gone.

Philip Emmons Isaac Bonewits, October 1, 1949 – August 12, 2010

This entry appeared on my blog, *Property of a Lady*, on August 13, 2010:

Isaac sits with the Shining Ones and eats from Dagda's Cauldron. The mortal world is a poorer place without him.

There will never be another Isaac. Those of us who knew him well could easily think of him as just Isaac: character, goofball, ladies' man, punster, life of the party, pain in the neck, singer, priest, friend, and ex-husband (in my case). But Isaac was so much more than that.

The press release gives you an inkling of his importance to the world. One of my favorite memorial posts comes from *The Wild Hunt:*

[The] vision of the ADF, written by Bonewits nearly thirty years ago, captures what was so vibrant and vital about him. The audacity of expecting excellence and success from himself, his coreligionists, and his peers.

"Audacity of expecting excellence"—Oh yes, that's Isaac.

I cannot begin to say how much I loved and love Isaac. As a husband, he drove me crazy. I don't regret ending our marriage, and I know he was very happy with Phaedra, whom he married in 2004. He loved her very much and I am so happy he had that. Still, Isaac and I were married for ten years (1988–98), and I'd qualify nine of those years as happy ones; only at the end did things break down, but our unhappiness was short-lived; we quickly became good friends.

Isaac was a wonderful, loving, proud father. He had a perverse sense of what made a good lullaby. Certainly, the baby slept better for him than for me, despite being sung to sleep with "The Internationale." As Arthur grew, Isaac always treated him as an intelligent being and spoke to him with a rich vocabulary even when he was a toddler. In the end, it was Arthur caring for Isaac. I am proud of my son, and I know that Isaac was and is as well.

He was an extraordinary High Priest in the Craft, as well as a Druid. He had a unique ability to move energy. When he called the Gods, They came. I was already a High Priestess of the Craft, albeit a young one, when we began dating in 1986, but I consider that only half my training was done. The rest I learned from him. He was a gifted teacher, exploring the nuances of every aspect of ritual and worship. *The Elements of Ritual* could not exist without Isaac's influence.

What Isaac loved the most was serving the Pagan community. He loved a good fight, he loved to get down and argue, to make trouble, to stir the pot. And he did it, always, on behalf of the community. He did it to make the world better, and more Pagan, and to serve the Gods. His love of the Gods was always at the forefront of who he was. His service to the community, to the Gods, and to his work as a priest was in every decision he ever made.

In the end, I look at Isaac, and I look at someone who was fundamentally good. He was not without his flaws, but he was without moral blemish. Isaac was honest, kind, charitable, generous, forgiving to a fault, open to new ideas, tolerant, attentive, amiable, and selfless. I assure you, I have thought over every one of those adjectives carefully, and every one applies to almost every moment of Isaac's life. I could list negatives if I wanted to, but none of them are moral failings. I believe, truly, that the Gods will look upon this man and embrace him as one of their own.

It was a privilege, Isaac. I hope we get to do it again.

Chapter 19

THE MIRACLE
OF THE SCABBARD

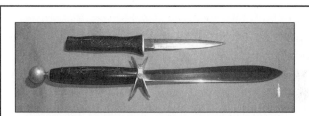

My athame (top) and Isaac's athame (bottom)

Athame. A Witch's personal, magical knife, traditionally
double-bladed with a black hilt, and fashioned of steel or iron.
The blade may be magnetized. Magical knives were said to be used
by witches in the Middle Ages.

According to the Gardnerian tradition,
the athame is used only for ritual purposes,
such as casting the magic circle, and never for cutting.
—The Encyclopedia of Witches, Witchcraft and Wicca,
by Rosemary Guiley[17]

Isaac had told me he wanted to leave his Gardnerian athame to Arthur.
He was one of those people with multiple athames—one for each tradition or practice. It's not an unusual habit; many people who work multiple traditions have different tools for each. Since I was his Gardnerian
initiator, he wanted to know if it was permitted to leave the blade to his
son. For his part, Arthur said he was ambivalent about the gift. Maybe
he understood how profound it was, but he didn't feel it was proper to
have a knife belonging to a tradition he didn't practice. Arthur is nothing if not proper and told his father no.

I promised Isaac that I would make sure, one way or another, that
the matter was handled appropriately.

By the time I received the knife in October of 2010, I'd already
researched ways I might ritually dispose of it. Ultimately, I decided
that destroying it was something I just couldn't do. I would hold it for

17. Rosemary Guiley, *The Encyclopedia of Witches, Witchcraft and Wicca,* 3rd ed. (New
York: Checkmark Books, 2008), p. 393.

Arthur in case he ever wanted it. But when the knife was in my hands, I was unexpectedly moved by it. I was almost shaking the first time I held it.

That was partly because it's a freakin' beautiful blade. I mean, absolutely gorgeous: about eighteen inches long, with leaf blade, Key of Solomon double-Moon crosspiece, round pommel, and ebony wood hilt. It was also partly because I was deep in the memory of the many rituals we'd done together. When Isaac asked me if there was anything of his that I wanted to inherit, I said I would be honored to possess some, or any, of the ritual tools that had been on our altar when we'd worked together magically. As it happens, I inherited exactly none of that stuff, and now, here was the athame that, so many times, had been dipped into my cup in the sacred marriage that is the cakes and wine ceremony.

What I felt, holding it, was, "WANT!" I wasn't sure, in that moment, if this was meant to be my blade. I knew I had too many entangled feelings to be clear about that. But it felt possible.

Complicating the whole thing further was that in a lot of small ways, I was becoming increasingly dissatisfied with my own athame. It had a paint smear, something like a thumbprint from when it was still new. I had dropped it a year earlier, and the wood had chipped in a small spot. Plus, a covenmate had dulled it for me "as a favor" when I was a new initiate. I didn't ask for that, and I was upset that it had been done, but many people considered it traditional to do so. An athame is never supposed to be used for actual cutting, and therefore many people dull the blade so it cannot cut and also to make it safer. Since you're not cutting with it, why risk hurting someone? Isaac, though, believed in Randall Garrett's maxim: "The best symbol for a sharp knife is a sharp knife."

When my friend dulled my blade, I was only twenty-one years old. He was older and more experienced, so I kept my mouth shut. Now, almost thirty years later, I'd come into possession of a beautiful, shiny, polished, sharp blade that I adored.

I agonized. I asked a number of Gardnerians whom I respected for their opinion. Everyone seemed to agree that it would be good and right for me to use this blade.

I sat down with Arthur and presented the issue to him. I told him that if he ever chose to be a Gardnerian, he could have his choice of blades. I would give him either Isaac's athame or my original one, and I'd keep the other.

Still ambivalent, I decided to use the blade in ritual and see how that felt. The difference was kind of ridiculous. Isaac's athame was twice the length of mine.

When Isaac and I first moved in together in 1987, he had two cars, a Fiat Spider and a Dodge cargo van. If I drove the Spider ("Li'l Honey") for a few days and then drove the van, I found I couldn't park it, couldn't gauge distances, and felt really disoriented. Isaac's athame was a Dodge van compared to my Li'l Honey of a knife.

What do you actually use an athame for? Consecrating salt and water involves putting the blade into a relatively small dish, so changing the size of the blade makes a real difference in coordination. We salute the quarters by kissing the blade and then sending the kiss by pointing the knife (like blowing a kiss off the end of the knife). Kissing something that's a disorientingly different size, something that's sharp, is funny only if you don't cut off your lips (I didn't).

So at the end of the first ritual, I was still ambivalent. Coven members were impressed by the beauty of my new knife, and they were touched when they learned where it was from, but I was back and forth and back and forth about it. I'd never discussed using it with Isaac. Wasn't it supposed to be buried? It felt so good. But I'd never discussed it with Isaac. Round and round I went.

I finally made a decision that wasn't quite a decision. Dave and I would repair my athame, and I would use Isaac's until then. (I wanted Dave to do the sharpening so it was really professional, and then I would do the wood and paint.) When my athame was ready, I would reconsecrate it, and once I had two consecrated athames, I would be able to choose between them.

The day before our next scheduled ritual, I went downstairs to clean the temple and to get my athame to give to Dave.

I was in the temple doing my thing, and I couldn't find the scabbard to my athame—a scabbard, by the way, that my initiator had made for me as an initiation gift. Since Dave was the one who always cleaned the temple after ritual, I called him on my cell.

"What did you do with my scabbard?"

"Nothing. I left it right where it always is: under the altar."

"No, it's not there....Oh, wait. Yes it is."

It was gone when I had called him, and then it was right there. I continued cleaning up, and five minutes later it was gone again. Just plain gone. When Dave and everyone else arrived for ritual the following day, no one could find it.

It's not like "Isaac stole my scabbard from beyond the grave" was the first thought that popped into my head, but eventually, my friend Melissa pointed out that the scabbard had gone missing immediately after I started using Isaac's knife. And it had gone missing in kind of a spooky way, and not from an ordinary place either: from under the altar.

This began a period of arguing with Isaac. I was intensely aware that I sounded like a crazy person. I was walking around the house talking to, cajoling, and negotiating with a dead person. I guess it's a good thing my son was over eighteen and the Department of Child Protective Services wasn't within earshot.

I laid it out for him. "Isaac, I don't know if you took the scabbard or what it means. If you want to let me use your athame, then put my scabbard back where it was. If you don't want me to use it, then put it upstairs in my bedroom." In other words, if you don't want me to change, then put it back naturally. If you want me to change, then make a big show of it by moving the sheath two stories above, where it was last seen.

Isaac had always been a great believer in the ability of inanimate objects to go "poof." He had several amusing and yet goose-pimply stories he liked to tell about his direct experience with things like disappearing/reappearing candles and spoon-bending, so there was a "this is just like him" quality to the whole incident. But also, I felt like it gave me some foundation from which to negotiate. "Here you are with an opportunity to prove these spooky things," I was saying. "So prove it." If he was going to assert his will and make me change my behavior, then he should do something impressive.

And again, yes, I know it sounds crazy. I've seen an awful lot of startling, supernatural things, but I've never been credulous. That's my girl-from-Jersey nature, I guess—naturally cynical.

No response. No sheath.

Now, let me break into this story to introduce you to Callisto. While Isaac was dying, I brought home a one-eyed kitten we named Callisto (Callie). With Arthur not living at home, I was lonely, and I was grieving; I needed the loving companionship. Callie turned out to be the most affectionate, most adorable animal I'd ever had, so I became interested in training her to be a familiar. I didn't know if that was in her nature, but there was only one way to find out. Finding lost objects is sort of Familiar 101, so I started giving her instructions to find my scabbard and put it back on the altar.

No response. No sheath.

It had been at least five weeks since the sheath had first disappeared. I know this because Dave had refused to bring my old athame home with him to sharpen if it wasn't sheathed, and at least two Moons had passed, during which time I had continued to use Isaac's athame. I was now quite enamored with the idea of getting my old athame repaired, so I didn't want to go back to it until that happened, and without a sheath, it wasn't going to happen.

I told my sister Roberta the whole story, and she said, "Deb, you gave Isaac a choice? Did that ever work when he was alive?"

Good point! There was simply no use negotiating with Isaac!

That's when the yelling started. Child Protective Services, you don't know what you missed!

"Isaac! GIVE IT BACK! Isaac! I want my sheath!" Yelling. I told him if he wanted to send a message, then he should hide his own damn sheath. I told him that he was actually delaying me from going back to my old athame, which I couldn't do until I had the sheath. I continued to ask Callie to find it, and I continued to yell at Isaac, and time passed.

At the Full Moon ritual for February 2011, Dave was setting up the altar and couldn't find the wand. "What do you mean, you can't find the wand?" Why would the wand be anywhere but with the ritual gear? Dave couldn't find it. I couldn't find it. We finally had to set up the altar with a substitute. I yelled at Isaac.

In a relaxed moment during the ritual, Dave asked me to explain the whole story about the sheath. He asked what Isaac had wanted done with the athame, and I told him he had wanted it to go to Arthur. But, I added, Arthur didn't want it. Dave just looked at me, and I said, "Oh." It dawned on me: Since when had Isaac cared about what Arthur wanted?

At this point, Dave said, "I've had it. Give Arthur the damn athame." As soon as the ritual was over, we sneaked into Arthur's bedroom (he was sound asleep) and left the athame on his dresser. A few minutes later, I realized where I had left the wand. Isaac hadn't moved it. Nonetheless, we were all quite clear that the athame had to go back to Arthur.

This all may sound really critical of Isaac. It isn't meant to be. He was a loving father and a wonderful man, but was willful and absolutely convinced that he was right. If he and Arthur disagreed on something, he had no doubt that Arthur would come around if he just put his foot down. Dave, who has four adult sons, the youngest of whom is Arthur's age, is fully on board with that kind of parenting and understood instantly.

So I was back to my old athame. And here's why I'd been ambivalent about it for so long. Other people have beautiful, magnificent, fancy knives—knives that could be in *Athame Collector Magazine*. Mine is kind of plain, kind of simple, kind of beat-up. But it feels so good. When I hold it, I feel like I'm holding my own hand. I was seduced by a fancy and beautiful knife that I had a lot of love and affection for, but when my own athame was back in my hands, I didn't miss Isaac's.

In April of 2011, I visited friends out of town and brought my athame, as we planned to do ritual. I wrapped it in a scarf for the trip. The day after I got back, Arthur and I were talking in my room and we both noticed a strong whiff of cat piss (a downside of cat ownership). I couldn't find a stain or puddle. As I walked around the room searching, the odor eluded me. I couldn't figure out where it was coming from. I looked under the bed and saw a dark object. It was vaguely mouse-shaped. As Callie had kindly left a dead mouse in a prominent place just two weeks earlier, I poked it gingerly with a stick.

It was my sheath.

There are a number of lessons I derived from this experience. First of all, it's absolutely true that everything that happened could easily be explained by coincidence and natural means. Cats do, after all, drag small objects around. I find Callie's toy mice in my bed all the time! Of course, Callie is a small girl, only six pounds, and the scabbard is almost as long as she is. I'd looked under my bed for something as recently as the week before, but it's not ridiculous to think that she was simply playing with an object and there was nothing mystical involved.

Similarly, the wand was right where I left it. I just forgot.

But pointing at coincidence and natural explanations misses the whole point of a Pagan life. Wicca isn't an episode of *Charmed*. Magic works through and with the natural world, not in opposition to it. In fact, the mystical events I'm talking about—communion with the dead and with animals—are considered perfectly natural and normal in a Wiccan worldview.

Hauntings are unpleasant communications from the dead. They are caused by unhappy ghosts. You hear about a place being haunted when a grave is disturbed or when someone has been murdered. Normal communication with normal, beloved dead doesn't have that creepy feeling about it, because there's nothing wrong. If the dead wish to communicate with us, they're not, as a rule, going to rattle chains or any of that nonsense. In fact, affecting the corporeal world at all is kind of difficult, what with the I Don't Have a Body thing, so Hollywood special effects are not an option.

Animals, especially cats, are commonly agents of magic and mysticism, which is why a companion animal is often an excellent familiar. So the fact that Callie might have dragged that scabbard upstairs doesn't mean the event wasn't mystically influenced. After all, I'd *asked* her to get the scabbard (although I'd asked her to put it on the altar, not drag it upstairs).

When I was taught about the magic circle, I was told that the circle forms a boundary "between the world of men and the realms of the Mighty Ones." No one, I was taught, can breach that boundary without making a magical doorway, with the exception of animals, children below the age of reason, and "idiots." (Sorry, I know that's offensive, but I'm quoting.) In other words, the only ones who can breach the boundary are beings without much rationality, because those beings move freely between the worlds all the time; for them, there is no boundary. Thus, an animal is an ideal agent for carrying an object back and forth between the worlds (if that's what happened) or receiving instructions from one world to be carried out into the other (if that's what happened).

Another common way that our world is influenced by other worlds is through attention, inattention, memory, and forgetting. For example, if I'm doing a Tarot reading, I allow my attention to simply relax, and I let my eyes fall on the cards as they will. Perhaps, as I look at the Queen of Pentacles, I notice the abundance of greenery around her, but perhaps I notice her downcast eyes and serious expression. Depending on what grabs me in the moment, my reading will change, and that's how I apply intuition and, perhaps, psychic knowledge to a reading. I tend to respect it if I suddenly "forget" the meaning of a card. I've studied Tarot for almost thirty years, so "forgetting" is more likely, I think, to be the way my subconscious has of telling me that the learned meaning isn't the right one for this situation.

It's a funny thing about that wand. When my coven members arrived that February night, I said we hadn't met since December, and they said, no, no way, we all hadn't missed the January ritual. I was sure there had been a cancellation due to a blizzard or something, but there were a bunch of them and only one of me, so I figured I was remembering it wrong. I wasn't, as I was later able to confirm by checking the coven diary I keep.

The reason that matters is, in December, we'd done a spell that, without going into details, required the wand to be washed afterwards.

There is no sink downstairs, so I'd brought it up to the kitchen. Of course, if we'd actually met again in January, as everyone insisted, then the wand would have been back on the altar. Where I ultimately found it, though, was in the spot where I always leave things that have been washed or polished or repaired and need to be brought back downstairs. So everyone's slightly screwy memory conspired to make us forget the wand. Maybe we're all screwy, but it might easily have been the method Isaac used to influence and communicate with us.

So the first lesson is, don't be fooled by natural explanations. The mystical world is as natural as a pile of laundry.

Similarly, communication with the dead doesn't have to feel spooky or magical. Talking with Isaac felt much like talking to myself. The hair on the back of my neck didn't prickle, the temperature in the room didn't change, and holograms didn't appear in my mirrors. It was very difficult to know if I was speaking with Isaac or fooling myself. This is the usual condition of many magical happenings. As a beginner, it disappointed me, and later confused me. But I learned to listen to my results more than to temperature changes.

The next lesson is something I was taught by my High Priestess very early on: The dead aren't superior beings, they're just people who happen to be dead. Isaac behaved exactly as one might expect Isaac to behave, exactly as he behaved in life. The series of incidents about the athames and the sheath were pure Isaac: funny, mischievous, stubborn, a little passive-aggressive, and a little flamboyant. Bless you, Isaac, you haven't changed a bit.

Another interesting thing is how the dead communicate. Dave and I have both experienced two major losses of loved ones. For me, it was John and then Isaac, and for Dave, it was his sister, Debbie, and then his brother, Gary. In both cases, the first loss was sudden and unexpected. John and Debbie each died almost instantly, and quite young. In both cases, the second loss was more prolonged. Gary and Isaac each died in middle age, after a long and painful illness. In both cases, we were able to communicate quickly and immediately with our loved ones when they died instantly. Debbie's death and subsequent communications left Dave feeling comfortable with the other world. He's often felt that she's not really gone—she's just somewhere else—because he was able to have that communication. He was disturbed, then, when Gary died, and he didn't hear from him.

My experience ran parallel to that. John came to me right after he died, and I've had dream messages from him from time to time over the years. But, until I found my sheath, I'd had no sense of communication from Isaac at all, nor had Arthur. I've come to suspect that, when someone dies suddenly, they feel a need to send a message and let the people "back home" know what happened. But when someone dies after a long illness, I think they're sick of the mortal body and not at all eager to reconnect to it. Plus, everyone already knows what happened. This whole communication with Isaac was nothing like what I might have imagined.

There are two more lessons that matter a lot to me. First, attachment, as the Buddhists teach us, isn't a great influence and tends to distort our thinking. My desire for Isaac's athame was full of attachment. I was under the influence of nostalgia for our ritual time together (attachment to memory), grief (attachment to Isaac as a living person), the desire to possess this beautiful knife (attachment to a thing), and frustration and envy that I hadn't inherited from Isaac the things we'd discussed him leaving to me (covetousness, which is attachment to other people's things). I was unable to determine if desiring that athame was right, or meant to be, or utterly wrong and greedy, because all those attachments distorted my thinking. Looking back, I know I should have seen my uncertainty itself as evidence that I was on the wrong track.

Finally, there's the specific desire for things that are beautiful and fancy. Coupled with that was my old demon: feeling inferior. My athame is absolutely ordinary looking. It's about nine inches long, the cross piece has no ornamentation of any kind and is flush with the hilt, and there's no pommel. It was made from a wood scrap and hand-painted.

On the other hand, I made the athame myself, with the help of my initiator. The wood is carved to the shape of my hand and fits into my palm exactly. I have used it in virtually every ritual I've attended since 1982.

I know people with Damascus blades, with kris blades, with dragons or pentacles in their crosspieces, with hilts of ebony, oak, or cherry, or even with embedded gems. I sometimes feel like a country cousin with my knife next to theirs on an altar.

None of that serves me. None of that means anything. None of that should inform my choices.

By the way, the smell of cat piss disappeared within a short time and did not return, nor did I ever find a stain.

About two months later, I ended up in a public dispute with ADF. It was a painful situation. I wrote and published an open letter of resignation, although I wished the organization much success. I said to a friend, partially joking, that if Isaac objected to my decision, he'd hide something.

About a week later, on a Wednesday, my debit card disappeared. The next day, my iPod disappeared.

Friday morning, driving to work, I had another crazy session of yelling at Isaac that went something like this: "Isaac, you are not allowed to run my life by stealing my things! That is NOT okay! The athame was different. The athame belonged to you, and you had every right to make your wishes known. But my relationship with ADF is *my* relationship. I paid for it with my money and it's none of your BUSINESS! I'm sorry you disagree, but you do not get to control me with my possessions. I RUN MY OWN LIFE!"

When I got out of the car, I opened the trunk, and the iPod was there.

Will My Pet Make a Good Familiar?

I was taught psychic exercises to determine the answer to this question, but I've discovered a preliminary test that teaches me more about a pet than any exercise: How does the animal behave in ritual?

In my experience, some animals will avoid ritual entirely. They'll disappear from view the moment a circle is cast, and suddenly be underfoot the moment it ends. These animals are declaring their discomfort with psychic work. Move along. The most beloved cat I ever had, the one most bonded to me as a person, was such an animal. I called her my "secular humanist cat."

Some animals are indifferent to ritual space. They'll move in and out with no change in their behavior. You might be able to work psychically with such animals, but don't count on it.

Finally, some animals are drawn to ritual space. They are the inverse of secular humanist animals—they may be nowhere to be found before ritual begins, but are suddenly underfoot as soon as energy starts to move.

This last category has the most potential as a psychic or magical assistant (a familiar). Carefully observe such an animal's behavior, and let that observation guide you as to how to proceed.

Does the animal sit at a quarter? Perhaps this is a companion who will make a good guardian. If it's always the same quarter, the animal may have a deep connection with the associated element. Does the animal sit directly under the altar? Perhaps it's more connected to the Gods and to spiritual work. Does it make its appearance during trance? During spells? During invocations? Each of these will tell you what role the animal wants to play in your spiritual life.

By respecting how the animal already behaves, you can have a mutually beneficial psychic relationship.

Chapter 20

HALF A CENTURY

May 2011: Happy birthday to me!

Oya is the guardian of the realm between life and death; as such,
She is not only the Goddess of spirit communication,
funerals and cemeteries but also the Goddess of clairvoyance,
psychic abilities, intuition and rebirth.
She can call forth the spirit of death,
or hold it back—such is the extent of Her power.
Because of Her affiliation to the dead,
and Her intense knowledge of the magick arts,
Oya is also known as "the Great Mother
of the Elders of the Night (Witches)."
—Oya: Lady of Storms, *by Heathwitch*[18]

Somewhere around April of 2011, I realized I was alive. I hadn't previously thought I was *not* alive, but when the feelings of aliveness and engagement came back, I sure noticed the difference.

When you grieve, restoration unfolds slowly, like a night-blooming flower. First, I had hours where I didn't cry, and then, sometimes, a whole day. At that point, I became impatient and was ready to say, "I'm no longer grieving," but the process itself, that stubborn unfolding flower, had other plans. In truth, despite my impatience, I was numb, and functioning only on a surface level. I wanted to play, to start dating again, to savor flavors, and to have adventures, but all of that was an arm's length away.

And then, I was alive.

---

18. *Oya: Lady of Storms,* by Heathwitch, www.orderwhitemoon.org/goddess/Oya .html, accessed November 8, 2012.

I was alive and grieving, to be sure. I will always miss Isaac, and my sorrow will always be complicated by the odd fact that I am grieving my *ex*-husband. I have had the strange karma of having to mourn two men who were not quite my husband: a fiancé and an ex-husband. It's one of those weird things that stands out for me as remarkable without the least whiff of explanation. It just is.

More concretely, I've lost the father of my child, and my love for each is wrapped up in my love for the other. Arthur looks, laughs, shrugs, smiles, jokes, and gestures like his father, and so I see Isaac every day, which makes me miss him both more and less.

But I am alive.

In May of 2011, I turned fifty years old. For several years, I'd said I wanted to throw myself a big 50th bash, and now it was around the corner. I started planning the party months in advance. When the time came close, it felt too soon after Isaac's death, and I was having financial struggles, yet putting it off wasn't an option—half a century comes but once. So I set aside all my concerns and rolled up my sleeves.

Party planning makes me anxious (which is one reason I never wanted another big wedding), but I got a lot of support. My mom helped me figure out the food, Tracy and Ray generously loaned their huge backyard, and Dave planned the music and set up a stage. Everyone pitched in, and the result was spectacular.

Instead of having the party the actual weekend of my birthday, I delayed it a few weeks in hopes of warmer weather, as Beltane in New Jersey can be cold. Unfortunately, a cold snap spoiled my weather fantasies. Nonetheless, there was lots of food, cake, wine, beer, soft drinks, good friends, and live music. It was thrilling to bring together the diverse parts of my life: Clan, family, Pagans outside the Clan, coworkers, and more.

Because I *am* so anxious about these things, I decided to give myself a break and not invite too many people from out of town, because having house guests seemed like added stress. Of course I invited Barbara—my first student, first initiate, and dearest friend. Barbara lives in Tennessee now, almost nine hundred miles away, and I invited her only out of love, not out of any idea she'd actually come, but she did.

Here's what happened: Another dear friend of mine, Melissa, lived about three hours from Barbara, and they decided they'd both come and share the driving. Barbara's brother was in the hospital, and she very much wanted to see him; she could visit us both on one trip. All of this was enough motivation to make my two wonderful friends drive over fourteen hours. They *almost* rang my bell without calling, as a birthday surprise, but Melissa realized I'd appreciate advance notice.

So, the night before my birthday party, I showed my Kentucky friend her first sight of New York City, and at my party, I got to share my beloved friends from far away with my beloved friends from home. It was truly a joy.

Is fifty different? In a way, yes. There were some "clicks" in my head, and I simply came to peace about certain things in a new manner. In some ways, I've fought myself my whole life, always wishing to be better or different. In the days following my birthday, a whole wave of that feeling fell away. I realized if I wasn't "that" person by fifty, I never would be. It felt great. Similarly, I found I felt differently toward my mother. I love her as much as ever, and *like* her as much, but somehow I care much less about what she thinks of me. It was like the inner me that was still a child, that still tried to please Mommy and rebelled against her, turned and saw that very big number, that 50, and said, "Oh, to hell with *that*." It was all very liberating.

In June, Arthur and I returned to Free Spirit Gathering. It was the kind of thing where you can see it coming down the road, and you steel yourself. This could be fine, I thought, or it could be another weeklong tearfest. Arthur was going to offer the classes he'd had to abruptly cancel the year before. I had an offer for another festival I wanted to attend, but I knew my son needed me with him.

It was not awful. It was not tragic. In truth, we had a great time. It was a lovely festival with Clan and many other friends, with fire circles and laughs and joy and some sad moments when we remembered how much we missed Arthur's dad. I attended wonderful workshops by Michael Brown of Simplicity Memorial. Michael is a Pagan funeral director committed to creating services (for any religion) that are personal, compassionate, and economical. He had handled Isaac's arrangements, and I was moved by his serenity and goodness at a time when we all really needed that. Michael's workshops were amazing, but I decided to skip the ritual honoring the dead; I was still too raw.

There was an unexpected miracle awaiting me at Free Spirit that year, courtesy of Izolda Trakhtenberg. Izolda is a singer and voice coach (among other things) who offered a three-part singing class called "Finding Your Sacred Voice," culminating in a choral performance on Saturday night, opening for the main concert.

I've been told my whole life that I cannot sing, that my voice is terrible, I wander off key, or sing every note in a different key. People cringed when I sang, and when I tried to teach a chant in the Pagan Way, people would say they didn't know what melody I was singing. I've been around musicians who despaired of teaching me—including Isaac. When Isaac's band, Real Magic, was active, I was the non-member member. Isaac, Roberta, Constance, and Jeff valued my input on arrangements and other things, but I neither sang nor played an instrument.

Izolda said I absolutely could be taught and challenged me to come to her class. A year later, I took her up on that challenge.

I can sing.

I can't express what a miracle this was for me. It's like I woke up one morning and found out I was Heidi Klum. This was something I always wanted, always longed for, that I knew was as far beyond my reach as being a six-foot supermodel. (Indeed, given a choice between the two, I'd much prefer to sing.)

I continue to struggle with a wandering pitch, but once Izolda placed me on the right note, I was able to stay on-pitch and on-key, and sing clearly and well. During the class I had to tolerate a lot of embarrassed feelings, being singled out when I was off-pitch and knowing

I was struggling in front of a bunch of people, many of whom were strangers to me. Yet, as promised, it was my *sacred* voice I found, and a sacred knowledge I uncovered. I performed confidently with the chorus in front of a large audience that Saturday night.

The joy of this discovery, the sheer wonder of it, caused a *lot* of tears to be shed. Another wall came down. I am that much freer.

Also at Free Spirit, I had my tattoo repaired.

Let me backtrack. During Isaac's illness, I told him I wanted to get a memorial tattoo for him. My denial was a powerful force; I never quite uttered the word "memorial," but he and I both knew what we were doing, and we planned the tattoo together.

The Laplantes (Christine, Orien, and the now-recovered Orien Rose) hosted several annual Winterspirit gatherings at their home, a weekend of sacred tattooing. The people being tattooed shared their intention with the group, and let the others know what they needed (drumming, silence, Om-ing, hand holding…each person is different). It was beautifully organized. There was a space for tattooing and holding a clear intention, and there was also a space for taking a break, hanging out, chatting, and resting. The room between the two allowed quiet chat; it was neither disruptive nor dedicated to ritual. People gathered to get tattooed or to support others, to share love, food, and the transformative meeting of body and spirit.

It was in this space, in January 2011, that I received my memorial tattoo. Naturally, it was painful and exhausting, but it was also beautiful and sacred. That same weekend, Arthur was tattooed as well—not a memorial, although he may get one. Arthur's tattoo is a personal symbol for the Archangel Uriel, his patron. Although we didn't realize it when we planned our tattoos, my son and I received "matching" work—pieces of approximately the same size on the same part of each of our right arms.

At the end of Winterspirit 2011, Christine announced it would be the last such event, which was bittersweet news.

My tattoo healed badly. I am well-experienced with tattooing; this was my thirteenth, but I'd never had any serious trouble before. My arm turned purple and was bruised all around. As a comparison, by the time the swelling finally went down and I could bear to be touched lightly, Arthur was fully healed. When I finally healed, after three months, the tattoo looked terrible. Lines were muddy, and sections were almost missing. This sort of thing can happen if you've been tattooed by an inexperienced or sloppy or unsanitary artist, but Captain Gordon of Time Bomb Tattooing and Piercing,[19] was none of those things. He'd tattooed half the Clan, including my own sister, and does beautiful work. It seemed that my body-heart-spirit connection was pushing an emotional healing process into my physical body, making the whole thing quite a mess.

At Free Spirit, Gordon reworked the tattoo. I was fully expecting another round of disastrous swelling, bruising, and pain, but apparently that part of my process was over. The session went smoothly, healing was swift, and the tattoo is now superbly rendered, a credit to the artist and an honor to Isaac. It was, again, a moving and transforming experience. I am blessed to have had many of those!

Also in June, I received an invitation to return to Brazil the following October. Claudiney Prieto and I had talked about my returning since my last trip, but it's an expensive and complicated journey to organize, and it took five years to pull it all together. This time I wanted to make up for my prior mistake, so we planned an extended stay where I'd have the chance to see some of the country.

One of my mottos in life is simply to say *yes*. I never know where opportunities or connections will arise. My mundane career came about by doing good work and having it noticed. I had no notion of becoming a technical writer, and was not even familiar with the job title, when I first began writing documents because my company was shorthanded. I showed a talent, a job opened up, and *voila!* It comes down to saying yes. Yes, I will try that new thing; yes, I am available; yes, I will do that—yes.

---

19. *Timebomb Tattooing and Piercing*, www.timebombtattoos.com.

I routinely do things I'm afraid of, because fear seems like a poor way to manage my life. I don't believe I've ever done a great job of planning my life. The dreams I had for myself have mostly not come true, because they turned out to be things I didn't want. I dreamed of becoming a midwife, but found myself ill-suited to that, instead finding a career I hadn't imagined. I dreamed of having three or four children and living in the country, but I found one child was the right number for me and I live in the suburbs. Some dreams worked out: I dreamed of being a writer, and of being a Witch, but I am not convinced my dreams are a good way to know myself or find what will fulfill me.

I have dreamed of a country with which I might have a complex, magical, and perhaps karmic relationship. That country is India. Despite my dreams, the country I seem to actually be developing such a connection to is Brazil. I never would have imagined it!

Often, I have visited a place, met wonderful people, had a marvelous time, and then that was that. I have never returned to Australia, nor have I kept in touch with the lovely people I met there, although who knows what the future holds? Other times I have visited a place, found myself at home, and returned annually or at least often. Starwood became a second home to me, and I've returned to Ontario many times. Brazil somehow seems different. I visited once, for only a few days, and somehow that was enough to convince me that I'd be back and that those people were my friends.

Because there had been so many setbacks to previous trips that I didn't end up taking, I thought little about Brazil at first. It was four months away, after all.

In July, a strange series of omens began. Some were alarming. Most had the quality of a near miss. A heavy object fell on me from the sky and cut my arm; the very minor scratch drew blood. A car backed into the outdoor café seat I'd considered taking and changed my mind about. It hit hard enough to make my table jump. There were many examples like these two, things that were both frightening (because they came so close) and relieving (because they didn't come closer). Alarmed, I got several readings in a hurry, and also read my own cards. At first, answers were obstinately vague, like "something you don't understand is happening." (Yes, *I know*.) Eventually, a reader helped me see these signs as messages from the goddess Oya.

For many years, I had experienced a kind of psychic block between me and the Yoruban pantheon. I would forget the names of orishas, even though remembering deities and myths from around the world is pretty much my specialty. I would be unable to hold simple things in my head, unable to be around rituals, and so on. After a while, I came to the conclusion that some kind of barrier had been placed there for a reason. Perhaps Kali's presence within me somehow denied an invitation to beings who seek an "open head." Around 2009, I began to sense that this block had lifted. I was able to hold ideas about Santería and Voodoo in my head with more clarity, and remember them the next day. It was as if I no longer felt *stupid* when the topic came up, and I wondered if it was time to attend my first open Voodoo ritual when I was next invited.

Oya and Kali have a kind of energetic kinship. Both have powerful, warrior-woman energy, and both are fearsome as well as beloved. A friend said to me, also around 2009, "You're an Oya woman, right?" I said, "No, I'm a Kali woman." But when the reading suggested I was connected to Oya, I remembered the conversation.

In the meantime, my history of psychic blockage left me ignorant about the orishas. I wanted further guidance. It's not at all a good idea, or proper, or respectful, to dabble with Yoruban deities—they require a reverent approach. I have several friends and acquaintances who practice Santería and Voodoo, so I was able to learn how to make an appropriate offering, to acknowledge that the message was received while I sought further advice.

In my typically skeptical way, I was not 100 percent convinced that this was really Oya. Nevertheless, I decided to leave an offering at a cemetery, as advised. (In fact, the *entrance* to a cemetery is what's called for, but the place I'd selected didn't have an entrance per se.) Arthur and I were in the car together, and we'd decided to take the back way home, which would take us past a tiny graveyard near his former high school. I asked him to point it out. Both in deciding to take the back way and in getting there, several weird things happened, and I wondered if they were more omens—the skin on my arms was certainly prickling.

The graveyard I was looking for was about the size of a large backyard, about a quarter of an acre. No more than two or three cars could park in front of it at once. There was no way I could have spotted it myself (I was actually looking on the wrong side of the road), but Arthur thought he could find it. We were both craning our necks to look when all of a sudden a utility repair truck flagged us to a stop... directly in front of the graveyard. Now *all* my skin felt prickly, and we just looked at each other. "Okay," I said, "I guess I'm coming back here with an offering."

That night I left an offering, asking only that future omens, when they came, be less frightening.

Gradually, I put together a daily practice of worshiping Oya. I was taught how to seek dreams from her, and messages began to come through, which I was able to respond to.

While shopping for things with which to set up my altar, I found a little ceramic serving dish shaped like an eggplant. (I *always* shop in Goodwill stores for altar supplies; they're full of strange treasures.) The altar includes a lot of purple (one of Oya's sacred colors) and a fan. (On the list of synchronicities goes this: A couple of days before being told I should set up an altar that included a fan, I won a gift basket in a raffle; the basket included a fan.) Going with the theme of the wind, I added wings, including butterflies and birds, to the altar.

The sum effect was very girly. Fans, the color scheme, wings... it all looked very feminine. That surprised me, because Oya is a fierce goddess, but it also pleased me. I have a reputation as a fierce woman, but it gives me great pleasure to express my soft, traditionally feminine side. I've always felt softer on the inside than people perceive on the outside, and I love being girlish. I wasn't sure this had anything to do with Oya, but I went with it.

Somewhere in all of this, someone mentioned to me that I was going to Brazil, the home of Candomblé, and perhaps my communication from Oya was connected to that.

After having a series of powerful dreams, to which I was able to respond, and some beautiful experiences, Oya came to me in a dream and told me to stop what I was doing. I was confused, because things had been going very well, but naturally I obeyed.

When Kali came to me, I knew her. She was my mother; I crawled into her lap. I didn't experience that with Oya; it was like we were getting to know each other. I longed to feel that connectedness, and I wondered if I'd find it in Brazil.

⁓

I left New York on October 6, 2011, flying a red-eye and arriving the morning of the 7th. Also arriving that morning was Jimahl di Fiosa, an Alexandrian Wiccan and an author of several books about Alex Sanders. Jimahl is a fascinating person with an unexpected depth. I had prejudged him harshly and, over the course of our time together, was pulled up short by how wrong I had been. He's the real thing!

Our translator, A., picked us up at the airport. Most of my friends from 2006 were still a tight and loving group, but shortly after we'd last seen each other, Lulu had fallen in love with a German man, and was now married, a mother, and living in Berlin.

That first day, A., Jimahl, and I visited a large Macumba shop. Both Jimahl and I noticed that there seemed to be no Oya statues at all, although all the other African powers were well represented.

I was in Brazil as a guest speaker at Mystic Fair São Paulo, a weekend event. The Mystic Fair was unlike anything I'd ever seen. It was massive, with approximately 22,000 people in attendance shopping at the vast array of booths, attending numerous workshops and lectures, listening to the in-house radio show, watching dance demonstrations, visiting the "living puja" (with people in Ganesha and Lakshmi costumes seated on life-size altars), and getting readings. It was essentially a huge New Age event, with a wide variety of New Age philosophies, healing modalities, and disciplines represented, including some unique to Brazil. I saw yoga, Theosophy, angel worship, Reiki, astrology, Tarot, and even a small Scientology table. Unlike any New Age event I'd ever heard of, it was run by a Wiccan (Claudiney) and had a strong Wiccan and occult component.

This was the second annual Mystic Fair, and it had thousands more attendees than the previous year; it had outgrown the college campus on which it was held. People were jammed together, barely able to move through the main intersections of the halls. Yet everyone was entirely civil and openhearted. Even though I required a translator, I still had excellent attendance at my lecture and was warmly received. I also gave a lot of readings, making deep connections to people through the cards.

Monday evening, Claudiney and I flew to Rio. If São Paulo was a whirlwind, Rio de Janeiro was an exercise in being laid back and enjoying the moment. It was pure tourism, with no obligations and no solid plans. Clau and I met up with two Cariocas (natives of Rio) who were friends of his. One, Valeria, I'd given a reading to at Mystic Fair and really liked, and the other, Alexsander, I was meeting for the first time (although he, too, had been at Mystic Fair).

Clau had sent his luggage home from our hotel in São Paulo and traveled light to Rio. When we arrived, he realized that the cable for his laptop was in the luggage he'd sent home. So, in addition to touring, we ran around Rio looking for a store that sold electronics. We found stores that didn't sell what he was looking for, stores that charged two or three times what he wanted to pay, and stores that had iffy cables that might or might not have fit his machine.

The first day, we got directions from someone to an electronics store. We arrived at the address, looked around, saw nothing, and suddenly realized we were standing in front of another Macumba shop. We went in, and while I shopped around, Clau surprised me with a statue of Oya as a present. When I saw it, I was shocked: She was red and black, and holding a sword in one hand. She was almost a mirror image of the idol of Kali on my altar at home—a metal statue with a sword in one hand, decorated in Kali's red and black. In fact, when I got home and said to Arthur, "Look what Clau bought me," Arthur's response was, "He bought you a statue of Kali?"

Clau explained that, in Candomblé, Oya is commonly referred to as Iansã, which is why Jimahl and I hadn't seen anything labeled "Oya" in our earlier explorations. Over coffee, I explained to Clau my strange history with the orishas, and described a little of the call I'd received from Oya. With my new statue and some guidance from Clau, I was able to see that this was a goddess with a natural place in my life, that my two altars to two goddesses were much more connected than I'd previously believed.

Dion Fortune famously said, "All gods are one God, and all goddesses are one Goddess, and there is one Initiator." Does that mean that Kali *is* Oya?

I don't think so. In some ultimate way, yes, all goddesses are one Goddess, just as all women are connected through womanhood, and all souls are one soul. On the other hand, it is respectful to individuals to *treat* them as individuals. Just as I don't want to be treated as if I were indistinguishable from every other woman, I don't think Kali, Oya, or any other goddess wants to be treated as if she were just a label.

In this case, though, the syncretism was helpful. Oya and Kali connect through *me*, through *my* red, storm, warrior energy. When I returned home, my girly Oya altar began to take on more and more warrior-woman characteristics, beginning with my fierce red statue. Soon enough, Drawing Down confirmed this information.

In Rio, I saw amazing sights. We rode the train to Corcovado and happened to arrive during the eightieth birthday celebration of the Christ the Redeemer statue. We took the cable car to Pão de Açúcar (Sugar Loaf Mountain) and saw the most glorious view. In addition, that cable car had been featured in the 1979 film *Moonraker*; I've been on James Bond location tours in New York and the Bahamas, so this was an extra thrill for me. We visited Copacabana, danced the samba on the street in Lapa, and drank "coconut water" at a kiosk on the beach at Ipanema.

In a samba club in Lapa, Alexsander began reading Claudiney's cards. He was just having fun, talking with Clau about his love life, but I could see that Alex was a skilled reader. I knew enough about what was going on in Clau's life to gauge the accuracy of the reading, and Clau's blushing gave away the rest.

I asked Alex to read me, and then I asked him if I had karma in Brazil—what was my connection to this country? "Oh, wait," he said, "you're being *serious!*" "Oh, sorry," I said, but I got my reading. It was the perfect opportunity: Alexsander knew nothing of my history, I knew nothing about the unique deck he was using, and the chaotic environment allowed the information to rush out without any of the ponderous seriousness that can be associated with a formal reading.

Alex said I did have a fate in Brazil. I was to teach there, and my teaching could have a profound effect on many people. It was gratifying to understand that, even though I didn't and still don't know what will come next, my sense that I was to keep saying *yes* in order to find my fate was panning out.

On Friday morning, we flew to Uberlândia in Minas Gerais, where we met a coven that was struggling to bootstrap themselves into deeper work, with a lack of formal training. They longed to provide teaching to the many people in their area who were interested in Wicca but had no access to training, but they didn't want to sacrifice the integrity of their group by growing too quickly. They were, in many ways, analogous to Pagans and Wiccans in the United States in the 1970s, but the Internet and the widespread availability of written materials today make everything different. We taught a *lot* of classes to a small group and left early Monday morning, giving me one last day in São Paulo before flying home, promising to return.

There were ways in which my Brazilian journey was a microcosm of my life. It was both more and less beautiful than I'd imagined. My fantasies did not come true, and my expectations were overblown. There were moments when I found I was standing next to the exact spot I needed to be, without realizing I was there. I had everything I needed, and met wonderful people, worked hard, laughed hard, relaxed, and allowed whatever would happen simply to happen. I found there was always more love than I could ask for, and that the Gods were present in accordance with their will.

I don't know what comes next. I don't need to.

EPILOGUE

I started my second half-century with a sense of completion. I'd even finished and delivered the manuscript for this book.

In March of 2012, Melissa flew up from Kentucky for another visit, one that would change my life. Her first night in town, she stayed in the guest room. Her second night, she didn't.

Melissa and I had met four years earlier, when I'd visited Louisville for Pagan Pride. She was a Gardnerian I'd known and admired from online groups.

My first night in Louisville, at dinner with about a dozen Witches, we were discussing movies. I pronounced that *Shrek* was "post-modernism for children," and Melissa stared at me with delight.

"Will you marry me?" she asked.

"Do I have to move to Kentucky?"

"Nope."

"Okay then."

At the time, I thought she was one of those people who popped off and proposed marriage every time they ate a chocolate bar, but I was wrong.

It was love at first sight for both of us, but for many reasons, we didn't act on those feelings, and settled instead into a good friendship. Despite an ostensibly platonic relationship, I couldn't stop thinking about that playful proposal, and I always flirted. Melissa, though, thought I was straight, and that I'd dally with her and break her heart.

At the age of fifteen I'd had a lesbian romance and believed I was gay. A year later, I met Ronnie. I came to understand that I was bisexual, but after that first love, I'd only had long-term relationships with men; my connections with women were few and transient. I often wondered, was I really bi? What did that mean? On dating sites, I realized I was only interested in looking at men. Didn't that make me straight?

Ultimately, I became comfortable with the ambiguity and stopped worrying about it. When I met Melissa, though, I began seriously reconsidering my orientation.

We chatted online often and occasionally on the phone. We saw each other about annually. We shared details of our lives that no one else knew, and grew to trust each other. She was a linchpin of the support that kept me going during and after Isaac's illness. Meanwhile, she'd met and moved in with someone else, filling me with what-if regret. I supported her through the realization that she was unhappy and needed to end her relationship.

And now this. Now we were in bed together.

The first thing we said was that nothing would change. We'd be "friends with benefits." She'd go back to Kentucky. Life would go on. But I was freaking out. How had I wanted this to happen for four years and never imagined what would come next? Six weeks later, she came back for my birthday, and it was clear that "nothing would change" was pure fiction. We had fallen in love.

I was terrified, even though that's not my usual reaction to love affairs. I was in agony; I was sure I would hurt her. If I rejected her because she was a woman, didn't that make me the bad actor in this? From March through June, I tore my heart out, tossed and turned, and questioned my every thought.

All of this, in the end, turned out to be a simple thing: I was coming out. "Bisexual" when it means I sometimes sleep with women, and "bisexual" when it means I am in love with a woman, are two entirely different orientations; this was a new chrysalis from which I had to break free.

"Do you really have to be bisexual?" she asked. "Maybe it's just me." But for me, it would never be enough to say that love transcended bodily form: I am not pansexual. Bodies matter to me. In fact, one thing I have always loved about Wicca is its earthiness, its roots in the physical. I needed to desire Melissa as much as I had desired any man; otherwise I knew that somewhere down the road, it would all fall apart. I had to look inside and see if that desire was there, and if it wasn't, I had to have the integrity to say so. To my relief, I found a deep well of desire and attraction that wasn't just soul-meets-soul, but encompassed body-meets-body as well.

Those weeks were painful for Melissa, who was already gay and sure of her feelings for me, but she was patient through my process.

Here, then, is the coda to my story. I have fallen in love with a good friend, someone I already trusted, someone who had already come through for me many times, someone I understand. She is the person I imagined I wanted: smart, funny, Wiccan, serious about magic, light-hearted about life, moral, and warm. We share values and opinions and hobbies. She and Arthur are buddies. The only unexpected part is her gender, and I have discovered I am more than happy with that. The next part of my story will be written with a partner who is, at this writing, packing her things to move from Kentucky to New York, where she and I, Arthur, my cats, and her cat will all form a family.

RESOURCES

This is not necessarily a recommended reading list. It is simply every book mentioned in these pages.

Adler, Margot. *Drawing Down the Moon: Witches, Druids, Goddess-Worshippers, and Other Pagans in America Today.* New York: Penguin Books, 1986.

Bolen, Jean Shinoda. *Goddesses in Everywoman: Powerful Archetypes in Women's Lives.* New York: Harper Collins, 1984.

Bonewits, Philip Emmons Isaac. *Neopagan Rites: A Guide to Creating Public Rituals That Work.* Woodbury, MN: Llewellyn Publications, 2007. Previously published as *Rites of Worship: A Neopagan Approach,* Earth Religions Press, 2003.

———. *Real Magic: An Introductory Treatise on the Basic Principles of Yellow Magic.* York Beach, ME: Weiser Books, 1989.

Butler, W. E. *Lords of Light: The Path of Initiation in the Western Mysteries.* Rochester, VT: Destiny Books, 1990. Note: Robin Goodfellow recommended "any books" by W. E. Butler. This is a sample.

Campbell, Joseph. *The Hero with a Thousand Faces.* Princeton, NJ: Princeton University Press, 1949.

Cunningham, Scott. *Earth, Air, Fire & Water: More Techniques of Natural Magic.* St. Paul, MN: Llewellyn Publications, 1991.

Daniélou, Alain. *Gods of Love and Ecstasy: The Traditions of Shiva and Dionysus.* Rochester, VT: Inner Traditions, 1992.

———. *The Myths and Gods of India: The Classic Work on Hindu Polytheism.* Rochester, VT: Inner Traditions, 1992.

Doniger O'Flaherty, Wendy. *Other Peoples' Myths: The Cave of Echoes.* New York: Macmillan Publishing Co., 1988.

Downing, Christine. *The Goddess: Mythological Images of the Feminine.* New York: Continuum, 1996.

———. *Gods in Our Midst: Mythological Images of the Masculine: A Woman's View.* New York: Crossroad Publishing Co., 1993.

Eliade, Mircea. *Myth and Reality.* Prospect Heights, IL: Waveland Press, 1998. First published in 1963 by Harper & Row in New York.

Eliot, Alexander. *The Universal Myths: Heroes, Gods, Tricksters, and Others.* New York: Truman Talley Books/Meridian, 1990.

Farrar, Stewart. *What Witches Do: The Modern Coven Revealed.* Rev. ed. Custer, WA: Phoenix Publishing Co., 1983.

Filan, Kenaz, and Raven Kaldera. *Drawing Down the Spirits: The Traditions and Techniques of Spirit Possession.* Rochester, VT: Destiny Books, 2009.

Fortune, Dion. *Moon Magic.* York Beach, ME: Samuel Weiser, 1978. Reprinted in 1980, 1981, and 1985. Note: Dion Fortune was another "any books" recommendation from Robin Goodfellow.

———. *Psychic Self-Defense.* New ed. San Francisco, CA: Red Wheel/Weiser, 2001.

———. *The Sea Priestess.* York Beach, ME: Samuel Weiser, 1978. First published in 1938.

Frost, Gavin and Yvonne. *Magic Power of White Witchcraft: Revised for the Millennium,* Paramus, NJ: Prentice Hall Reward Books, 1999.

Gardner, Gerald B. *High Magic's Aid.* Hinton, WV: Godolphin House, 1996.

———. *The Meaning of Witchcraft.* York Beach, ME: Red Wheel/Weiser, 2004.

———. *Witchcraft Today.* New York: Citadel Press, 2004.

Graves, Robert. *The White Goddess: A Historical Grammar of Poetic Myth.* Rev. ed. New York: Farrar, Straus and Giroux, 1975. Originally published in 1948.

Guiley, Rosemary. *The Encyclopedia of Witches, Witchcraft and Wicca.* 3rd ed. New York: Checkmark Books, 2008.

Hamilton, Edith. *Mythology.* Boston, MA: Back Bay Books, 1998.

Harding, M. Esther. *Woman's Mysteries: Ancient and Modern.* Boston, MA: Shambhala Publications, 1971.

Higginbotham, Joyce and River. *Paganism: An Introduction to Earth-Centered Religions.* St. Paul, MN: Llewellyn Publications, 2002.

Hopman, Ellen Evert. *Being a Pagan: Druids, Wiccans, and Witches Today.* Rochester, VT: Destiny Books, 2001.

Huson, Paul. *Mastering Witchcraft: A Practical Guide for Witches, Warlocks and Covens.* New York: Perigree Books, 1970.

Johnson, Robert A. *He: Understanding Masculine Psychology.* New York: Harper & Row, 1974.

———. *She: Understanding Feminine Psychology.* New York: Harper & Row, 1976.

———. *We: Understanding the Psychology of Romantic Love.* San Francisco, CA: Harper & Row, 1983.

Laplante, Christine. *Sirens from across the River.* Unpublished.

Leeming, David, and Jake Page. *God: Myths of the Male Divine.* New York: Oxford University Press, 1996.

———. *Goddess: Myths of the Female Divine.* New York: Oxford University Press, 1996.

Le Guin, Ursula. *Always Coming Home.* Berkeley, CA: University of California Press, 2001.

Leland, Charles G. *Aradia, or The Gospel of the Witches.* Translated by Mario and Dina Pazzaglini. Blaine, WA: Phoenix Publishing Co., 1998.

Lethbridge, T. C. *Witches: The Investigation of an Ancient Religion.* London: Routledge and Kegan Paul, 1962.

Lipp, Deborah. *The Elements of Ritual: Air, Fire, Water and Earth in the Wiccan Circle.* St. Paul, MN: Llewellyn Publications, 2003.

———. *The Study of Witchcraft: A Guidebook to Advanced Wicca.* San Francisco, CA: Red Wheel/Weiser, 2007.

————. *The Way of Four: Create Elemental Balance in Your Life.* St. Paul, MN: Llewellyn Publications, 2004.

————. *The Way of Four Spellbook: Working Magic with the Elements,* Woodbury, MN: Llewellyn Publications, 2006.

Martello, Dr. Leo Louis. *Witchcraft: The Old Religion.* Secaucus, NJ: Carol Publishing Group, 1991.

Monaghan, Patricia. *The Book of Goddesses and Heroines.* St. Paul, MN: Llewellyn Publications, 1990.

Murray, Margaret A. *The God of the Witches.* New York: Oxford University Press, 1970.

————. *The Witch-Cult in Western Europe.* Oxford: Clarendon Press, 1962.

Neumann, Erich. *The Great Mother: An Analysis of the Archetype.* New York: Pantheon Books, 1955.

Roberts, Jane. *Seth Speaks: The Eternal Validity of the Soul.* Englewood Cliffs, NJ: Prentice Hall, 1972.

Roberts, Susan. *Witches U.S.A.* New York: Dell Publishing Co., 1971.

Sheba, Lady. *The Book of Shadows.* St. Paul, MN: Llewellyn Publications, 1971.

————. *The Grimoire of Lady Sheba.* St. Paul, MN: Llewellyn Publications, 1972.

Shuttle, Penelope, and Peter Redgrove. *The Wise Wound: Menstruation and Everywoman.* London: Marion Boyars, 2005.

Starhawk. *The Spiral Dance: A Rebirth of the Ancient Religion of the Great Goddess.* San Francisco, CA: Harper and Row, 1979.

Sulak, John, and V. Vale. *Modern Pagans: An Investigation of Contemporary Pagan Practices.* San Francisco, CA: RE/Search Publications, 2001.

Valiente, Doreen. *An ABC of Witchcraft Past and Present.* New York: St. Martin's Press, 1973.

————. *Natural Magic.* New York: St. Martin's Press, 1975.

————. *Where Witchcraft Lives.* London: Aquarian Press, 1962.

————. *Witchcraft for Tomorrow.* Blaine, WA: Phoenix Publications, 1988.

Weinstein, Marion. *Earth Magic: A Book of Shadows for Positive Witches.* Franklin Lakes, NJ: New Page Books, 2003.

————. *Positive Magic: Ancient Metaphysical Techniques for Modern Lives.* Franklin Lakes, NJ: New Page Books, 2002.

Wolkstein, Diane, and Samuel Noah Kramer. *Inanna, Queen of Heaven and Earth: Her Stories and Hymns from Sumer.* New York: Harper & Row, 1983.

TO WRITE TO THE AUTHOR

If you wish to contact the author or would like more information about this book, please write to the author in care of Llewellyn Worldwide Ltd. and we will forward your request. Both the author and publisher appreciate hearing from you and learning of your enjoyment of this book and how it has helped you. Llewellyn Worldwide Ltd. cannot guarantee that every letter written to the author can be answered, but all will be forwarded. Please write to:

Deborah Lipp
℅ Llewellyn Worldwide
2143 Wooddale Drive
Woodbury, MN 55125-2989

Please enclose a self-addressed stamped envelope for reply,
or $1.00 to cover costs. If outside the U.S.A., enclose
an international postal reply coupon.

Many of Llewellyn's authors have websites with additional
information and resources. For more information,
please visit our website at http://www.llewellyn.com.